IMAGES of America

GRAND RAPIDS

FURNITURE CITY

On the cover: The Robert W. Irwin Company was one of the many Grand Rapids companies offering collections of pieces with hand-painted finishes. Artists like Frank J. Davidhazy (center, back to camera) produced original designs that were then painstakingly copied onto the furniture. Here the decorating department applies those final artistic touches that were a hallmark of home furnishings destined to become family heirlooms. This photograph was taken in 1925, during the time the company specialized in living room and bedroom pieces. (Collections of the Public Museum, Grand Rapids.)

IMAGES
of America

GRAND RAPIDS
FURNITURE CITY

Norma Lewis

ARCADIA
PUBLISHING

ISBN 978-0-7385-5200-2

Published by Arcadia Publishing
Charleston, South Carolina

Printed in the United States of America

Library of Congress Catalog Card Number: 2007939956

For all general information contact Arcadia Publishing at:
Telephone 843-853-2070
Fax 843-853-0044
E-mail sales@arcadiapublishing.com
For customer service and orders:
Toll-Free 1-888-313-2665

Visit us on the Internet at www.arcadiapublishing.com

For Jay de Vries and in memory of Raymond Lewis

Contents

ACKNOWLEDGMENTS

A big thank-you to everyone whose generosity helped make this book a reality. I could not have done it without you. For everyone in the History and Special Collections Department of the Grand Rapids Public Library, especially Karolee Hazelwood and Christine Byron: you always came through! Also, Jeanne Larson at the Public Museum, Grand Rapids who did not have time but helped me anyway: I am aware of the effort you made.

My appreciation, too, for the companies that took time with me and shared archival photographs. The Kindel, Herman Miller, Steelcase, American Seating, Guardsman, Haworth, Irwin Seating, Knape and Vogt, and Howard Miller images have greatly enhanced this book, and I am in your debt.

To those of you who offered images from your private collections: your contributions are all the more special because you saved and cherished those images, and they could not have been obtained elsewhere.

My heartfelt thanks to Anna Wilson, my editor at Arcadia Publishing, and everyone else at Arcadia who contributed to this project.

I am ever grateful to my family for their ongoing love, support, and encouragement: my son, David Harris; and my daughter and her family, Rhonda, Pat, Shelby, and Shane Ayers. My husband, Jay, kept me on track and did the "high-tech" chores at which I fail miserably. Thank you!

Also a thank-you to the Lewises, Fay Lewis Reilly, Jerry Lewis and Gwen Werner, Debby Buckman, and Kelly, Nick, and Joey Ellinger. And the De Vries clan I more recently married. There are too many of you to name individually, but I appreciate you all. A special thank-you to Jill (De Vries) Berry for the map on page 24.

INTRODUCTION

In the year 1836, Antonio Lopez de Santa Ana's army massacred Davy Crockett at the Alamo, Martin Van Buren was elected to replace Andrew Jackson in the White House, and in Grand Rapids, William "Deacon" Haldane opened the city's first cabinetmaking shop. Scores of others followed and created home furnishings of such distinction that Grand Rapids and fine furniture were synonymous for more than a century.

Grand Rapids was well on the way to becoming "Furniture City" when the 1876 Philadelphia Centennial Exposition made it official. Furniture made here appeared in more and more of the country's greatest houses and even graced the White House. Desks were given to presidents, and tables, chairs, bookcases, and sofas were prominently displayed in the Oval Office. Pieces made in the city adorned Theodore Roosevelt's Red Room.

There was no Grand Rapids furniture, or even a Grand Rapids, when George Washington furnished Mount Vernon, but when his great-great-great-grandniece Anne Madison Washington furnished a Mount Vernon replica for the French International Colonial and Overseas Exposition in 1931, she turned to Grand Rapids and Kindel Furniture Company for Colonial-style canopy beds. When another George, Pres. George W. Bush, conferred with French president Nicolas Sarkozy in November 2007, they met at Mount Vernon and with their entourages sat around a Kindel-made table.

Kindel was not the only company making reproductions. Baker Furniture Company, with factories in both Grand Rapids and Holland, Michigan, reproduced fine English pieces. The family that owned the original of one Baker cabinet was British nobility and could trace its roots to William the Conqueror.

Local products went to Hollywood. Clark Gable bought furniture for his home, then came back to chose furnishings for the *Gone with the Wind* set. The movie was a sensation and prompted Macy's Department Store to introduce "Miss Pitty-Pat's Boudoir Suite."

When Edith Taliaferro, a popular actress in the 1920s, appeared in a local play, the Sligh Furniture Company asked her to pose with its furniture. She agreed but insisted on bringing her leading man. He was an unknown, but Spencer Tracy soon enjoyed enormous success. Years later, Tracy's wife, Louise, posed with her Sligh-made "Coleridge" desk.

Sometimes the furniture makers played an important role without fanfare. Fireproof metal desks, chairs, and bunks outfitted United States Navy submarines. Church pews, train seats, school desks, and sports and entertainment seats were more taken for granted than admired, but they too came from Grand Rapids.

Not all the early players remained in the game. After a few years, Haldane sold his shop in favor of a second career in real estate. The Pullman brothers, George M. and A. B., made custom furniture in Grand Rapids in the early 1850s. By 1855, they had moved to Chicago where they built an empire with their Pullman Palace passenger railcars.

The Grand Rapids map confirms the impact the industry had on the city. Streets are named for the companies and the men who made them great: Berkey, Davis, Gay, Hall, Hastings, Nelson, Richards, Sligh, Widdicomb. A college is named for designer David W. Kendall, and the downtown YMCA bears David D. Hunting's name.

One

The Early Years

Michigan already boasted a booming lumber industry. Perhaps seeing logs floating down the Grand River gave William "Deacon" Haldane the idea of opening a cabinet shop. Others had the same idea and soon factories dotted both sides of the river. Grand Rapids became Michigan's first one-industry town—decades before Henry Ford's horseless carriage made Detroit the second.

By 1858, the Detroit and Milwaukee Railroad reached the city, and factory owners were no longer limited to river and wagon train shipment. Their newfound ability to ship to New York, St. Louis, Cleveland, and Buffalo made Grand Rapids competitive with the better-known Chicago and Rockford, Illinois, manufacturers.

Waves of immigrants, most from the Netherlands, made up a reliable work pool, one with a strong Protestant work ethic. Company owners helped the newcomers assimilate by offering classes in citizenship and English. Some allowed weekly lunch-hour hymn sings for all who wished to participate.

Poles came too, along with Lithuanians and Germans, all thankful to have jobs in their adopted country. They repaid their employers with superior work and loyalty—sometimes staying with the same company until retirement. It was not unusual for their sons and daughters to go to work in the same factory.

But the immigrants did not just supply labor. Some were skilled carvers, craftsmen, and designers. Little by little, word got out that there was a wealth of talent in what most outsiders considered an unremarkable Michigan backwater.

Manufacturers held nothing back when preparing for the country's 1876 centennial exposition in Philadelphia. The larger companies exhibited their finest, and Grand Rapids walked away with all the major awards. Those awards brought world-wide recognition. Furniture City, USA, was off and running and would dominate the home furnishings industry until the mid-1900s.

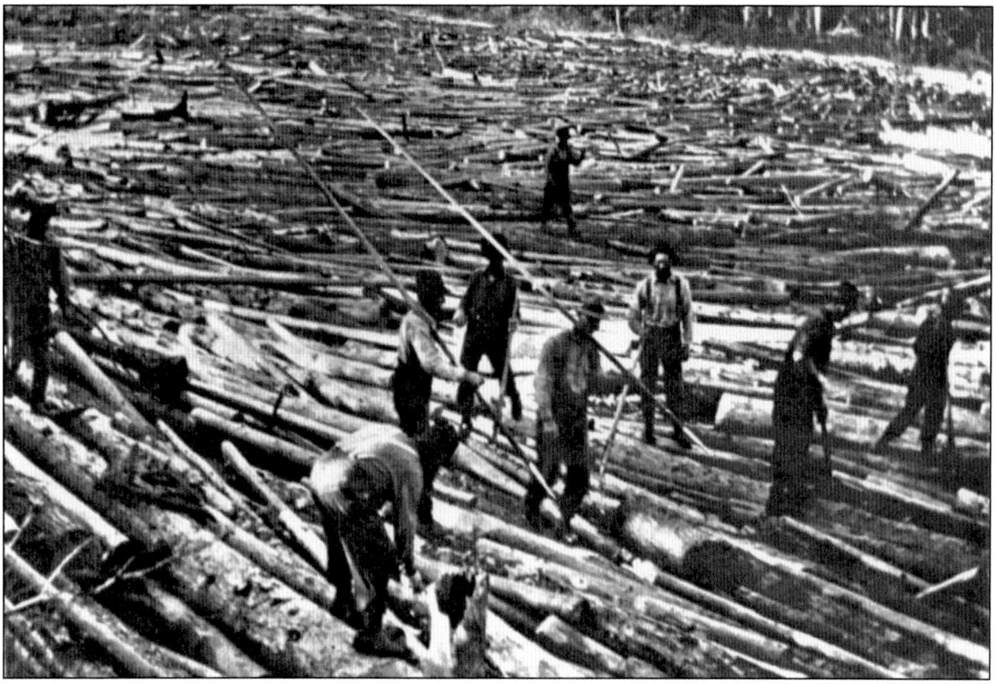

Men risked their lives in dangerous log drives long before the furniture factories appeared in Grand Rapids. With timber abundant here and throughout Michigan, scenes like this were common during the months the Grand River flowed ice-free. (Grand Rapids Public Library.)

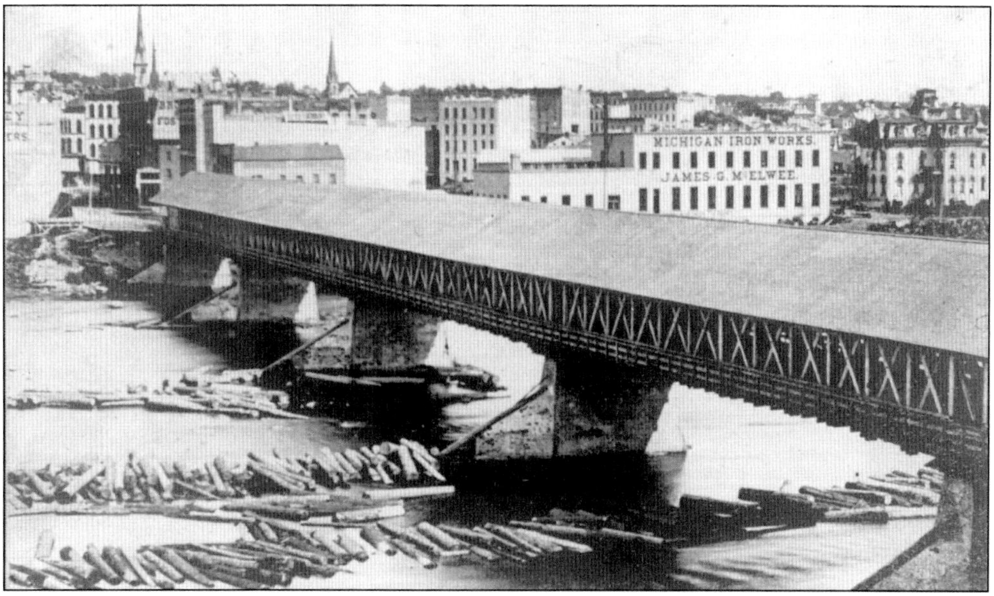

Grand Rapids began as a three-building trading post and did not incorporate as a city until 1850. In 1836, the combined population of the village and the township of Grand Rapids numbered less than 1,500. Every day lumberjacks floated logs down the Grand River to Grand Haven and, from there, Lake Michigan. It was only a matter of time until someone associated the logs with furniture. William "Deacon" Haldane was the first person to act on that association. (Grand Rapids Public Library.)

In 1836, cabinetmaker William "Deacon" Haldane opened a shop in his home on the southwest corner of Pearl Street and Ottawa Avenue. By the end of the year, he had so much work he had to relocate. At his new site, on the bank of the Grand River, he harnessed waterpower and had space to train apprentices. He earned his nickname by praying and reading the Bible with his employees at the start of each day. (Grand Rapids Public Library.)

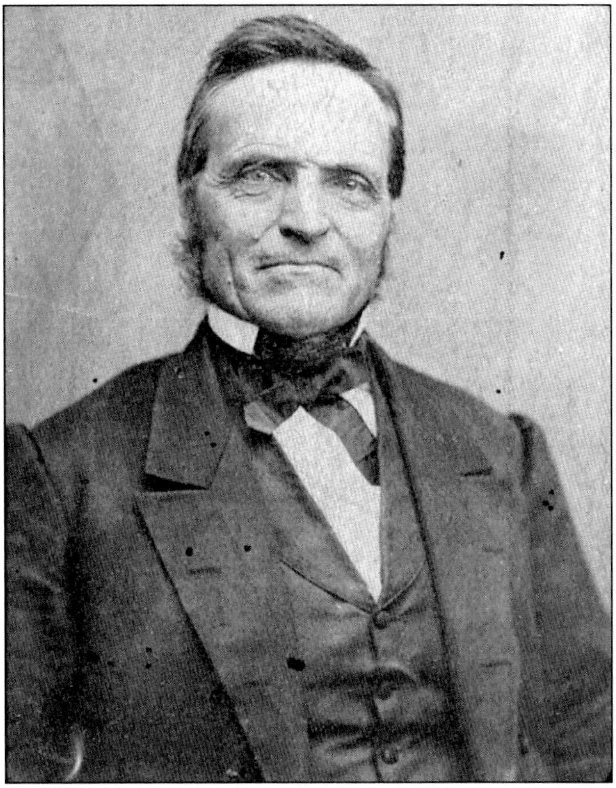

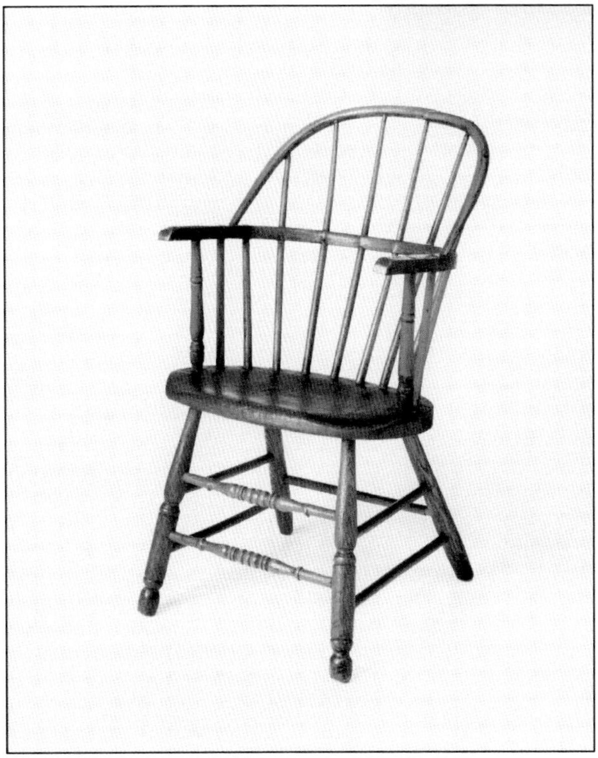

This hoop-back Windsor chair was one of Haldane's best sellers. He also offered beds, tables, cabinets, and coffins "a man would be proud to be buried in." Chairs started at $3; the coffins ran as high as $7. Others, spurred by his success, began making furniture, and the industry that would put Grand Rapids on the map had begun. (Collections of the Public Museum, Grand Rapids.)

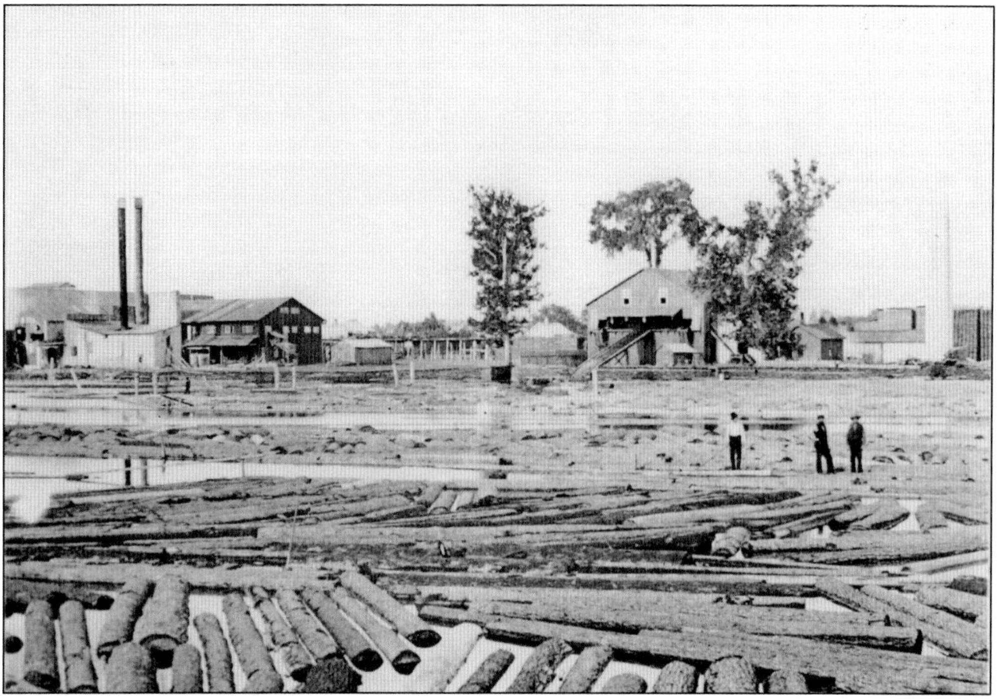

In 1870, this lumberyard stood where the Grand Rapids Water Filtration Plant was later built, on Monroe Avenue between Michigan and Leonard Streets. The constant demand kept them all busy. (Grand Rapids Public Library.)

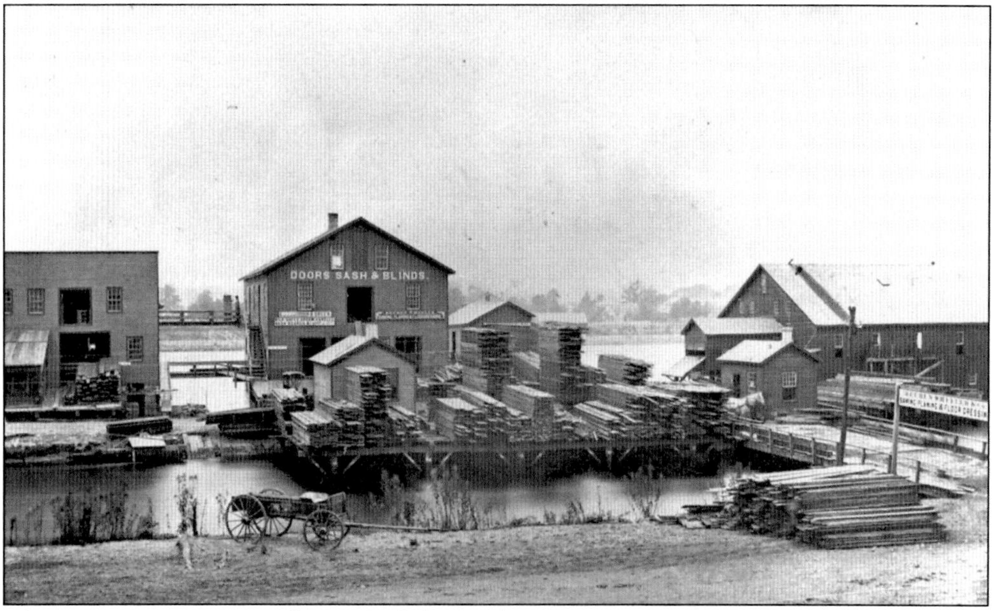

The city's numerous sawmills supplied the lumber needs for the furniture companies and for smaller operators like Rueben Wheeler, who provided doors, sashes, and blinds on the west bank of the Grand River. But nothing lasts forever, and as logging in the state lessened, the number of sawmills decreased as well. This photograph was taken around 1870. (Grand Rapids Public Library.)

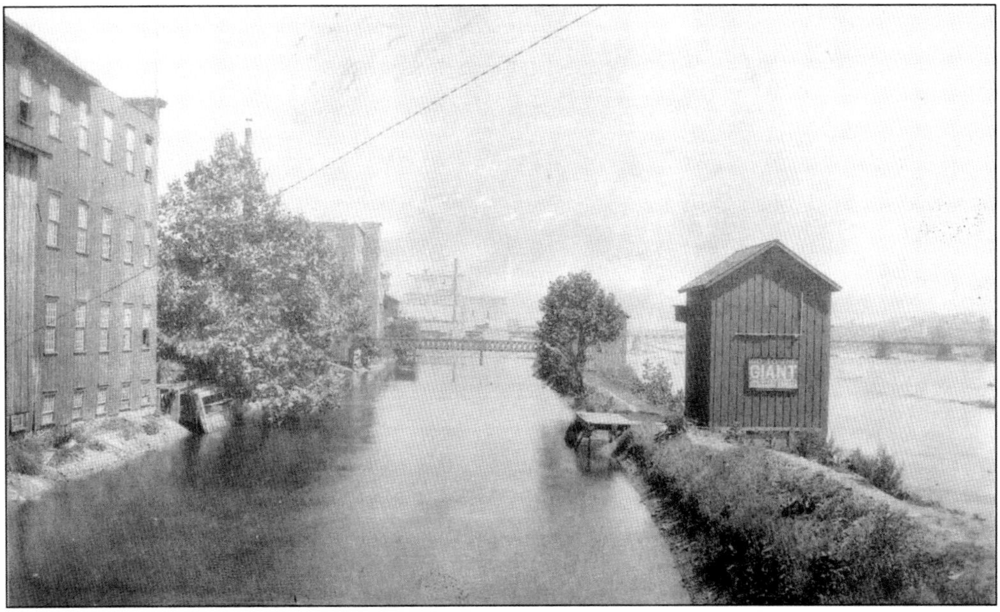

Factory owners began building these canals in 1842 to carry water along each side of the river above the rapids. Water ran through millraces placed between the canals and the river. When it fell to the river's level below the rapids, it powered machinery inside the factories. The canals were completed in 1867. (Collections of the Public Museum, Grand Rapids.)

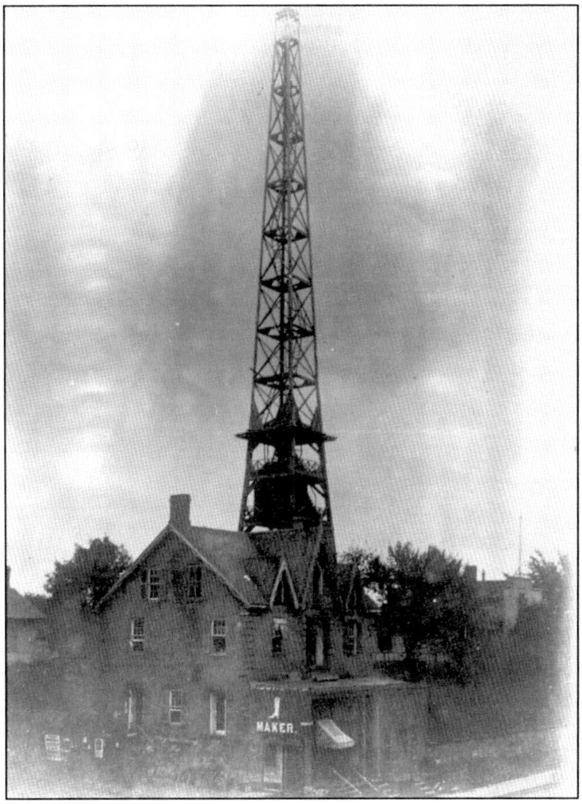

The city bought William "Deacon" Haldane's Pearl Street house in 1872 and used it as offices for the departments of justice and waterworks. The tower was added in 1878 and held a bell that served as a fire alarm. In 1890, the house was demolished. (Grand Rapids Public Library.)

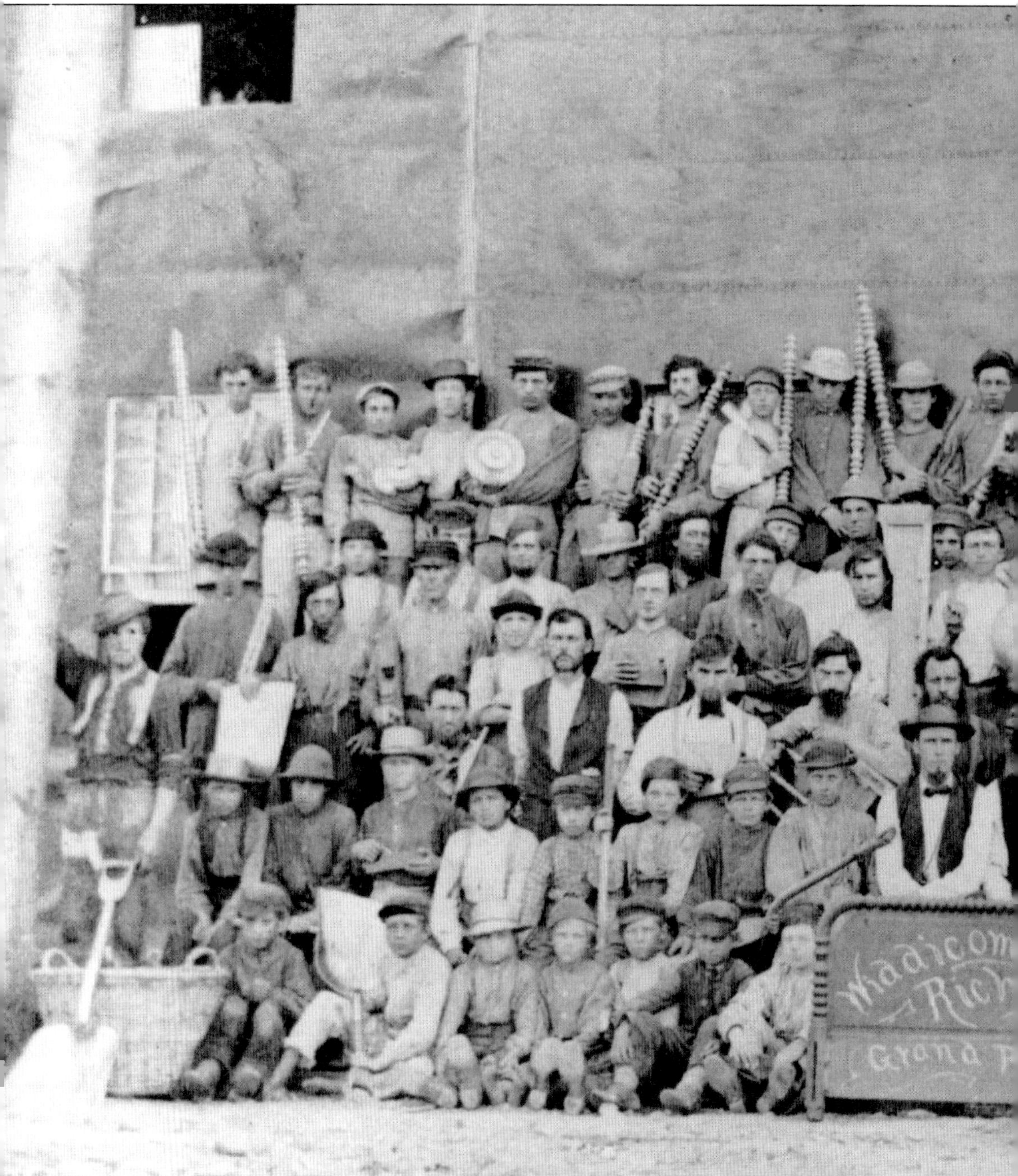

John, Harry, and William Widdicomb are pictured from left to right in the first row, center, with their factory employees in 1871. Part of the image's charm is that many workers are holding the pieces they were working on when called outside to pose. The company name is painted on a headboard. Furniture makers took great pride in their products and worked 10 hours a day,

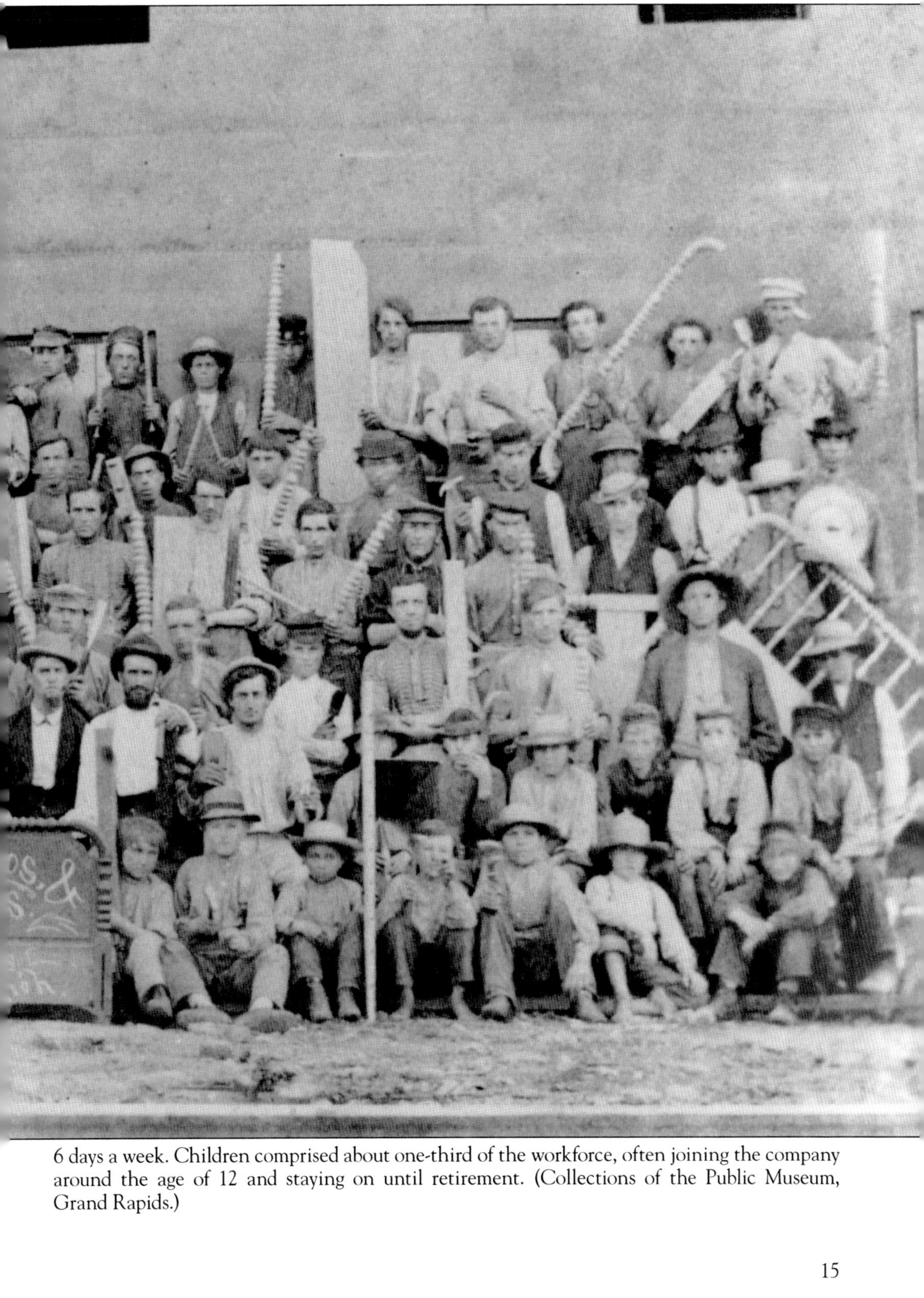

6 days a week. Children comprised about one-third of the workforce, often joining the company around the age of 12 and staying on until retirement. (Collections of the Public Museum, Grand Rapids.)

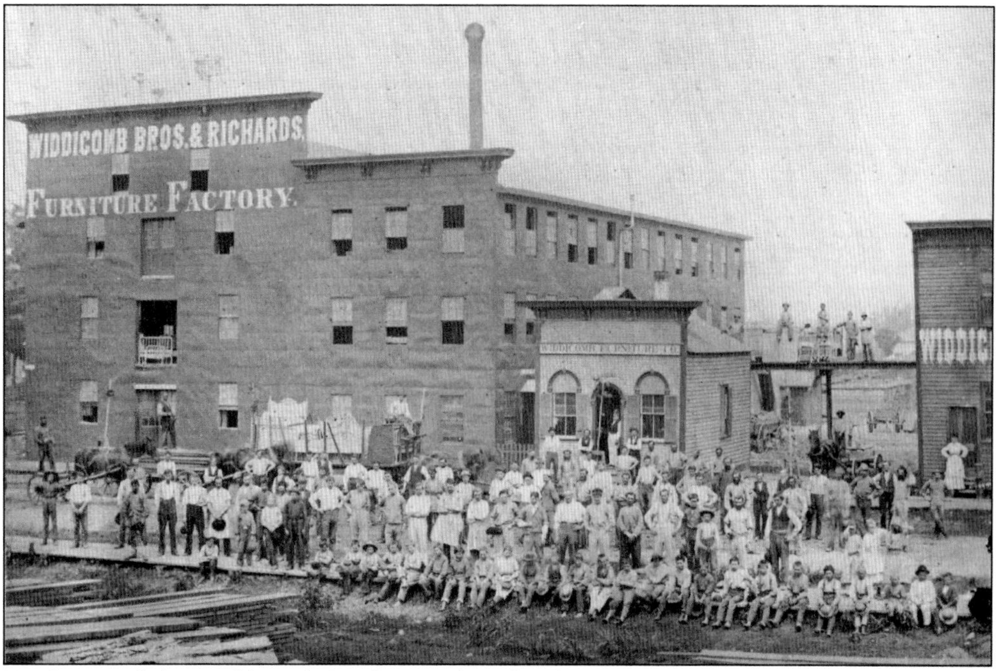

Employees of the Widdicomb Brothers and Richards Furniture Factory located at 436 West Leonard Street pose with a few pieces of furniture and a company horse. The company existed from 1869 to 1873, then dropped Richards from the corporate name. Here too one-third of the workers are children. Today the Widdicomb brand is produced and sold by the Stickley Company in Manlius, New York. (Grand Rapids Public Library.)

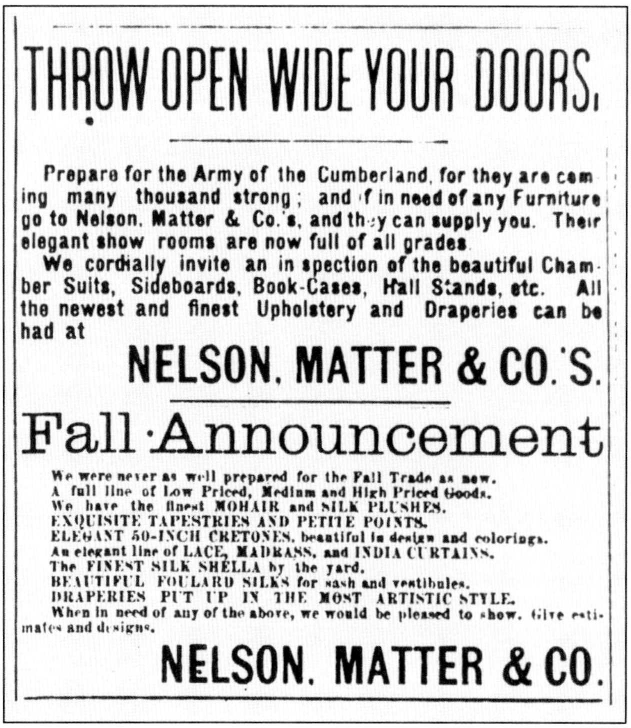

THROW OPEN WIDE YOUR DOORS.

Prepare for the Army of the Cumberland, for they are coming many thousand strong; and if in need of any Furniture go to Nelson, Matter & Co.'s, and they can supply you. Their elegant show rooms are now full of all grades.

We cordially invite an inspection of the beautiful Chamber Suits, Sideboards, Book-Cases, Hall Stands, etc. All the newest and finest Upholstery and Draperies can be had at

NELSON, MATTER & CO.'S.

Fall Announcement

We were never as well prepared for the Fall Trade as now.
A full line of Low Priced, Medium and High Priced Goods.
We have the finest MOHAIR and SILK PLUSHES.
EXQUISITE TAPESTRIES AND PETITE POINTS.
ELEGANT 50-INCH CRETONES, beautiful in design and colorings.
An elegant line of LACE, MADRASS, and INDIA CURTAINS.
The FINEST SILK SHELLA by the yard.
BEAUTIFUL FOULARD SILKS for sash and vestibules.
DRAPERIES PUT UP IN THE MOST ARTISTIC STYLE.
When in need of any of the above, we would be pleased to show. Give estimates and designs.

NELSON, MATTER & CO.

Nelson Matter and Company posted this newspaper advertisement to acknowledge the homecoming of the Kent County soldiers who fought in Cumberland during the Civil War. (Grand Rapids Public Library.)

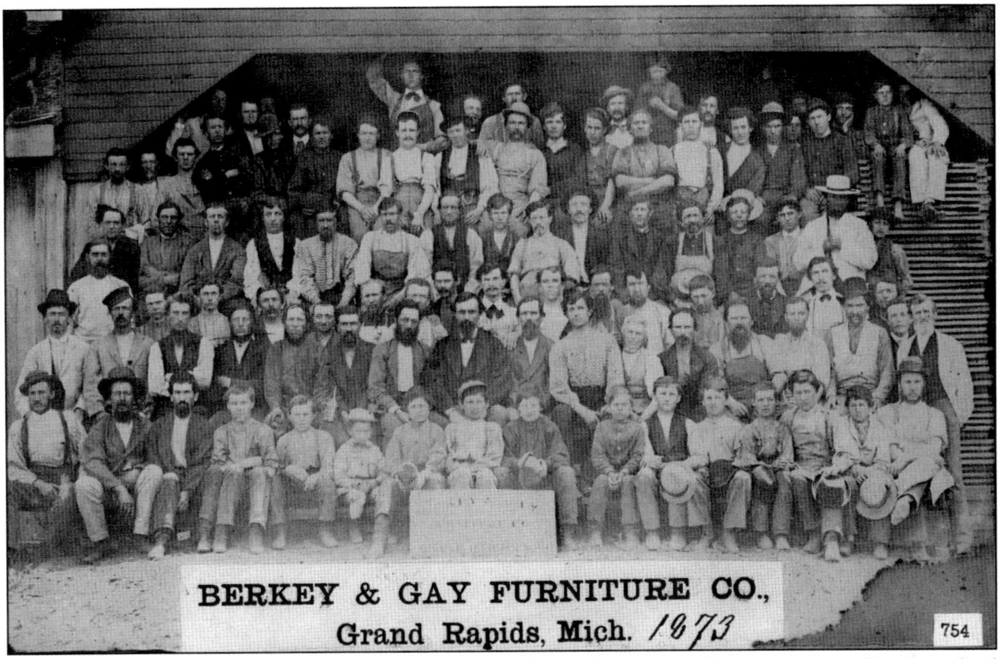

This group of factory workers from the Berkey and Gay Furniture Company was photographed in 1873. Like Widdicomb, the company was one of the early industry stalwarts. (Collections of the Public Museum, Grand Rapids.)

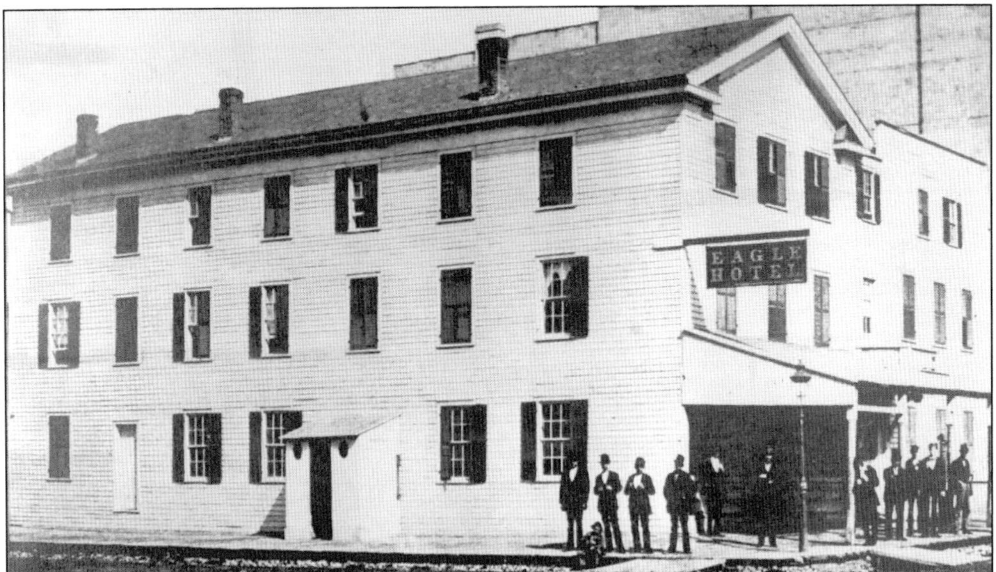

The Eagle Hotel, built in 1834, was the city's first. The need for hotel rooms rose significantly when the growing furniture industry began hosting markets. By 1928, 6,000 buyers descended upon the city, all needing a place to sleep. The city planned no other events during these conventions, and hotels reserved all their rooms for the hordes of buyers. Along with the popular Pantlind Hotel and the Morton House, lesser-known establishments also hosted the twice-annual visitors. Among those was the Cody Hotel owned by Darwin Cody. Darwin's famous cousin "Buffalo Bill" Cody visited frequently. (Grand Rapids Public Library.)

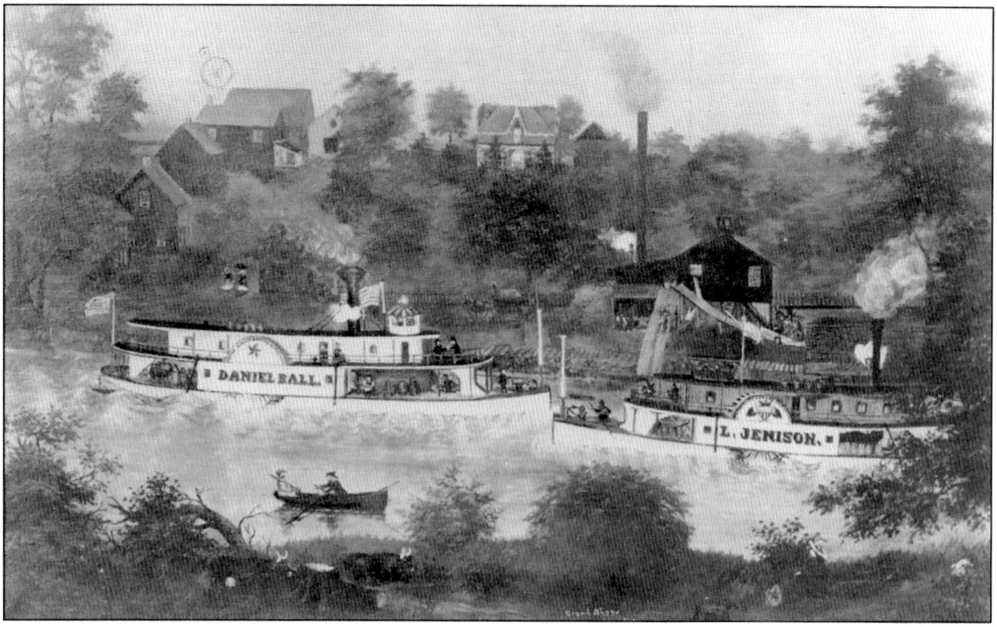

A Grand Rapids side-wheeler, the *Daniel Ball* was photographed near Wealthy Street in 1861. Wealthy Street marked one of the original city borders when incorporated in 1850. Until the railroad came in 1858, riverboats were the only way to ship furniture to Grand Haven, where it would then be ferried across Lake Michigan. (Grand Rapids Public Library.)

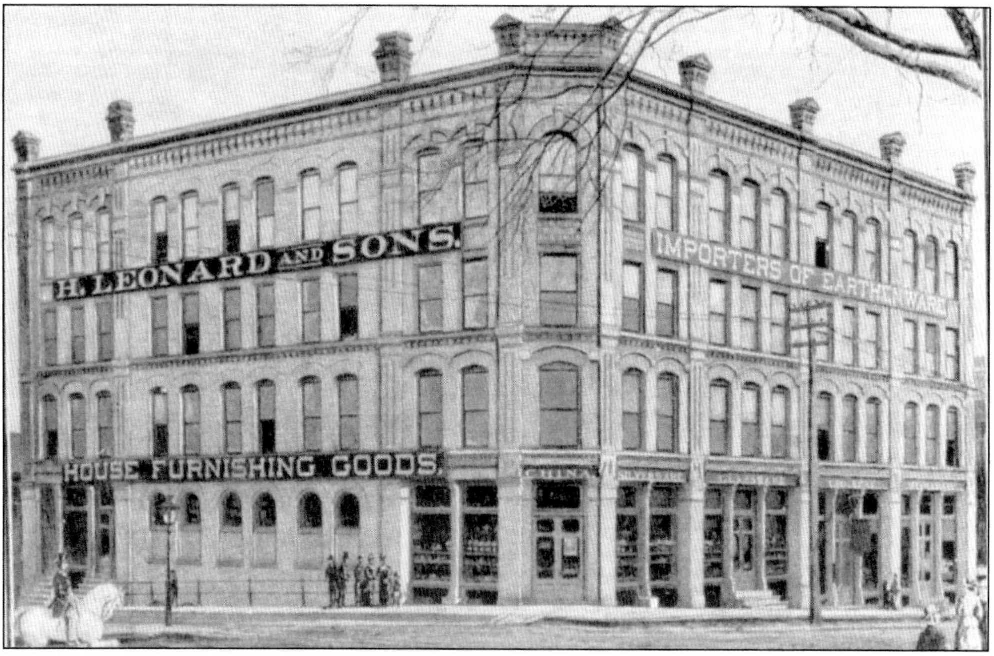

Retailers H. Leonard and Sons sold house furnishing goods on the corner of Fulton and Spring Streets. The city that made the goods also needed retail establishments to serve local residents. The company opened in the 1860s. Although undated, the men's top hats, along with the high-stepping white horse and absence of automobiles, place this early in the city's history. (Grand Rapids Public Library.)

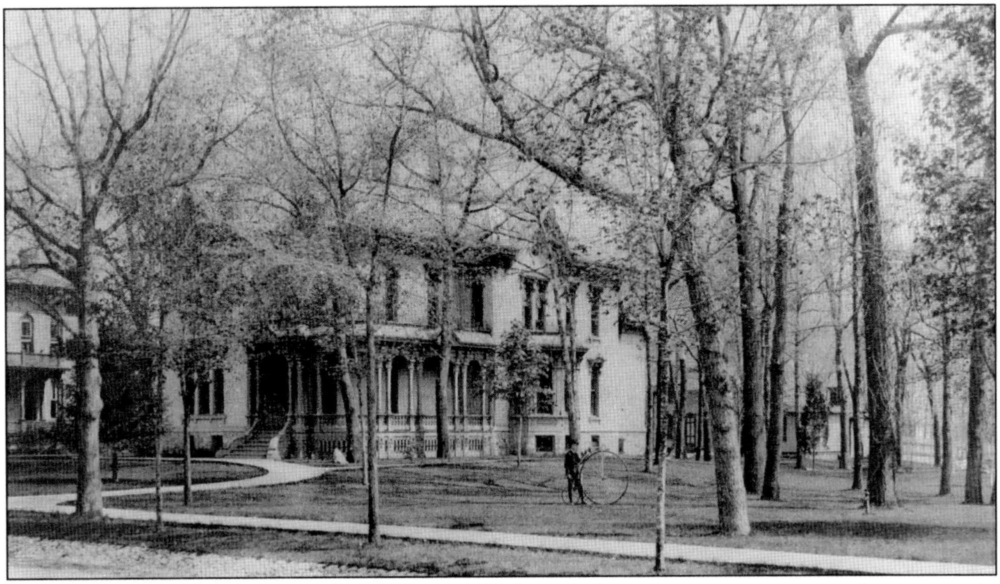

Furniture made some men rich. William Widdicomb built his mansion near downtown in the Hill District. Now called the Heritage Hill neighborhood, it includes the late president Gerald R. Ford's boyhood home. The Widdicomb residence was at 260 Fountain Street. William Widdicomb Jr. built at 248 Fountain. The neighborhood was convenient to the factories and attracted other owners as well. An unidentified young man shows off his high-wheeler bicycle. (Grand Rapids Public Library.)

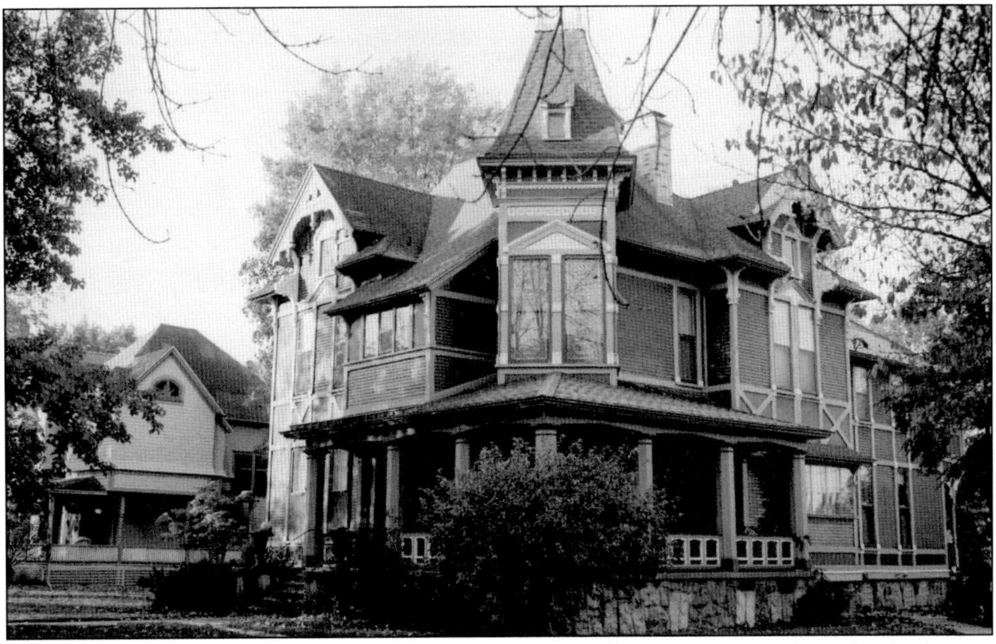

Austin E. Stockwell and his wife, Myra, also built in the Hill District. He was first a lumber baron, then furniture entrepreneur. His 515 Madison Avenue Southeast home is stick style/Eastlake and was built in 1882. The style is defined by the "sticks" of the false structural members. Its angled tower, hipped roof, and dormers give it further character. The house's exterior appearance remains unchanged. (Norma Lewis.)

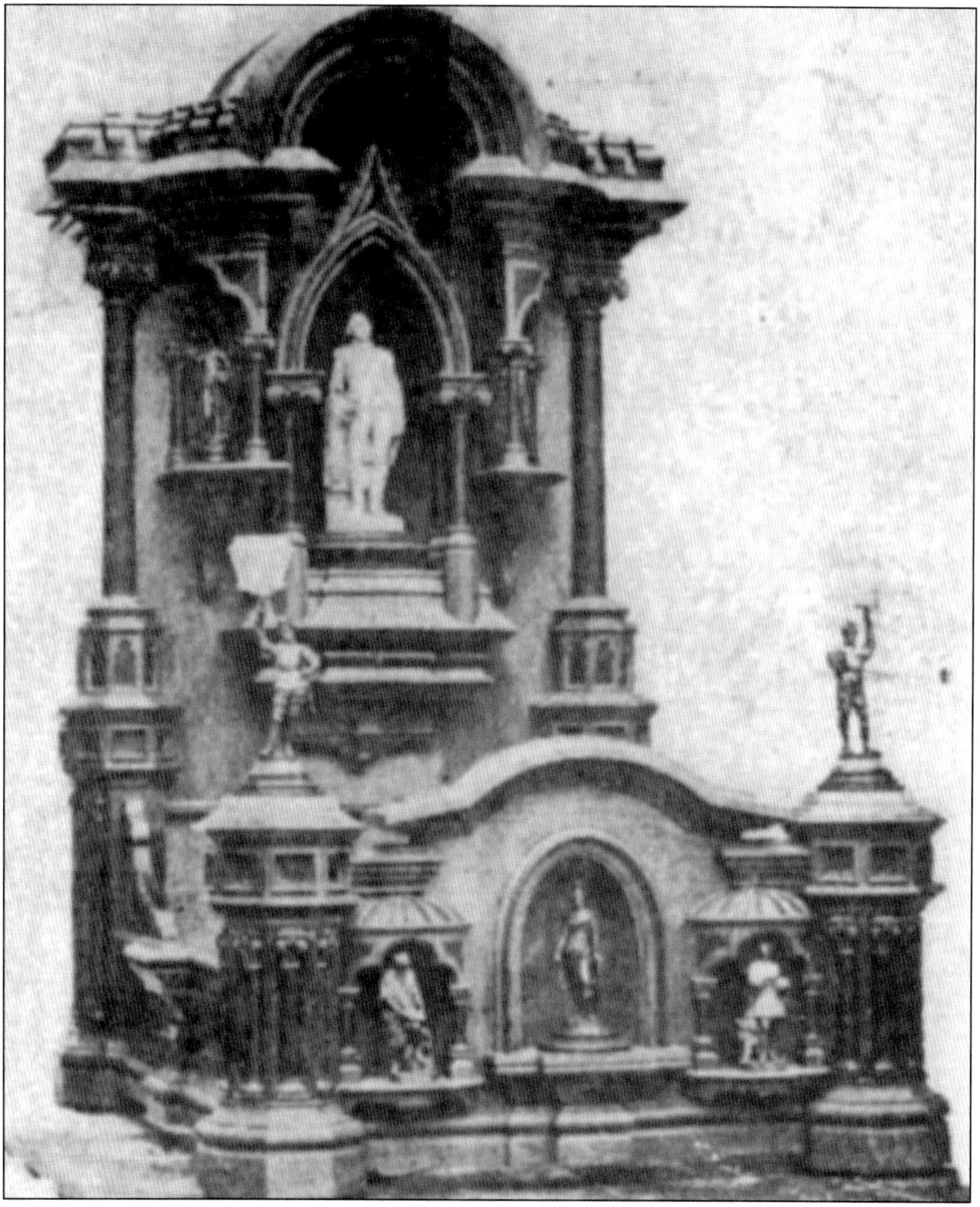

When America celebrated its first 100 years at the 1876 Philadelphia Centennial Exposition, this bed proved conclusively that Grand Rapids was the country's furniture-making capital. Although other local companies also displayed award-winning pieces, the showstopper was made by the Nelson Matter and Company. This ostentatious bed and its matching dressing table were made of more than 6,000 pieces of walnut, ebony, onyx, and tulipwood. Niches held exquisitely carved figures of George Washington, Thomas Jefferson, and other patriots. It took the $10,000 prize, but more important, all who saw it became aware of the capabilities of the factories in the city from which it came. Other photographs show a life-size bald eagle perched atop both pieces but lack the finials. The behemoths must have been shipped in separate pieces, assembled on site, and photographed at various stages. (Grand Rapids Public Library.)

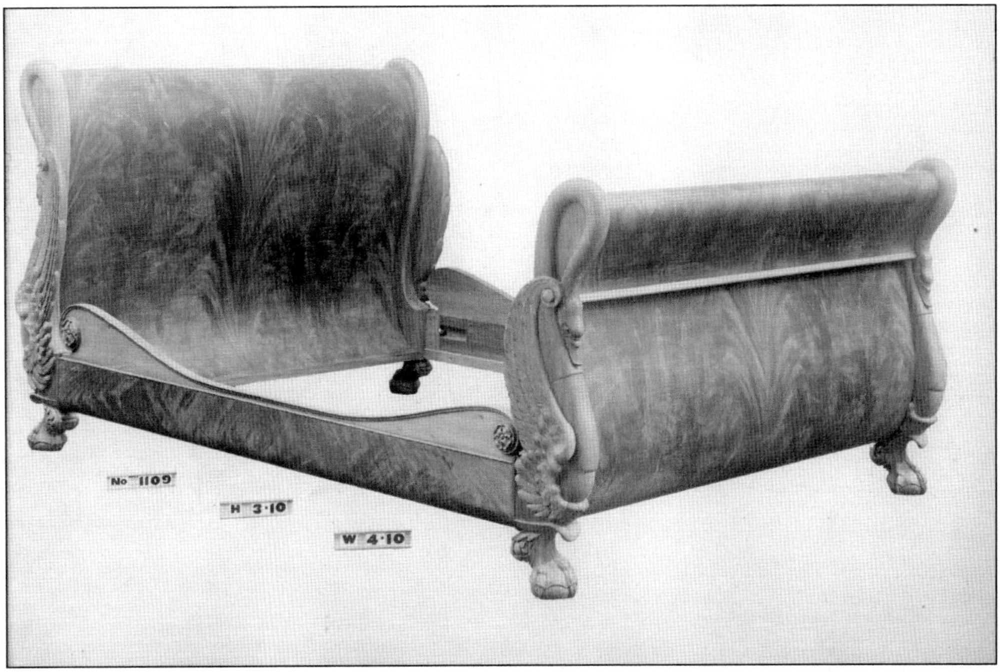

The bed on the preceding page may be what Nelson Matter took to Philadelphia, but there was little market for that much splendor. This photograph represents what it offered for sale. A catalog of that year lists its bedroom suites as ranging in price from $25 to $500. (Grand Rapids Public Library.)

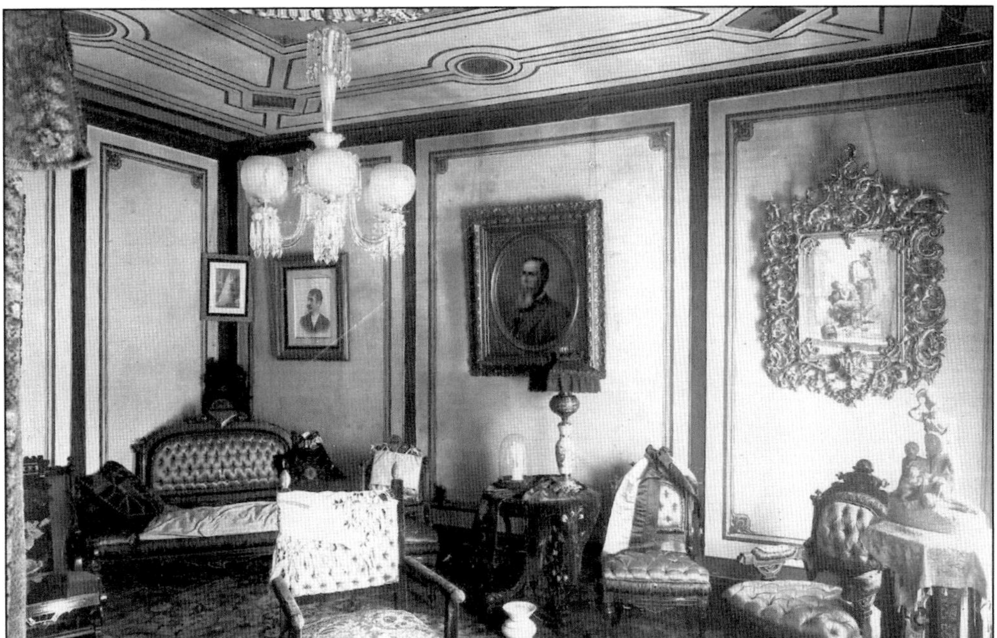

The Berkey and Gay Furniture Company displayed these parlor pieces at the 1876 centennial. Here, a few years later, they are proudly displayed in the home of the William Hoke family. (Collections of the Public Museum, Grand Rapids.)

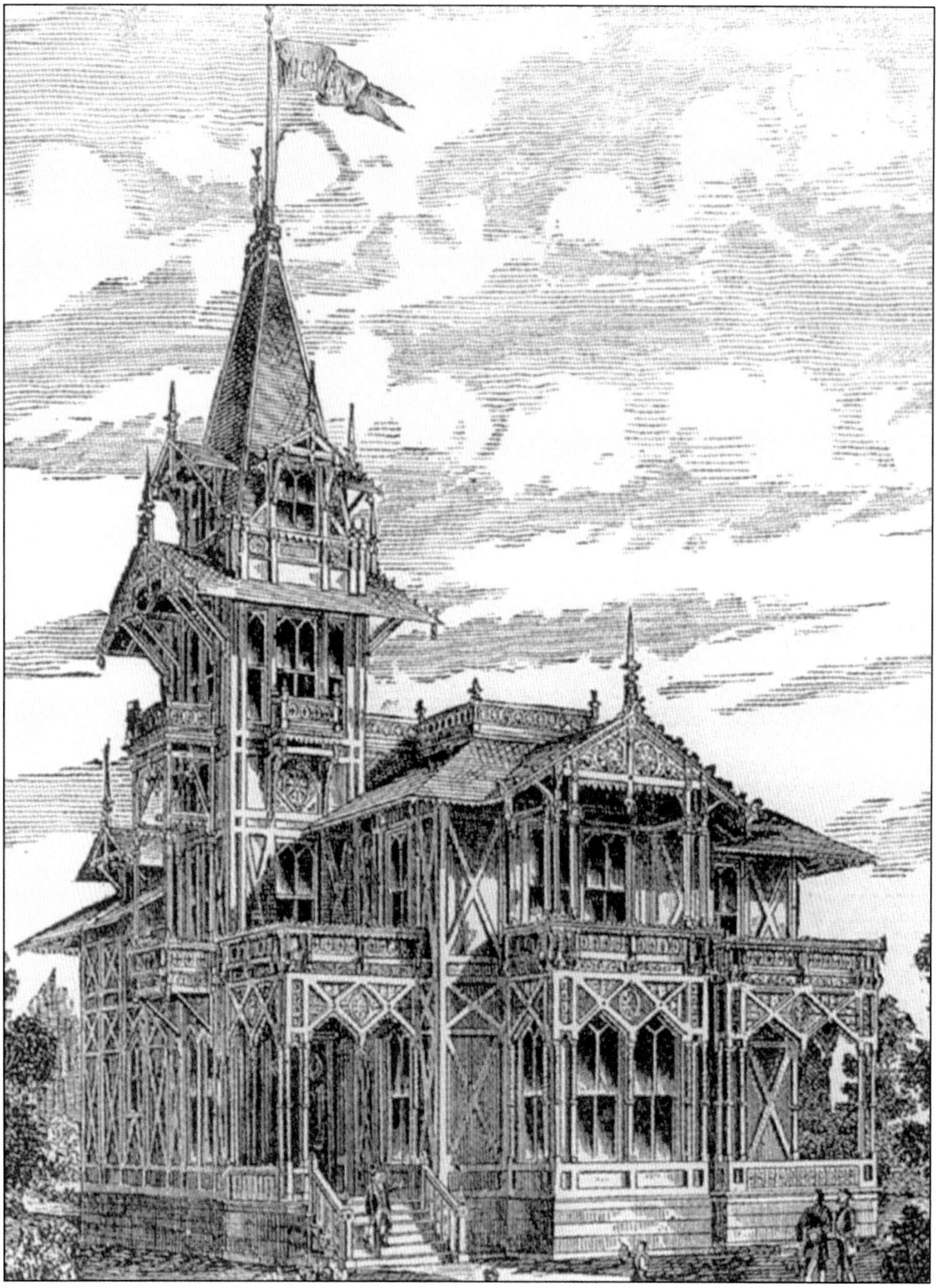

The Michigan Building shown above was where many of the local furniture companies displayed their wares in Philadelphia. The Gothic building was reported to have been visited by more than 30,000 Michigan residents alone. Gypsum paneling was used on the interior. Among Berkey and Gay's offerings was a parlor organ and suites complete with draperies. By 1884, when the World's Industrial and Cotton Centennial Exposition opened in New Orleans, 20 local furniture companies built their own pavilion. Grand Rapids was the only city to have a separate furniture building, again enhancing the local reputation with buyers nationwide. (Grand Rapids Public Library.)

Two

The Glory Years

The golden age of Grand Rapids home furnishings is generally said to be from 1870 to 1930. Those were the years the semiannual markets brought thousands of buyers to the city. Additional hotels and exhibition halls were built to accommodate the rising demand.

More than one-third of the city's workers were employed either in the factories or in furniture-support companies. Peripheral industries included the production of springs for mattresses, chairs, and sofas; brass hardware for drawer pulls and ornamentation; and lacquers, shellacs, and waxes for smooth, shiny surfaces. Independent designers and carvers set up shop. Lumber mills boomed, and woodworking machinery companies flourished.

Grand Rapids offerings were held in such high regard that manufacturers in other states began advertising "Grand Rapids style" pieces. A company in Grand Rapids, Minnesota, neglected to mention *Minnesota* in its advertisements. A lawsuit ended those practices.

Although 1870–1930 defines the glory years, in reality many of the companies hung on through the 1950s and 1960s, some even longer. Baker Furniture Company and Hekman Furniture Company remained in Grand Rapids until the beginning of the 21st century, although the Hekman company had a factory in Lexington, North Carolina, by the late 1960s. Sligh still has its headquarters in Holland, Michigan, but all the manufacturing is done in Asia. Today only Kindel remains in Grand Rapids serving a worldwide niche market that demands the best and is willing to pay for it.

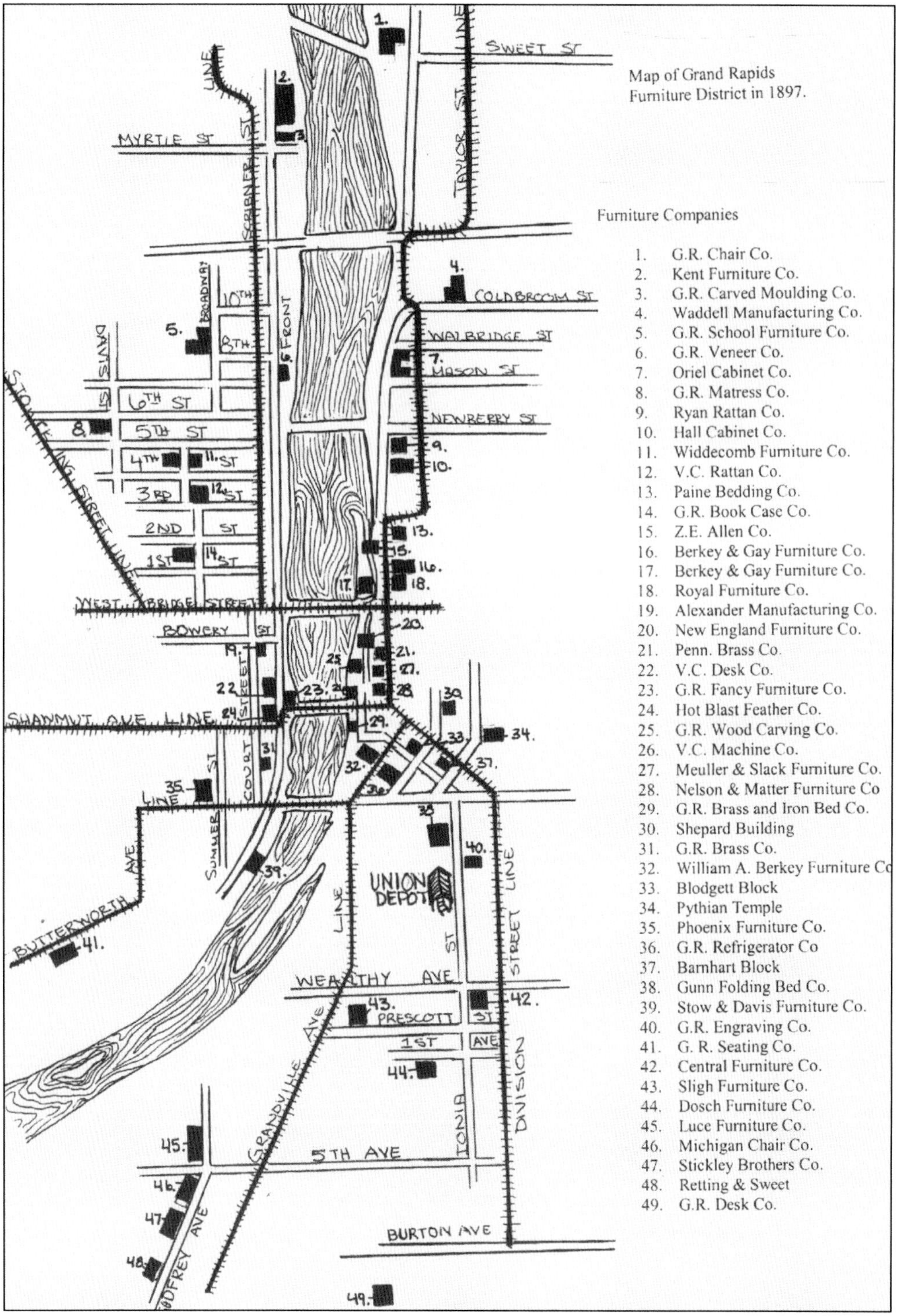

This map shows the concentration of the Grand Rapids furniture district in 1897. Manufacturers, industry suppliers, and exhibit buildings line both sides of the Grand River, although by then the railroad made it possible for newer companies to locate elsewhere in the city. (Jillian Berry.)

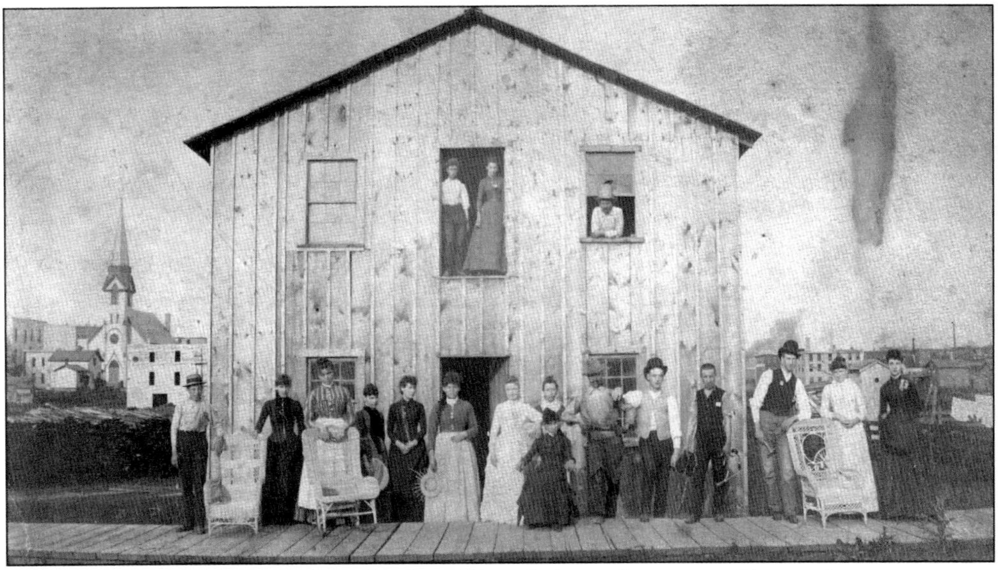

Although the industry giants brought Grand Rapids fame, there was still room for entrepreneurs like John W. Lawrence, who opened a small factory and specialized in wicker products like these chairs. While some Lawrence employees line up outside, others pose playfully in the windows in this 1896 photograph. (Grand Rapids Public Library.)

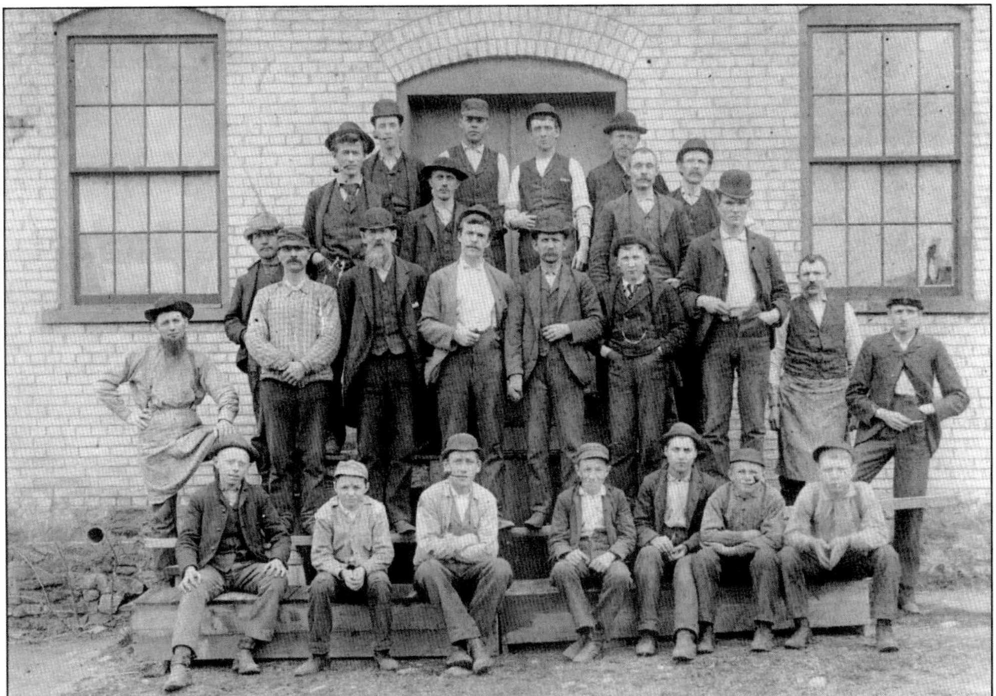

Grand Rapids Fancy Furniture Company workers pose in the late 1800s. One of the smaller manufacturers, the company produced oak and mahogany desks, bookcases, tables, and benches. About one-third of the employees were teenage boys. The products reflected mission and revival styles. In 1940, the company was sold to Metal Office Furniture Company, which in turn became office furniture giant Steelcase, Inc. (Collections of the Public Museum, Grand Rapids.)

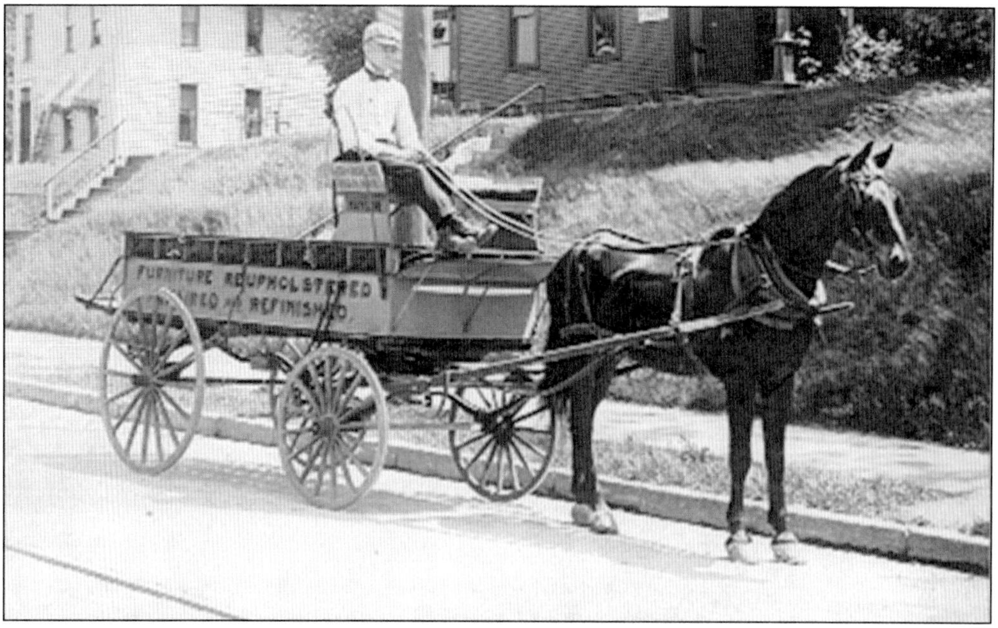

By the time this photograph was taken in 1900, about one-third of the city's population worked in the industry. Larger companies created opportunities for entrepreneurs like Samuel J. Naylor to start their own industry-support businesses. Naylor, proprietor of Naylor's Upholstery Company, was assisted by his son, Leonard, shown here driving the company's horse-drawn delivery wagon. (Grand Rapids Public Library.)

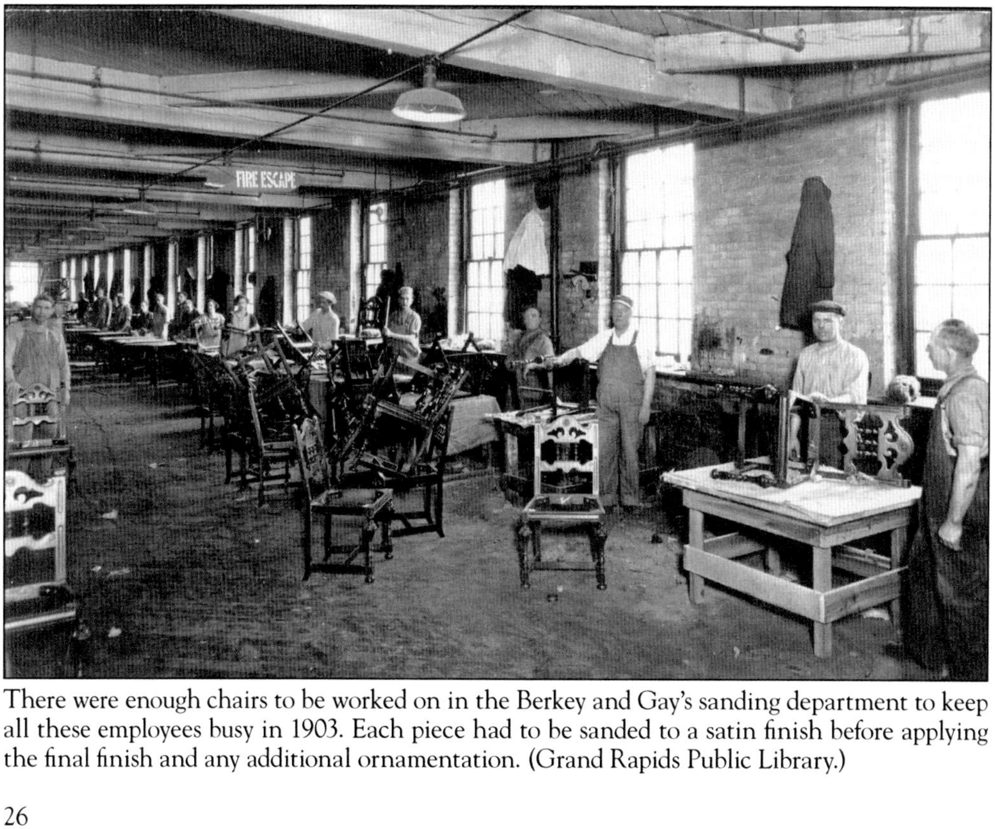

There were enough chairs to be worked on in the Berkey and Gay's sanding department to keep all these employees busy in 1903. Each piece had to be sanded to a satin finish before applying the final finish and any additional ornamentation. (Grand Rapids Public Library.)

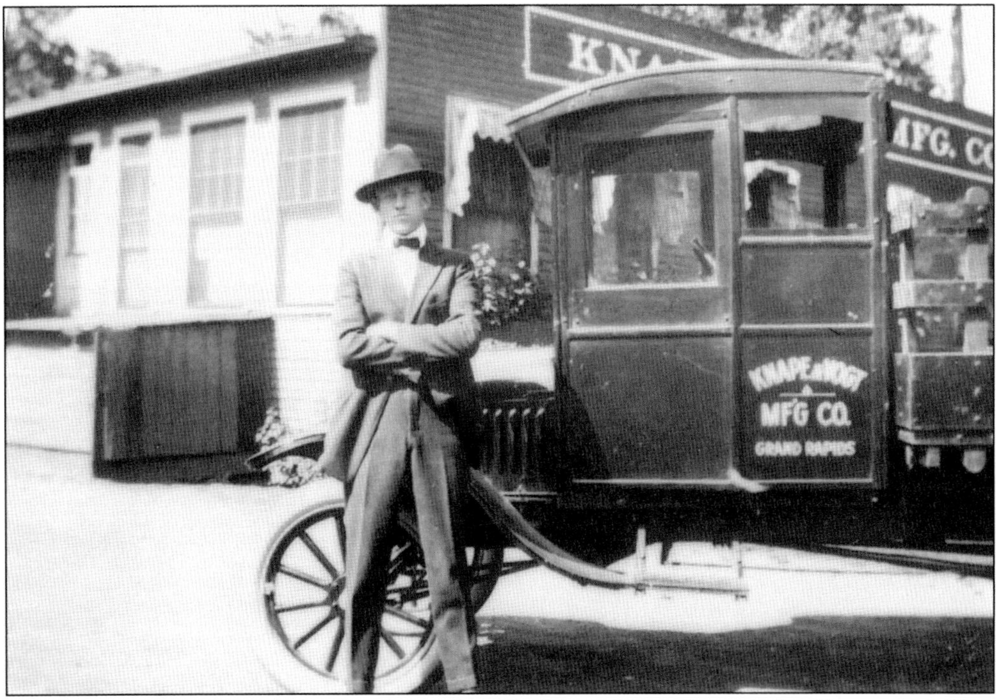

John Knape (above), with his brother-in-law Englebert Vogt, formed the Knape and Vogt company in 1898. They made a good team. Knape provided the engineering know-how and Vogt the business savvy. Their company has remained in continuous operation in Grand Rapids although their product line changed from their initial offering, bicycles, to drawer slides, clothing racks, and other hardware items for the furniture industry. Dedicated employees like the ones in the photograph below helped build the company's success. In the years leading up to World War II, the company focused on shell casings and bayonet clips, as well as fuselage ribs for the Boeing Flying Fortress. (Knape and Vogt.)

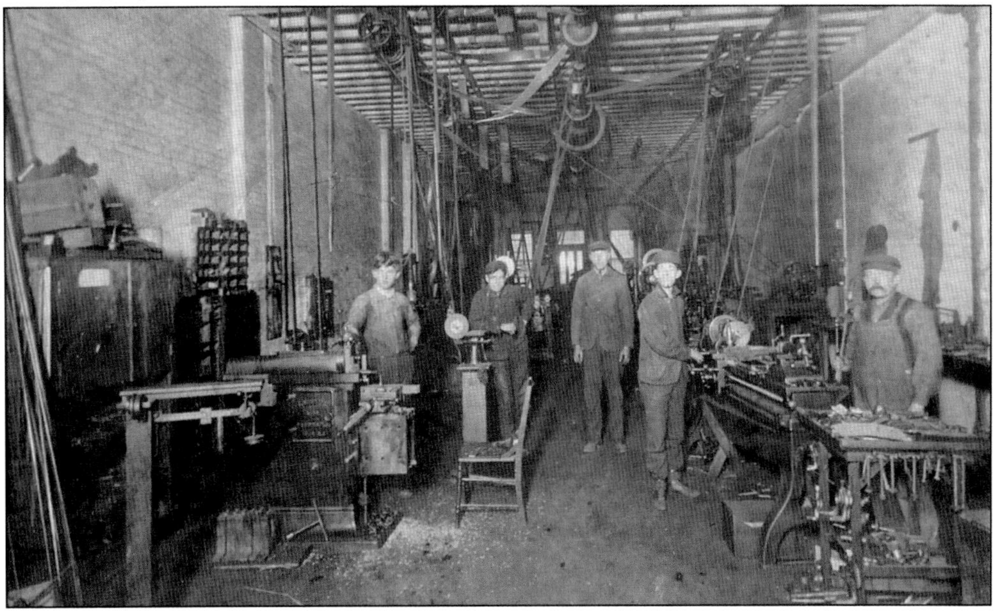

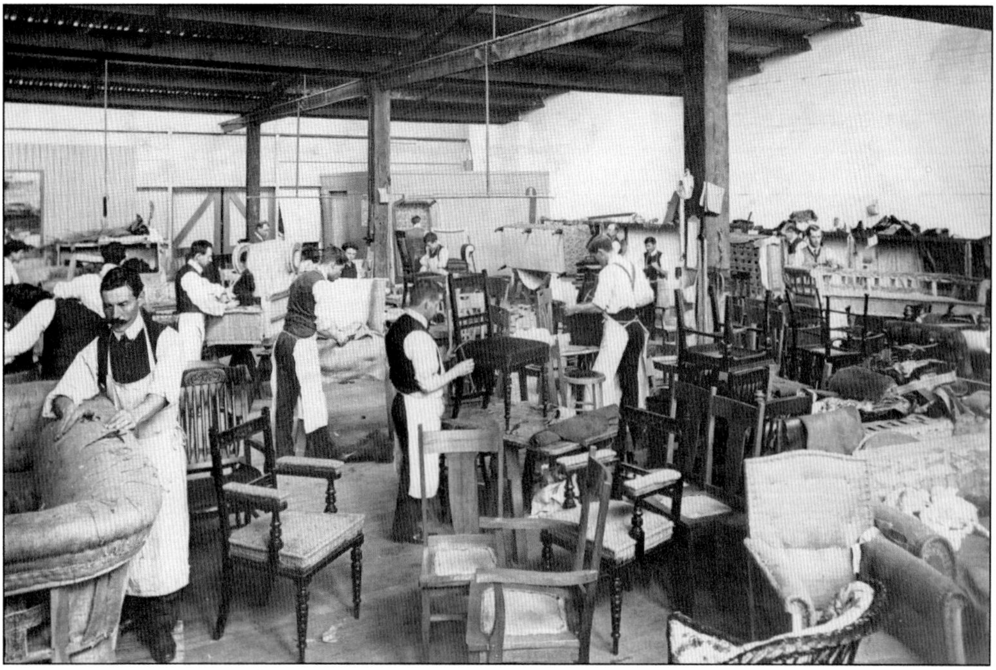

Upholsterers were called spitters because they held tacks in their mouths and spit them at magnetic hammers, then pounded them into the sofa or chair. When the worker occasionally swallowed a tack, he quickly swallowed a small amount of upholstery batting to lessen the risk of internal damage. This upholstery room is at the Century Furniture Company, around 1903. (Collections of the Public Museum, Grand Rapids.)

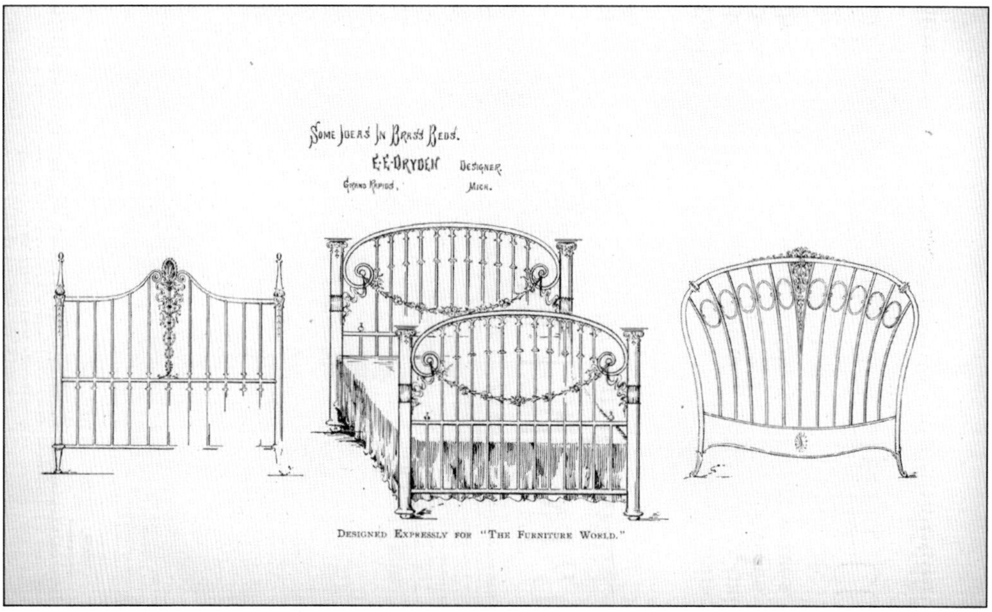

Furniture designer E. E. Dryden came up with these three brass beds expressly for the March 25, 1897, issue of the *Furniture World* trade magazine. The airy, open headboards must have been welcomed by those who sought a change from the usual heavy, carved wood offerings. (Grand Rapids Public Library.)

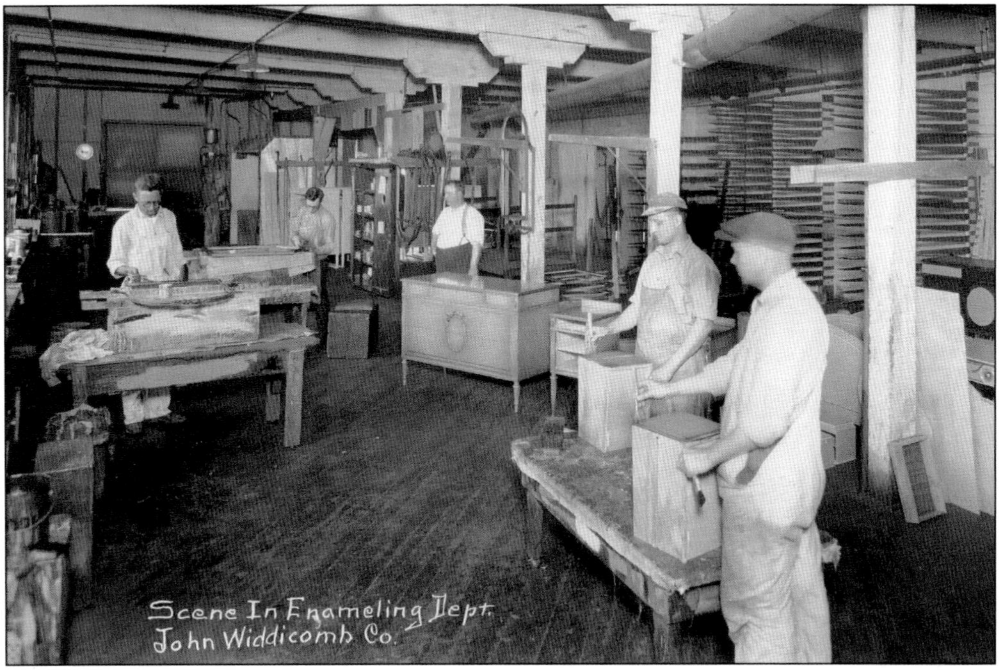

Fine furniture like the pieces produced by the John Widdicomb Company were labor intensive, and many functions still had to be done by hand as shown in these photographs depicting the rubbing and enameling departments, around 1904. A smooth-as-satin surface required hands-on application, and each piece received meticulous attention to detail. Employees took great pride in turning out the highest-quality work possible, thereby insuring these bedroom pieces would last through generations of proud owners, a far cry from today's throwaway society. Not surprisingly, some furnishings remain in the families that first purchased them. (Grand Rapids Public Library.)

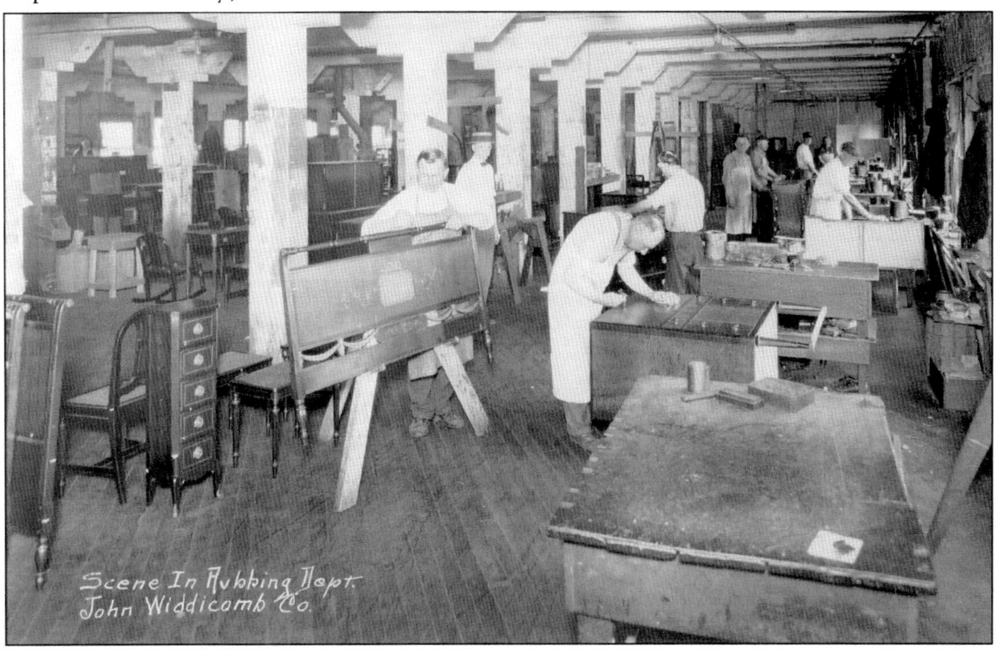

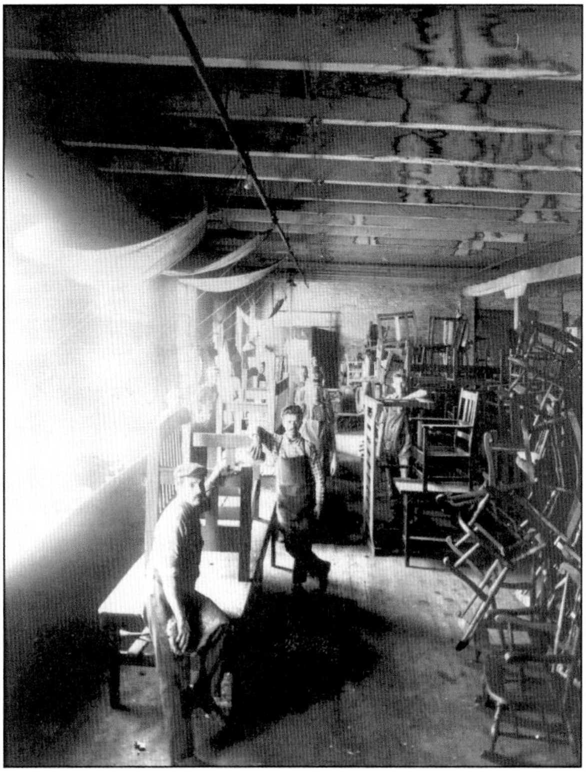

Gustav Stickley may be the name most often associated with the arts and crafts style, but his brothers Albert and John George also left their mark on the furniture industry. They founded the Stickley Brothers Furniture Company in Grand Rapids in 1891. This photograph of their factory interior, taken around 1905, shows the mission-style chairs still coveted by collectors. John George left the city in 1900, but Albert ran the company until his death in 1928. Two other brothers were also in the business. Charles and Leopold made Stickley a name to be reckoned with both here and in New York. (Grand Rapids Public Library.)

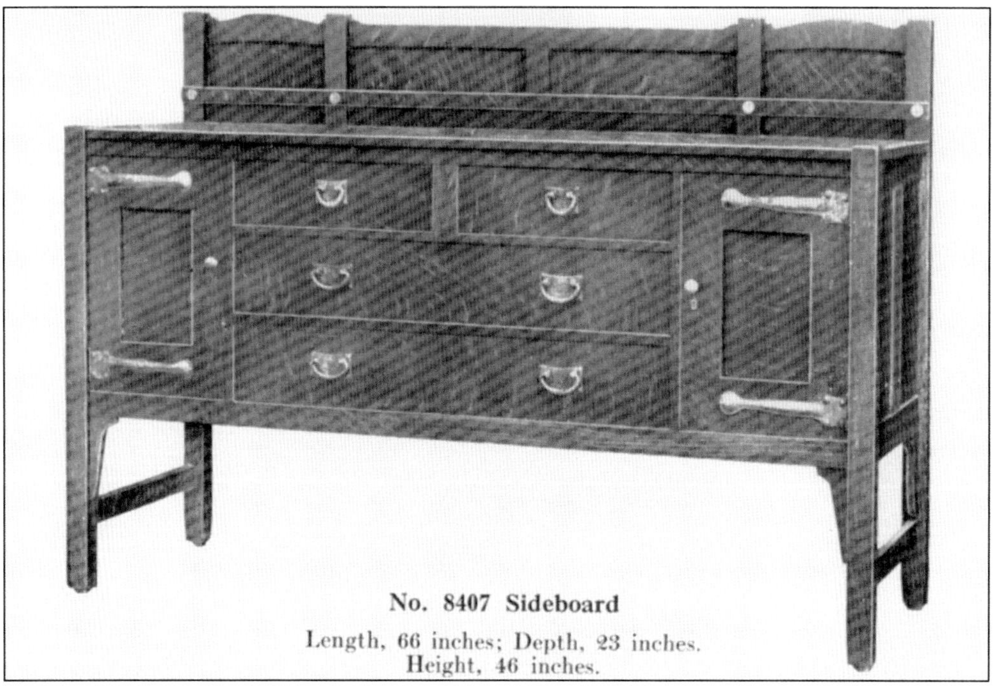

Stickley Brothers specialized in mission and in arts and crafts styles. Those lines blurred when it merged the styles into the Stickley/Quaint line. This sideboard, with its clean lines, is a prime example of the enduring style. (Grand Rapids Public Library.)

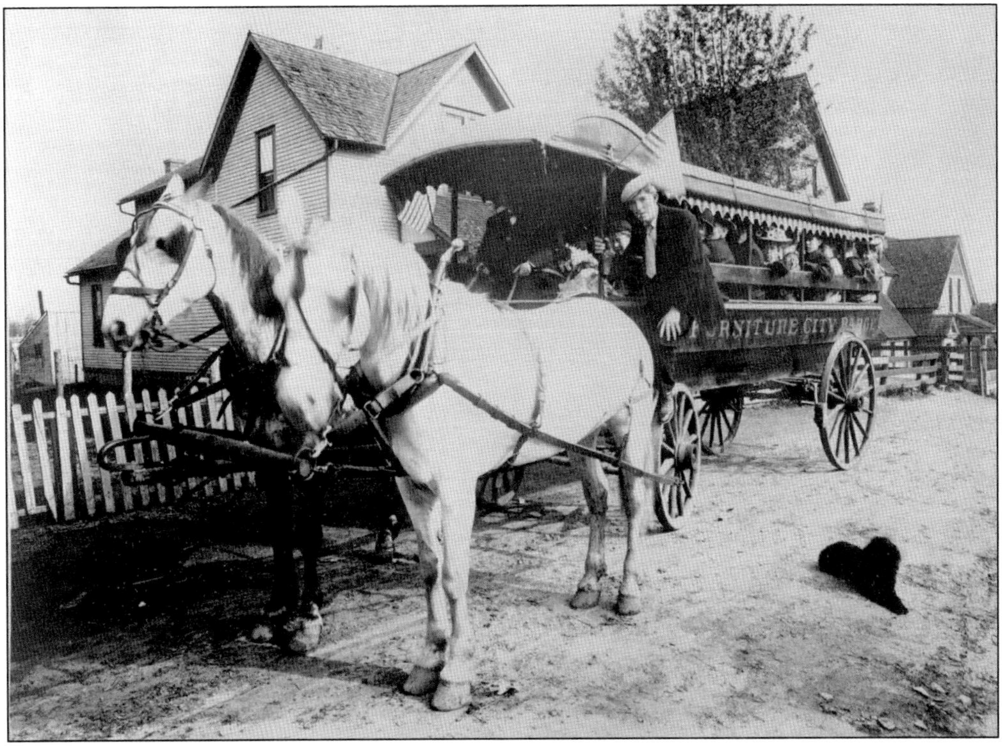

Everyone wanted to be identified with the growing fame of Grand Rapids as Furniture City. This horse-drawn passenger conveyance is named the Furniture City Barge. (Grand Rapids Public Library.)

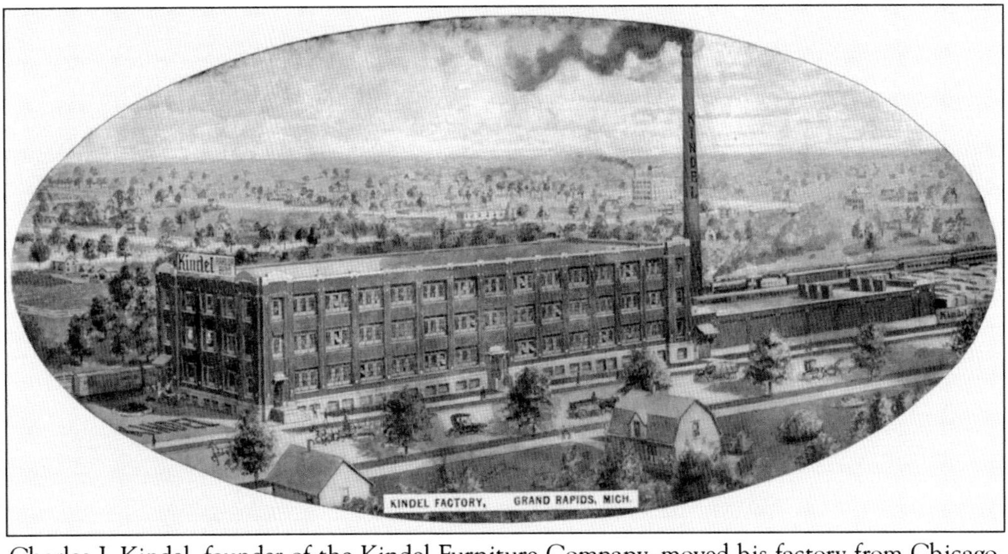

Charles J. Kindel, founder of the Kindel Furniture Company, moved his factory from Chicago to Grand Rapids and built this factory in 1912. The Garden Street building still stands and still houses the only remaining Grand Rapids home furniture manufacturer. (Grand Rapids Public Library.)

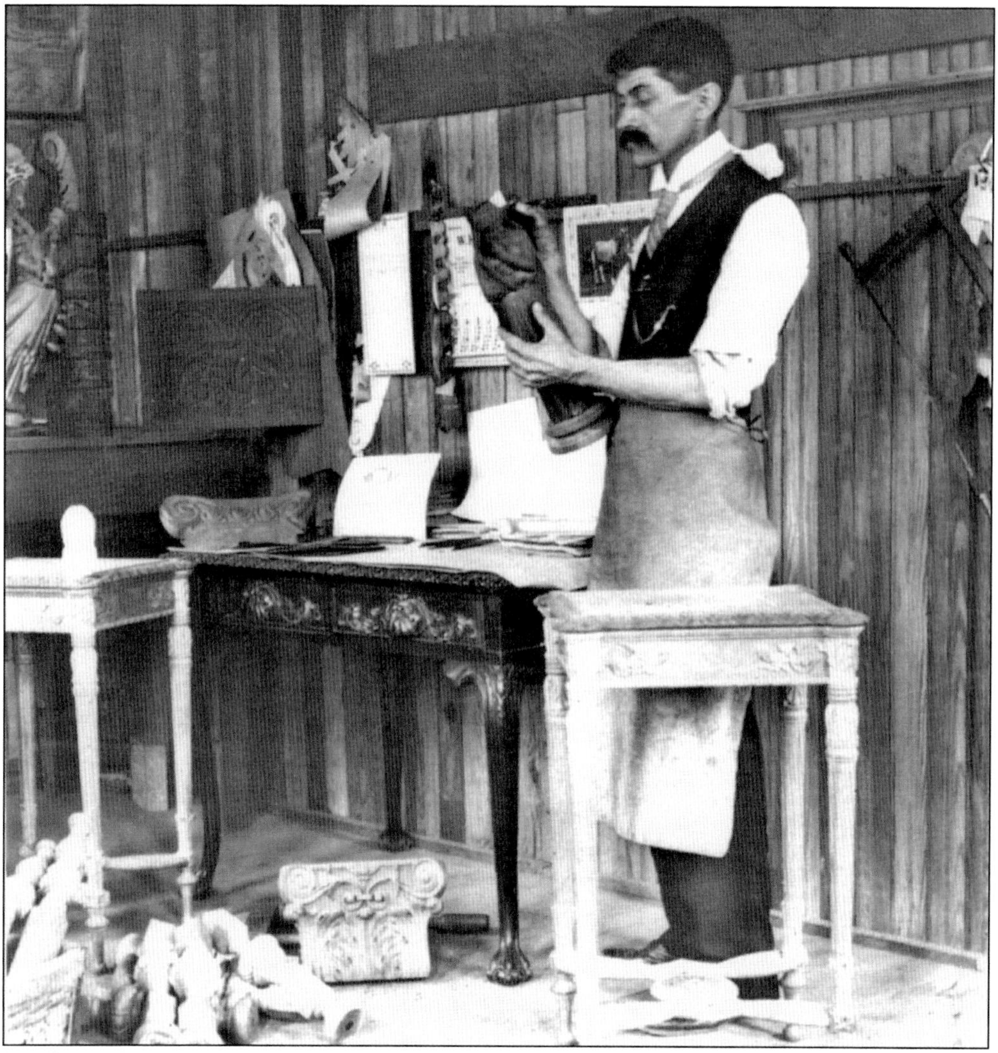

Boudewyn DeKorne came to Grand Rapids from the Netherlands in 1879 at age 14 and soon found work as a hand carver in the Berkey and Gay factory. In the early 20th century, he and a friend opened the DeKorne and Lindhout Carving Company near Berkey and Gay on Ottawa Street. He carved patterns from original sketches, and his clients included Berkey and Gay, Widdicomb, Kindel, Colonial Clock, and local architects, among others. In addition to furniture designs, he carved cornices, stairs, and ceiling medallions for the Pantlind Hotel and mansions in the Hill District, including the Voight House, which is now a part of the Public Museum, Grand Rapids. Churches hired him to carve life-size statues of biblical figures such as the 12 apostles. He is about 40 years old in the photograph above. (Jack DeKorne family.)

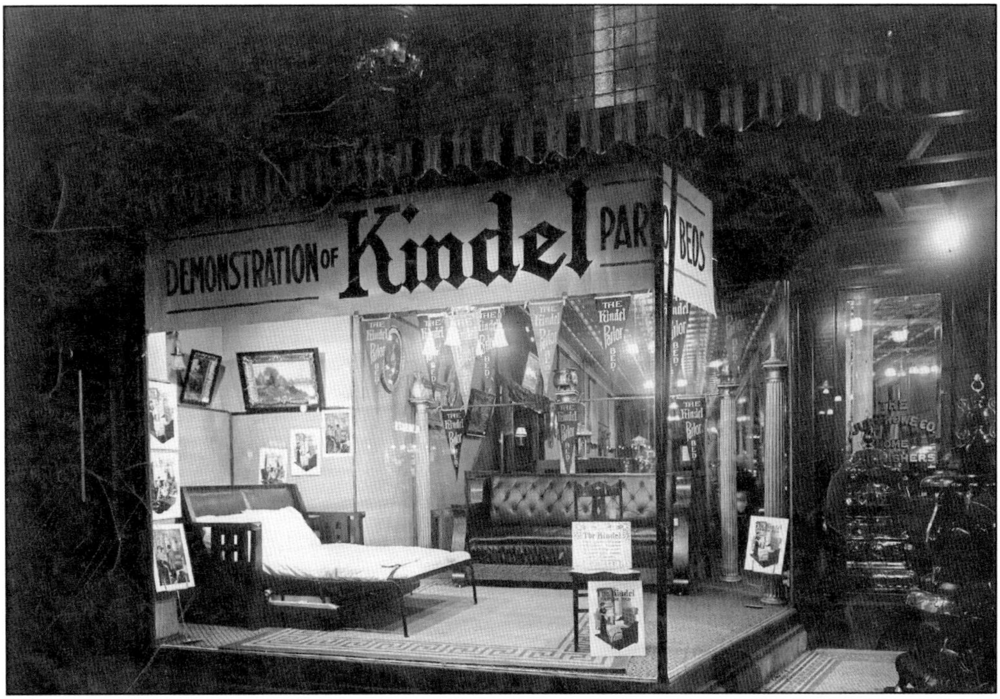

Kindel Furniture Company, a Grand Rapids fixture since 1912, first made a name for itself with its parlor bed, a forerunner of the perennial sofa bed. Then operating under the name Kindel Bed Company, the firm made convertible beds for retail giants, including Chicago's Marshall Field and Company and Barrs Dry Goods Store in St. Louis. (Kindel Furniture Company.)

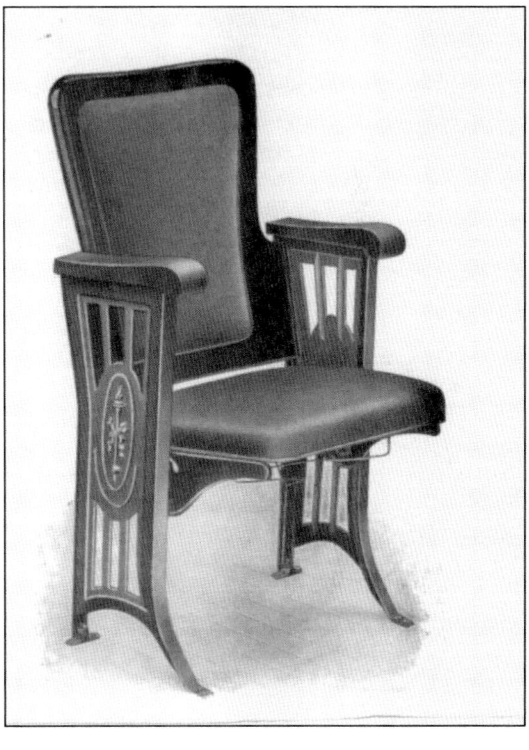

Today's Irwin Seating Company was founded in 1907 as the Steel Furniture Company. Its earliest products included opera seats like the one shown at right, as well as school desks, church pews, folding chairs, and the ubiquitous park bench. This opera chair was shown in a 1912 catalog. (Irwin Seating Company.)

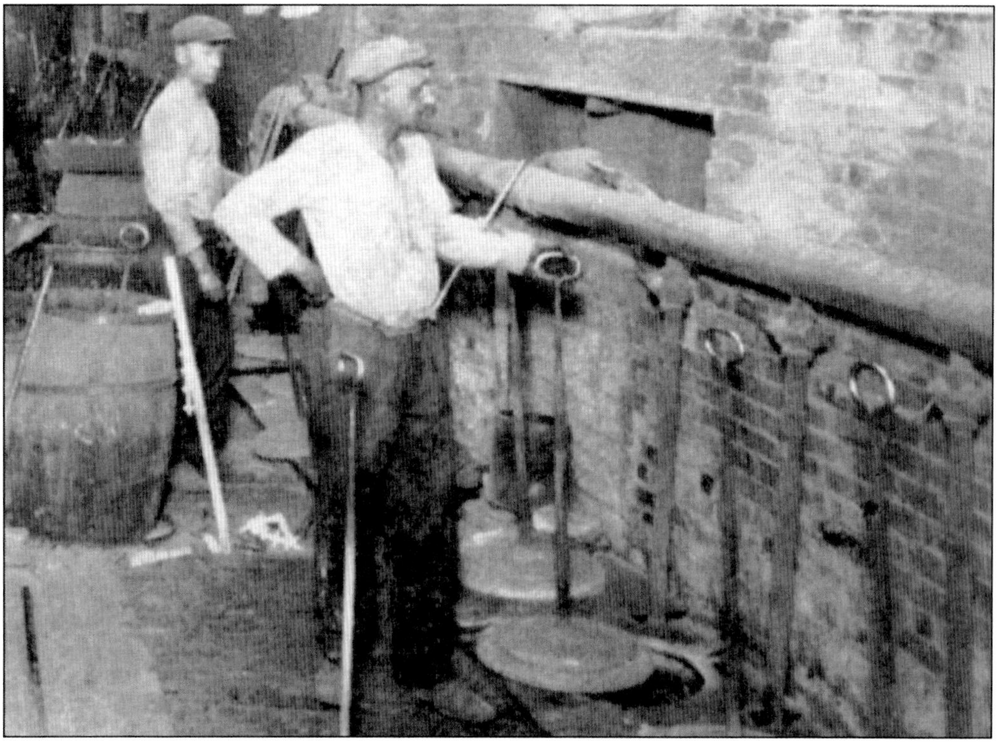

Along with the furniture manufacturing companies, other companies were founded to supply them. Daniel Tower worked for Nelson Matter and Company as a wood carver. He noticed management's increasing frustration over the difficulty of finding the right hardware to complement the pieces produced. Not one to pass up an opportunity, he quit his job in 1882 and, with Thomas Farmer, started the Grand Rapids Brass Company. Here two employees tend the furnaces where the brass was melted. (Grand Rapids Public Library.)

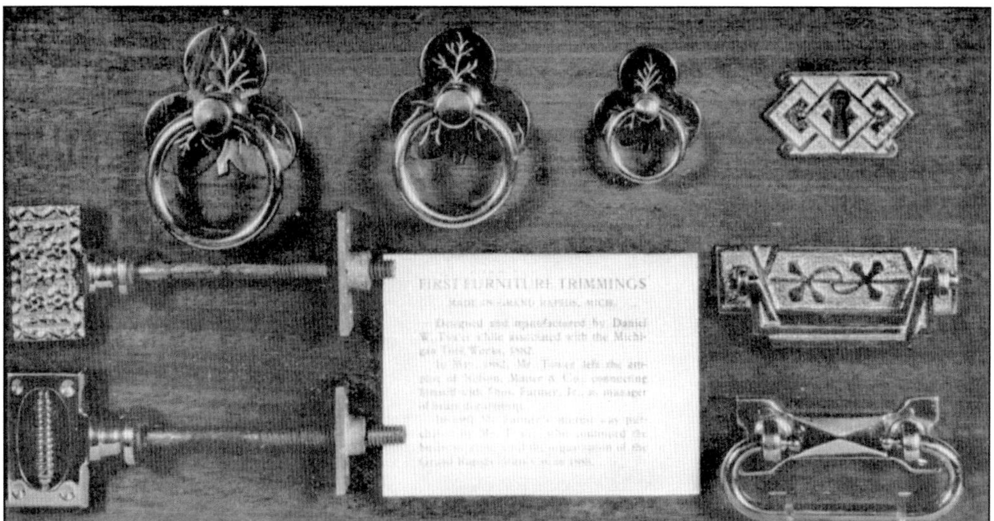

The Grand Rapids Brass Company specialized in traditional drawer pulls and decorative brass trimmings for fine furniture. The company also produced a line of modern trimmings made of Bakelite, Formica, and Micarta. (Grand Rapids Public Library.)

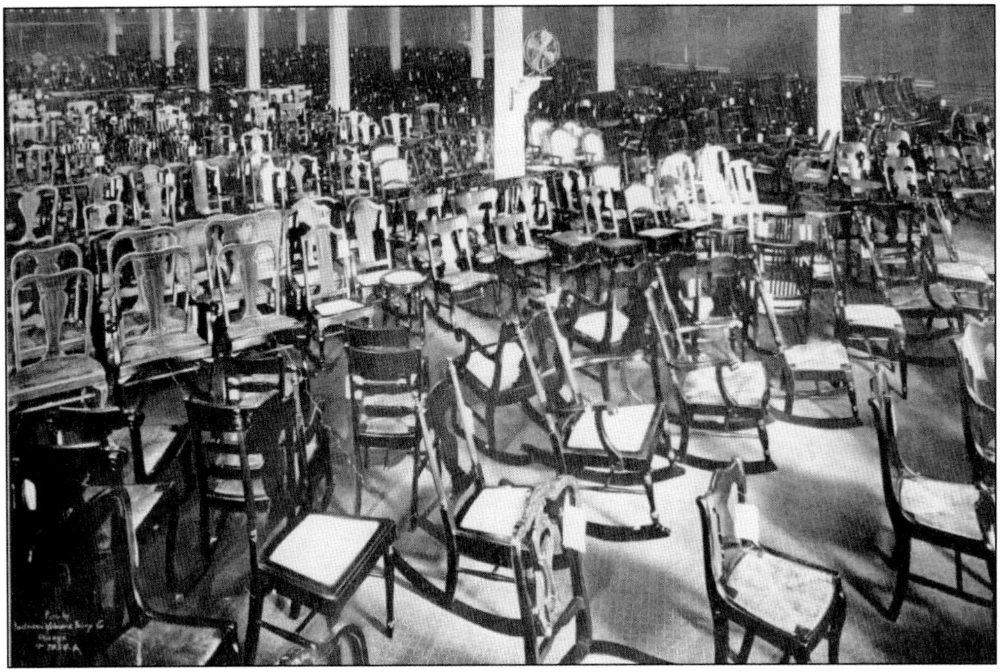

Michigan Chair Company started business near Lansing in Grand Ledge. The company moved to Grand Rapids in 1890 and amassed this display of nearly 2,000 chairs in 1911. Like most companies of the day, Michigan Chair concentrated on one product—chairs. Other companies made beds exclusively. (Grand Rapids Public Library.)

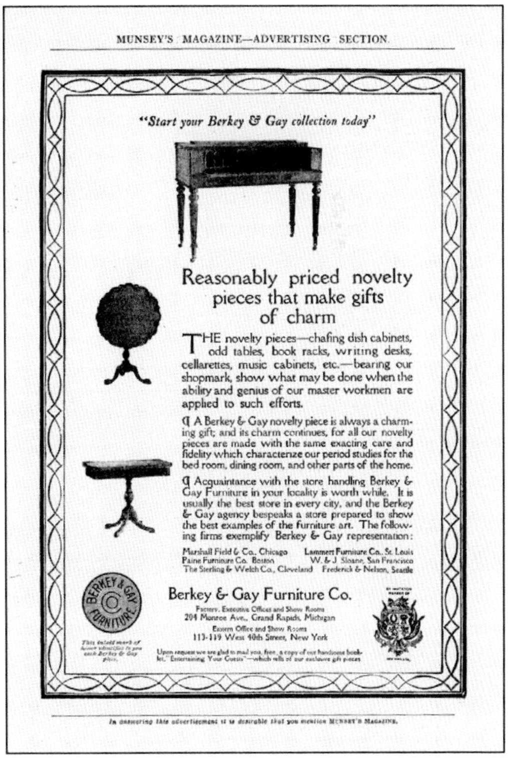

This Berkey and Gay advertisement from *Munsey's Magazine* in 1915 highlights the company's occasional pieces like the writing desk pictured at the top. They were sold at company showrooms, furniture stores, and select department stores like Chicago's Marshall Field and Company. The Berkey and Gay mark on the lower left identifies the manufacturer. Member companies of the Furniture Manufacturers Association began using a Grand Rapids triangular registered trademark when factory owners elsewhere hawked their wares as "Grand Rapids style" to cash in on Furniture City's sterling reputation. It took a lawsuit in 1919 to end that deception.

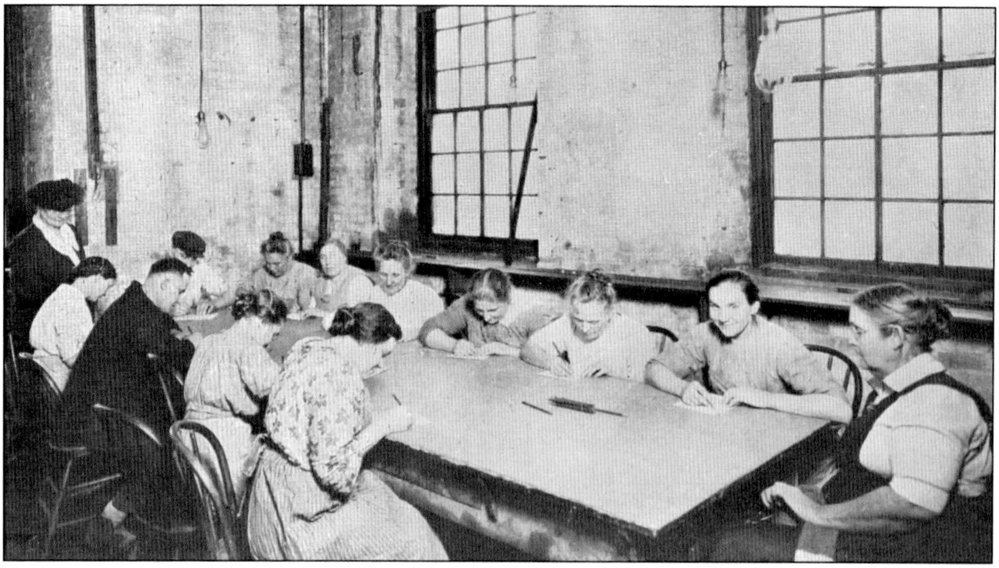

With immigrants making up a major portion of the labor pool, company owners felt a responsibility to help them assimilate. Lunch breaks became learning experiences, and classes sometimes followed 10-hour shifts. These women study English at the Oriel plant in a photograph published in an industry paper, the *Shop Mark*, in February 1920. Although still called the Oriel plant, the Oriel Cabinet Company had been taken over by Berkey and Gay in 1912. (Collections of the Public Museum, Grand Rapids.)

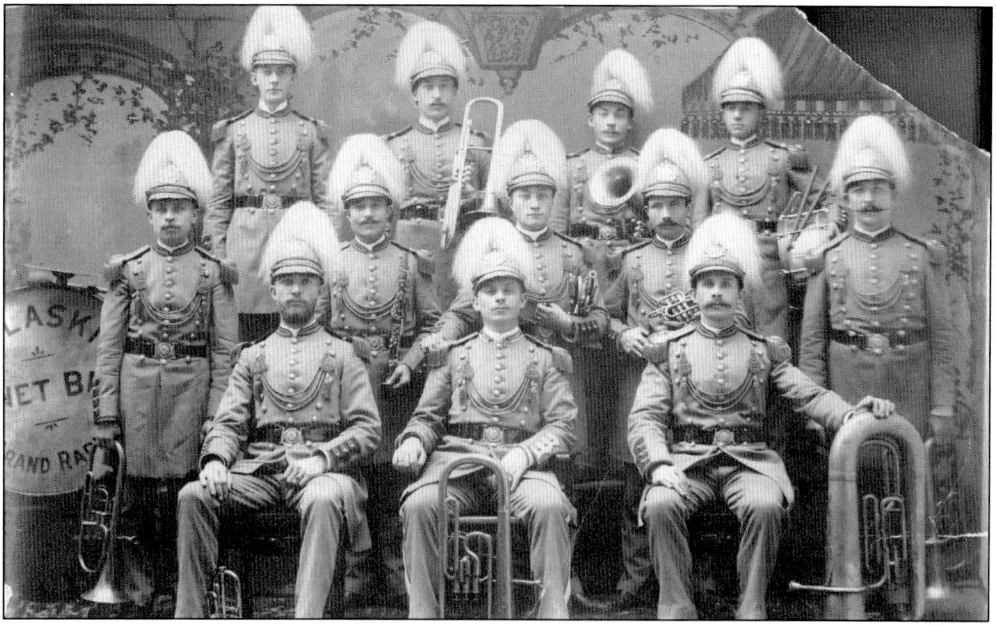

The immigrants in the furniture factories were predominantly Dutch, but southwest Michigan also attracted large numbers of Poles, Lithuanians, and Germans. These groups formed communities and retained their old country customs by socializing with those who spoke their own language and with whom they had a common background. More than half the members of this Polish marching band worked in the furniture industry. (Collections of the Public Museum, Grand Rapids.)

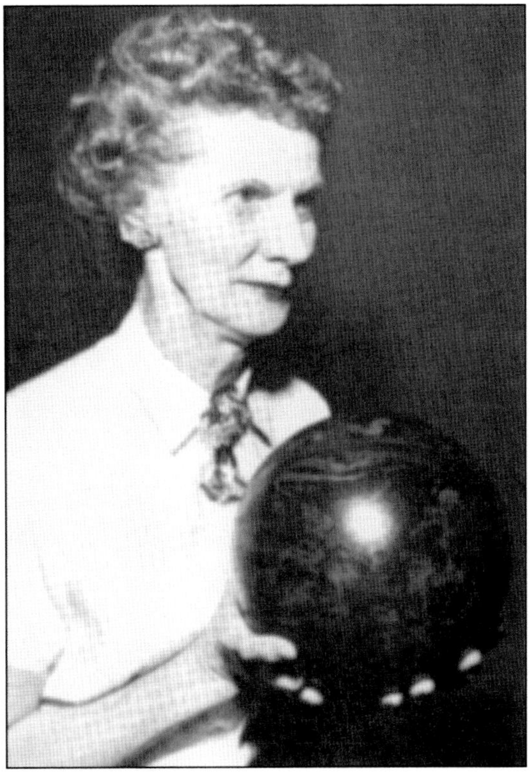

From the beginning women were valued employees in the furniture industry. Strong friendships formed when workers spent long hours together in the factories. American Seating Company encouraged a sense of community by sponsoring athletic and social activities, like the women's bowling team shown below. Nell Smith winds up to roll a strike (right). The whole team says "cheese" in the photograph below. (American Seating Company.)

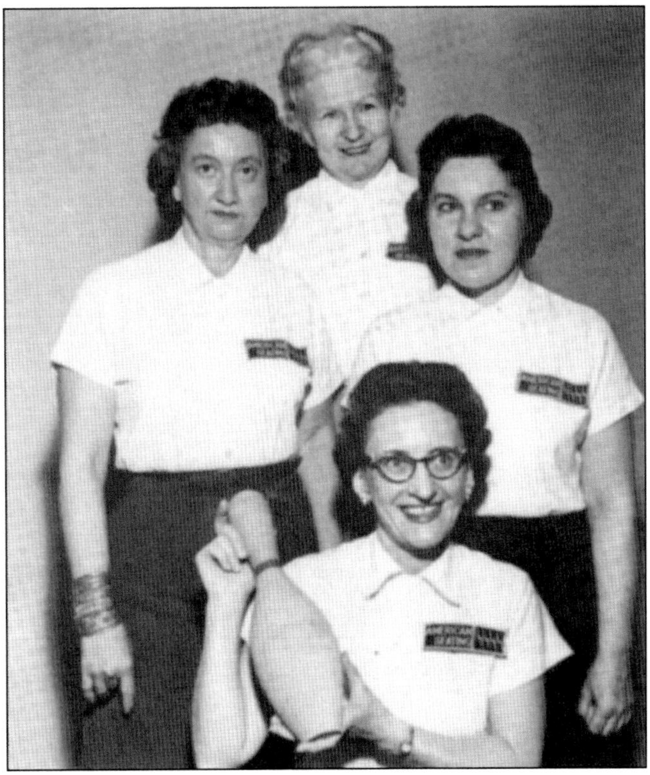

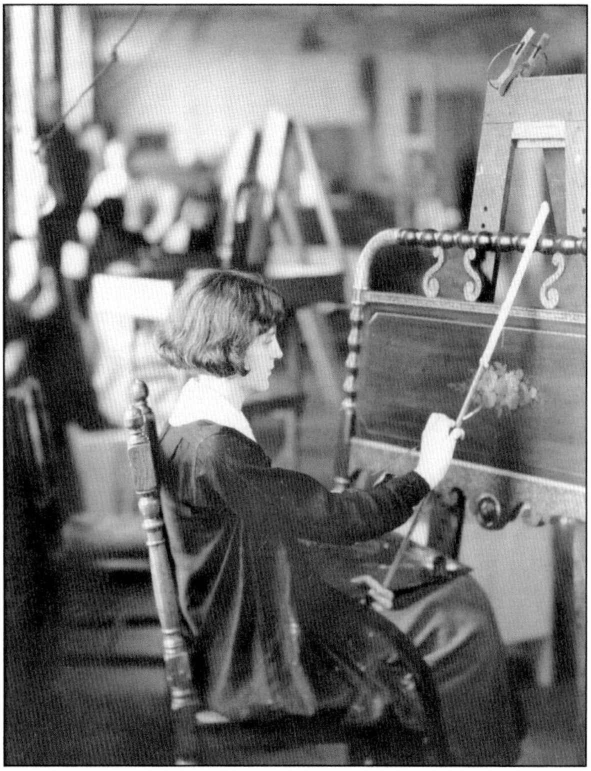

This decorator uses an artist's maulstick to steady her brush hand as she paints designs on the headboard. The undated photograph is believed to have been taken in the Phoenix Furniture Company factory. (Collections of the Public Museum, Grand Rapids.)

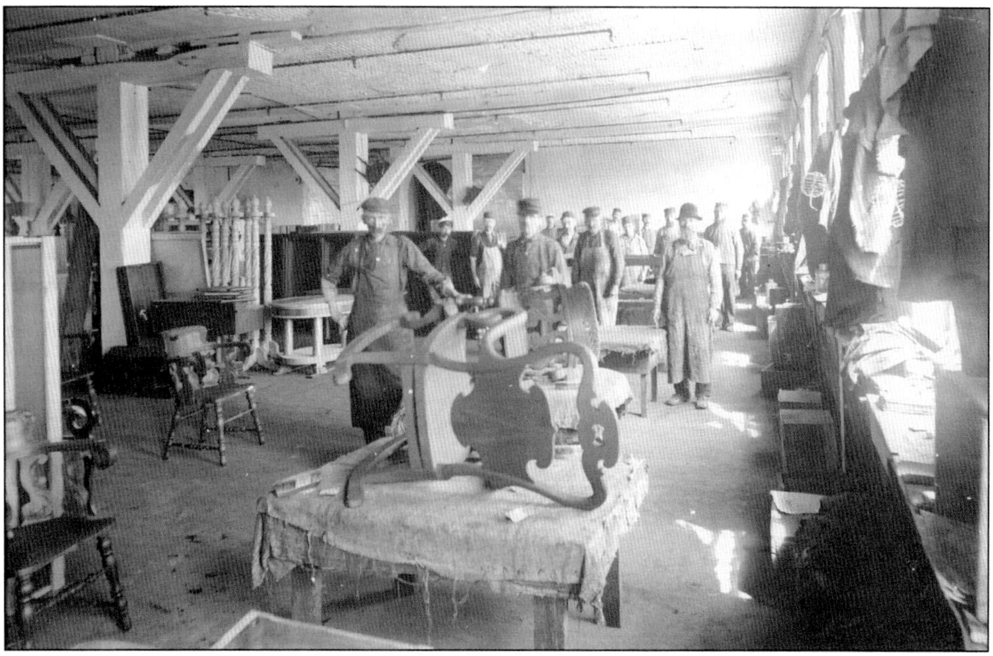

Robert W. Irwin Company employees are shown with their chairs and tables in progress. The company went out of business in 1953, but in 1994, a section of the old factory was reconstructed in the Public Museum, Grand Rapids' Furniture City exhibit. This photograph was taken around 1925. (Grand Rapids Public Library.)

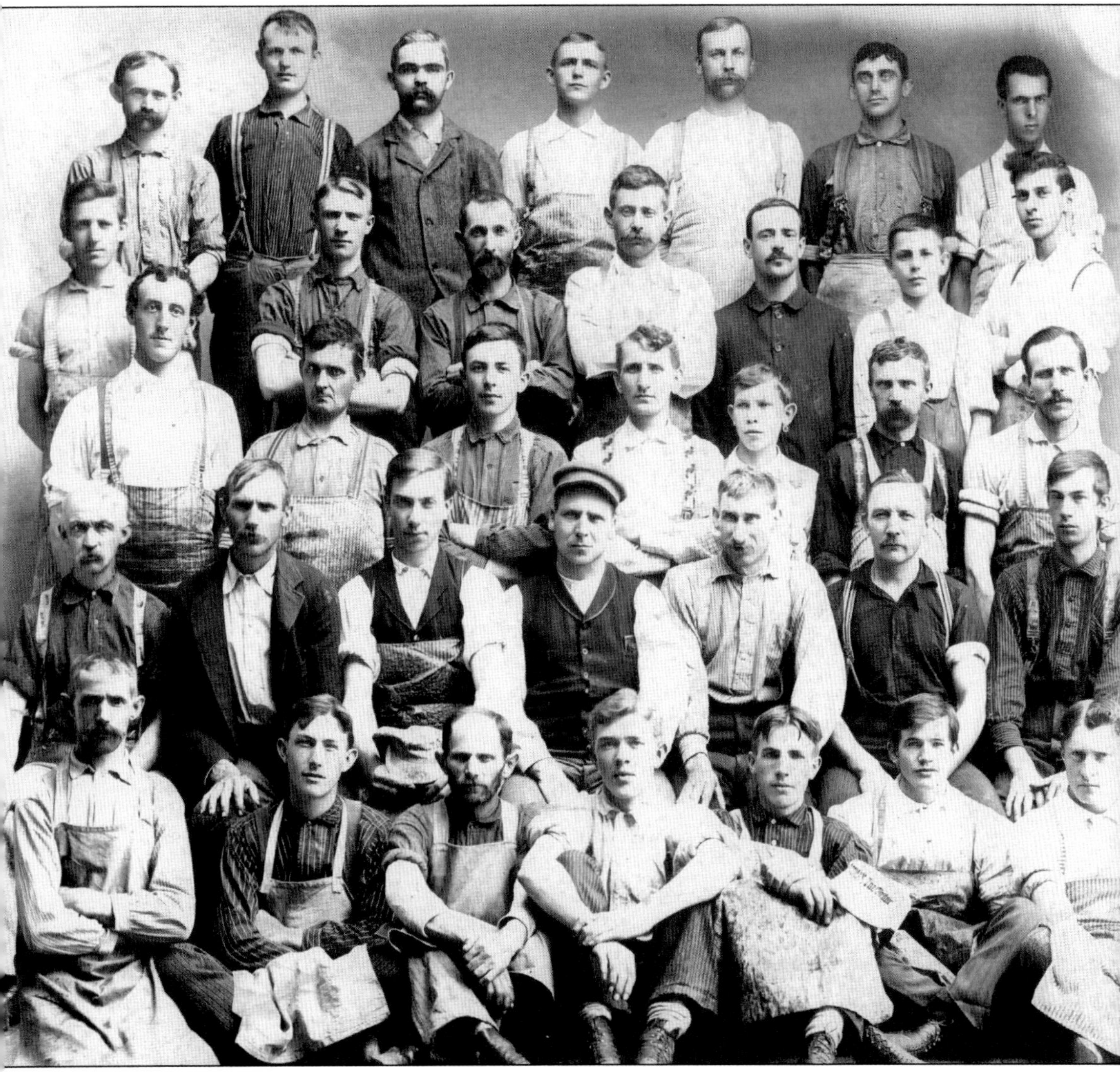

West Michigan Furniture Company employees were photographed in the 1920s. From left to right are (first row) Corndal Dalman, unidentified, Peter Elhart, three unidentified workers, and Cornelius Yakes; (second row) two unidentified workers, George Steffens, Henry Brusse, William Kardux, unidentified, and Tony Ver Hulst; (third row) ? Visscher, Neal Kiuken, Ecko ?, ? Karsten, and three unidentified workers; (fourth row) four unidentified workers, Henry Van Ry, and two unidentified workers; (fifth row) Cornelius Waldering, unidentified, Dick Hoodeman, Bill Vandenberg, unidentified, Peter Slagle, and John De Kooyer. The Holland-based company was bought by the Mueller Company in Grand Rapids. (Holland Museum Archives and Research Library.)

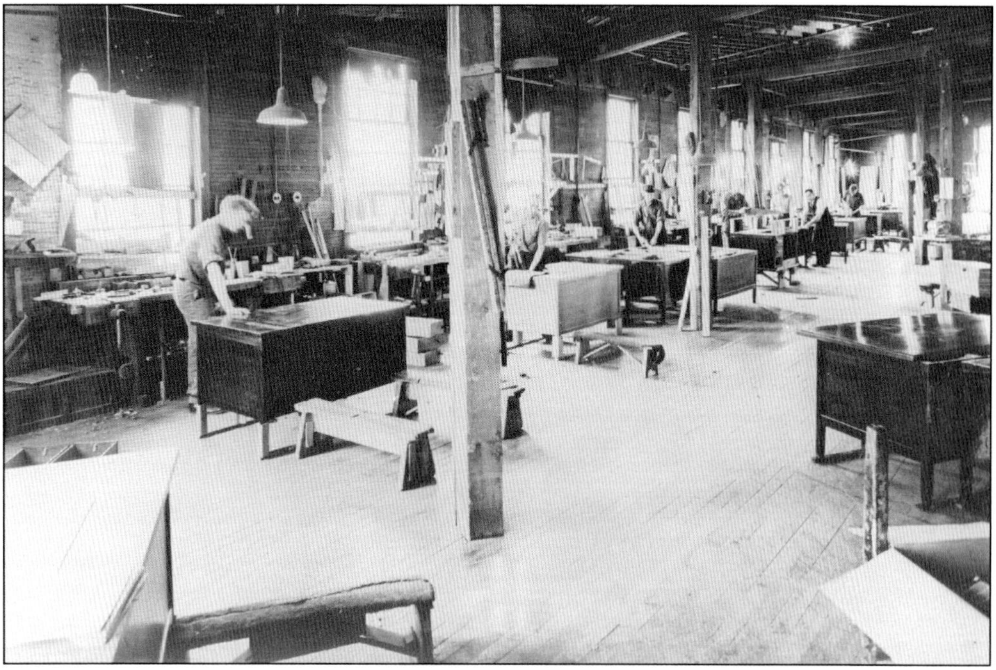

Lithuanians did not just find work in the furniture factories, they found opportunities for advancement. John Yurkinas (sixth from left, wearing vest) went to work at age 17 cleaning desks at the Gunn Furniture Company for 25¢ an hour. By 1934, when this photograph was taken, he had worked himself up to factory superintendent. Imperial Furniture Company employed more than 150 Lithuanians in the 1930s. Some were laborers, but many were master wood finishers. (Grand Rapids Public Library.)

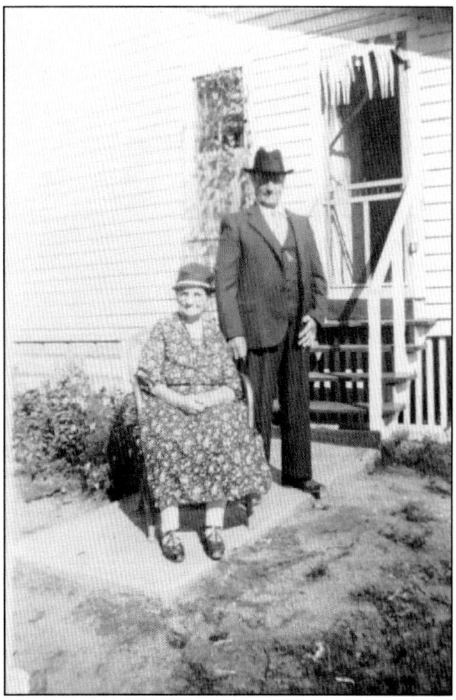

Of all the immigrants in the furniture industry, the largest number came from the Netherlands. Taeke Van Dyke, pictured in 1930 with his wife, Hiltja, arrived in 1881 and worked as a laborer at the Widdicomb factory. The Public Museum, Grand Rapids displays the Widdicomb bedroom furniture Van Dyke bought—one piece at a time. (Collections of the Public Museum, Grand Rapids.)

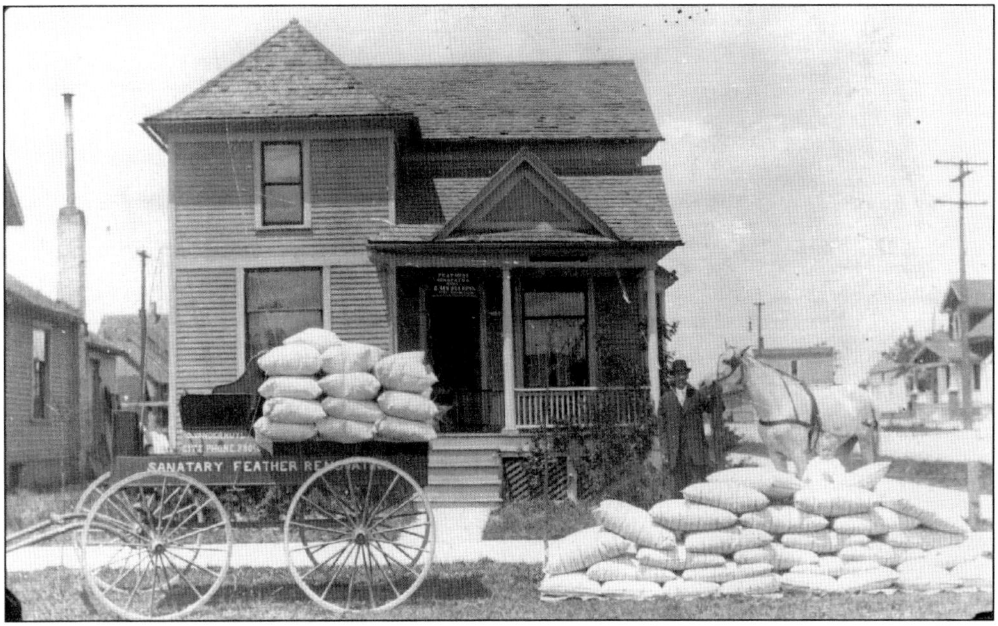

In the 1920s, the Sanatary Feather Renovating Company made feather mattresses and pillows. Here owner Dennis VanderKuyl leads his horse to the delivery carriage. The VanderKuyl home and business was at 901 Courtney Street, in the West Side of Grand Rapids. A few years after the photograph above was taken, the company had a fancy new truck and a new name, Feather and Mattress Renovating, to go with it. It was a time when hardworking entrepreneurs could start their own businesses and enjoy the freedom of self-employment. (Marcia VanderKuyl.)

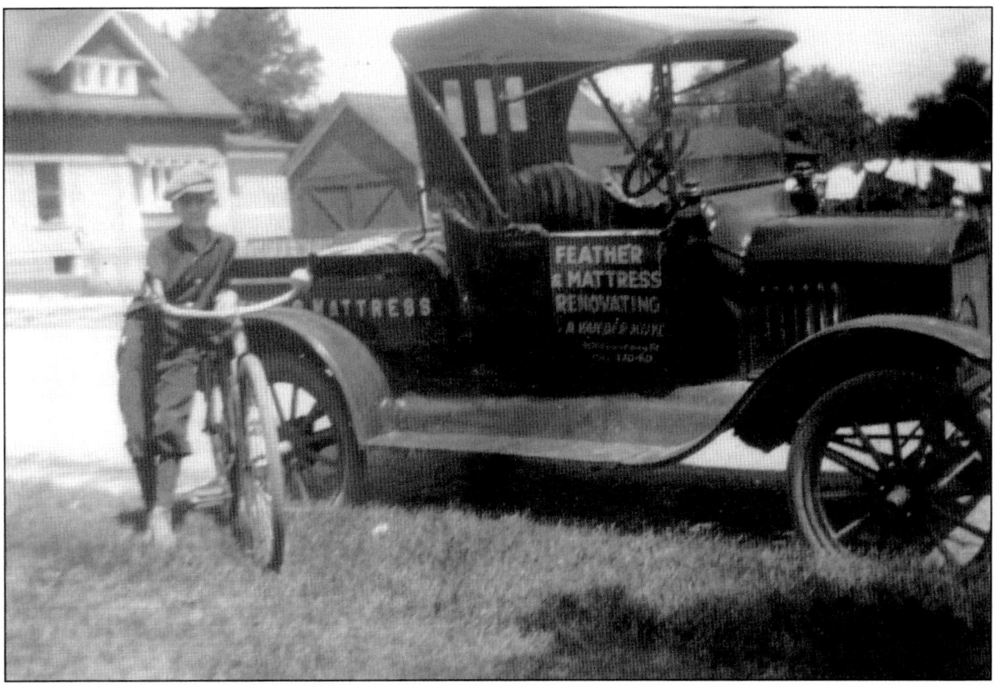

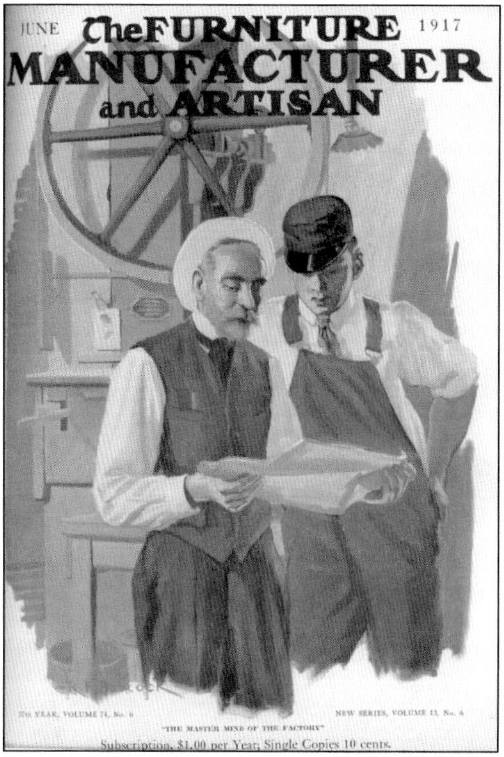

The cover on the June 1917 issue of the *Furniture Manufacturer and Artisan* shows a scene played out all over Grand Rapids as designers and managers communicated their vision to the workers charged with making it a reality. (Grand Rapids Public Library.)

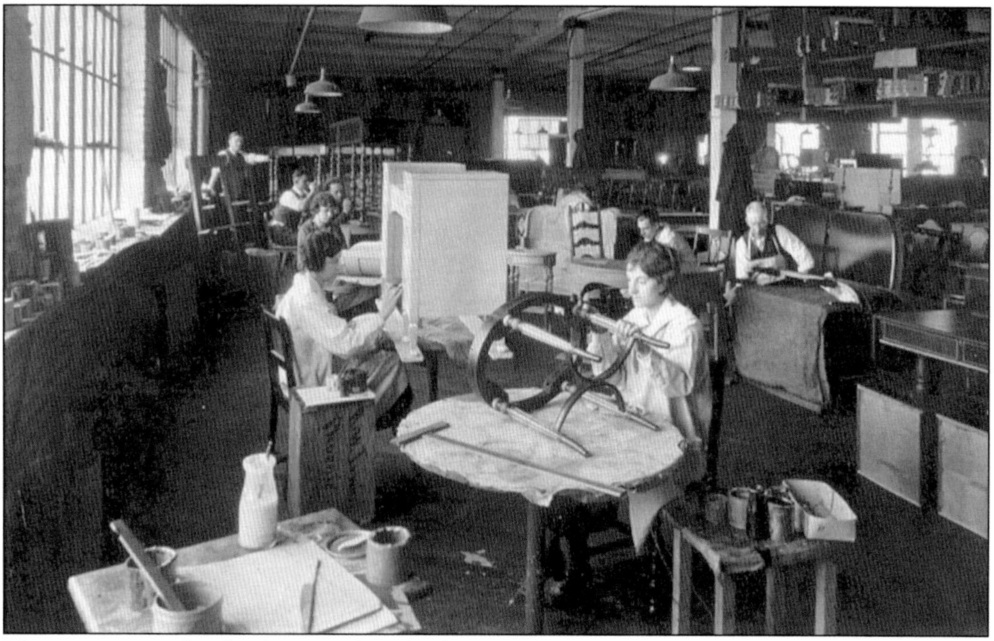

The woman in the forefront applies finish to a chair while another paints a cabinet front. Other employees perform various tasks in the background. Phoenix Furniture Company was bought by the Robert W. Irwin Company in 1920, but Phoenix products were marked "Phoenix Furniture/made by Robert W. Irwin Company." It made sense to continue using a name long associated with quality products. (Collections of the Public Museum, Grand Rapids.)

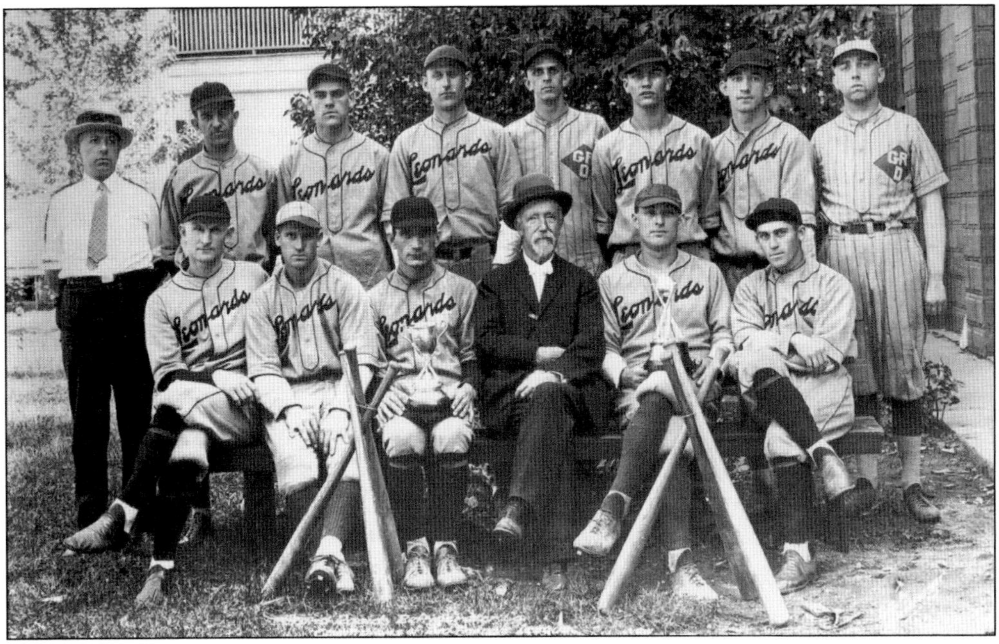

Company-sponsored athletic teams have long been an American tradition, and the furniture industry was no exception. In 1925, the Leonards, the Leonard Refrigerator Company team, defeated the Standard Oils to clinch the City Red Triangle League title. They won 12 of their 14 games. Team members are, from left to right, (first row) L. Wescott (pitcher), C. McCoy (second base), F. Schultz (third base), C. H. Leonard (president), F. Sullivan (catcher), and F. McCoy (shortstop); (second row) H. Van Sluyters (manager), T. Van Drummal (first base), C. Klonkyke (pitcher), J. Sherman (left field), E. VanderSwag (right field), J. Hudnut (right field), I. Schultz (center field), and P. Kol (captain). When the Leonards were not winning baseball games, they produced wooden iceboxes. In 1926, the company merged with Kelvinator to become the Kelvinator-Leonard Company. (Grand Rapids Public Library.)

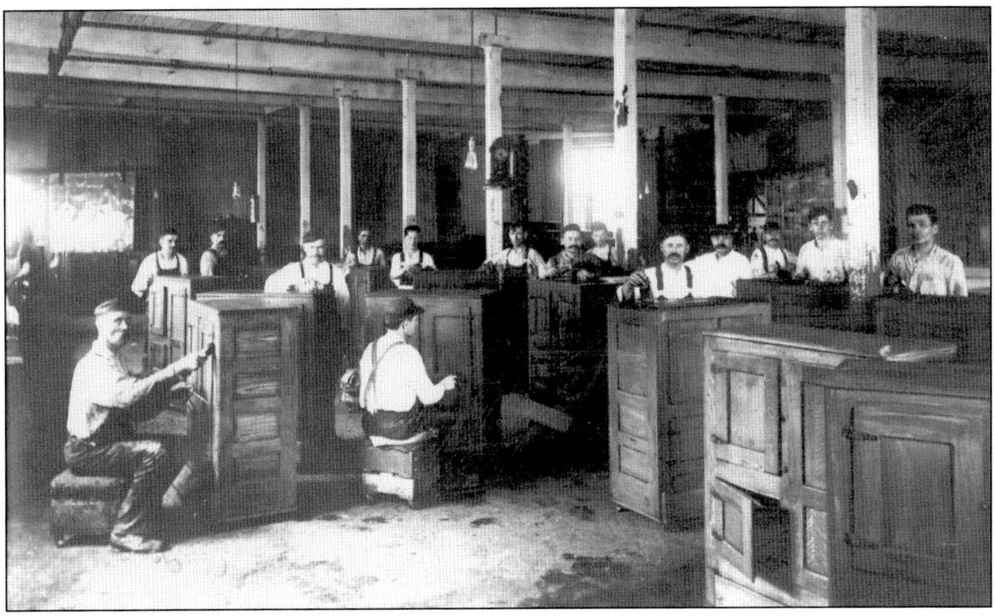

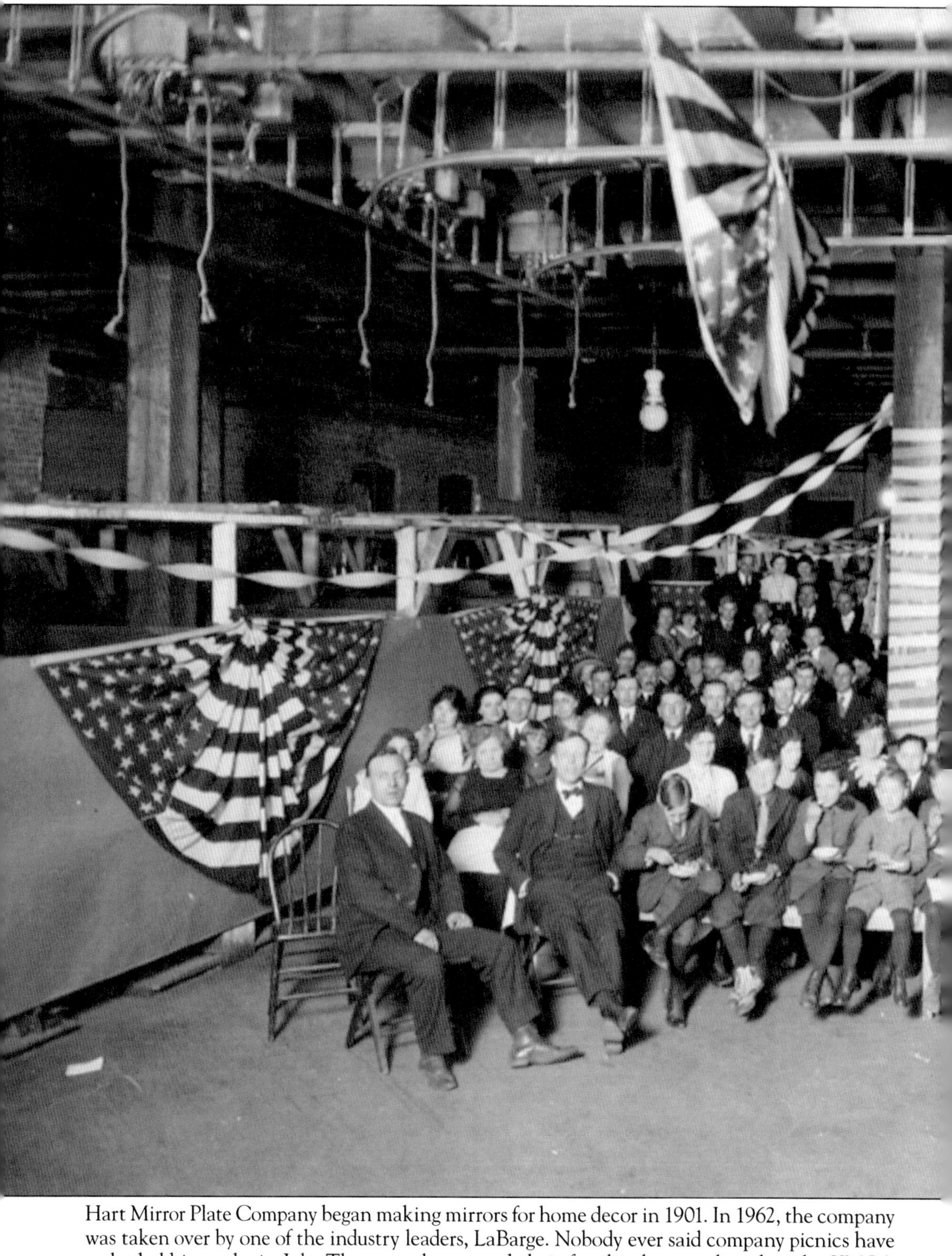

Hart Mirror Plate Company began making mirrors for home decor in 1901. In 1962, the company was taken over by one of the industry leaders, LaBarge. Nobody ever said company picnics have to be held in parks in July. These employees and their families have gathered at the YMCA

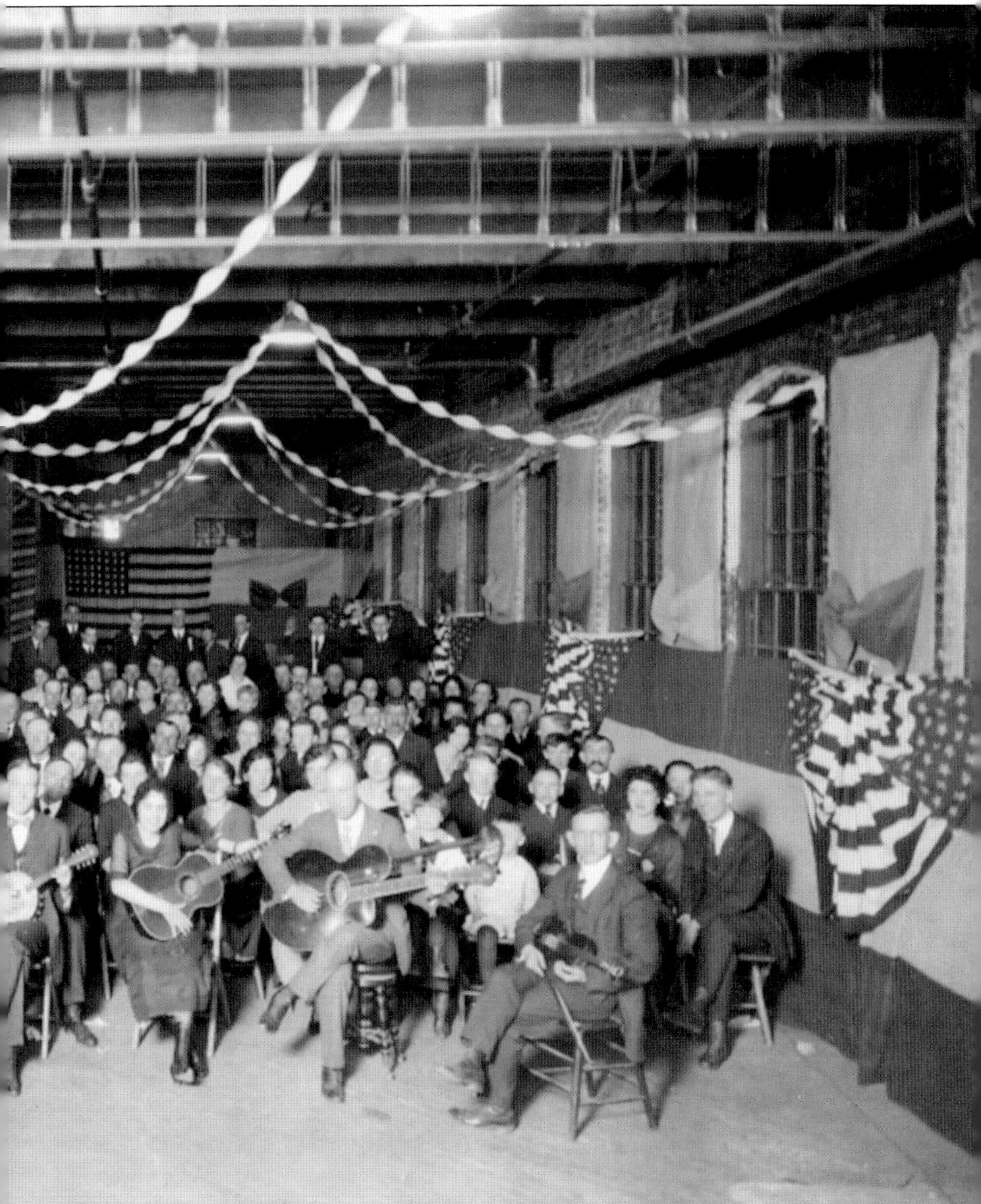

for a company-sponsored winter picnic in January 1921. They might be a little overdressed for the occasion, but the flags and streamers, along with the musicians in the front row, indicate a successful event. (Grand Rapids Public Library.)

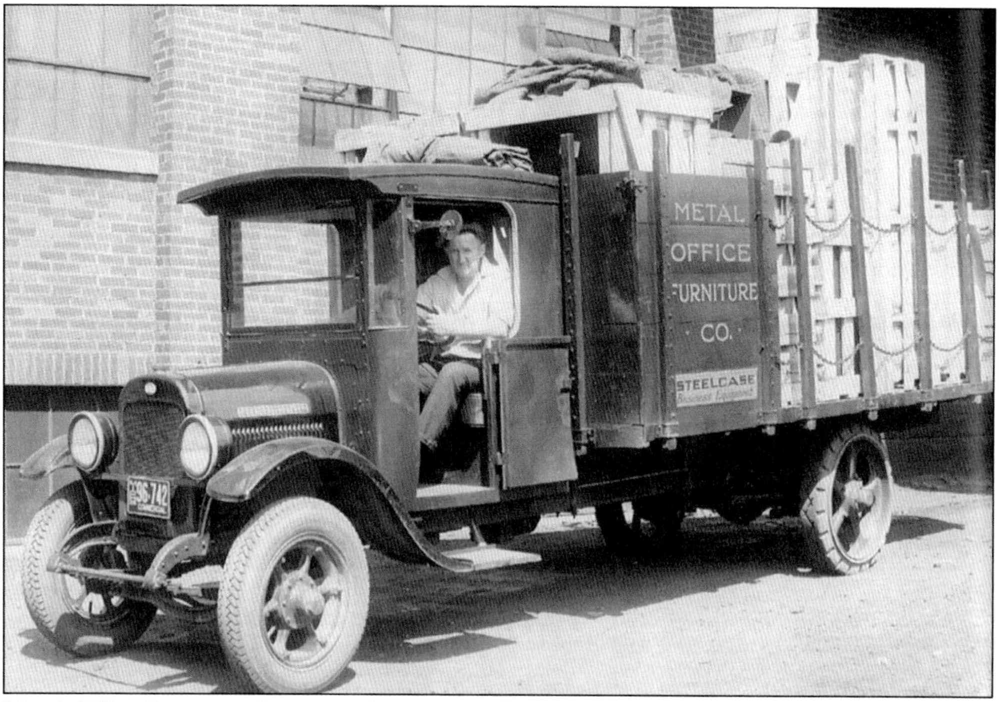

Metal Office Furniture Company, forerunner of Steelcase, Inc., delivered products in Federal Knight trucks. This rather utilitarian 1924 vehicle is a far cry from the rainbow-hued Steelcase trucks on the road today. Company lore has it that actor Burt Reynolds once insisted on using the blue of the current logo for his boat. Steelcase accommodated him. Reynolds piloted the only Steelcase-blue boat on the Atlantic Ocean. (Steelcase, Inc.)

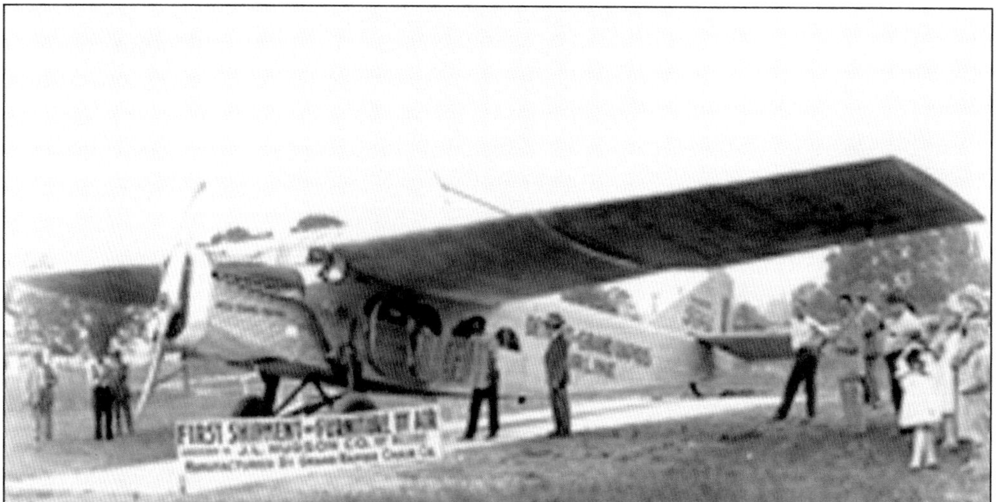

Although many still clung to the idea that "if God wanted me to fly he would have given me wings," air travel gained grudging acceptance. Stout Air Service first provided passenger service to the city in 1926. Two years later, Grand Rapids Chair Company hired the airline to make the country's first furniture shipment by air. Detroit's J. L. Hudson department store received this historic delivery. (Grand Rapids Public Library.)

David Wolcott Kendall has been called the "Dean of Furniture Designers." In 1928, his widow, Helen, after her death, provided in her will to establish the Kendall School of Art as a memorial to her husband. It has since become part of Ferris State University and offers a curriculum in furniture design. The school was first housed in the former Kendall home at 145 Fountain Street and is currently located downtown on Division Avenue. Note the intricate carvings on the sideboard he designed while working for the Phoenix Furniture Company. A devotee of the arts and crafts style, he also designed the McKinley chair, so named because Pres. William McKinley owned one. That chair was so widely copied that Kendall patented it in 1897. (Kendall Visual Resource Collection.)

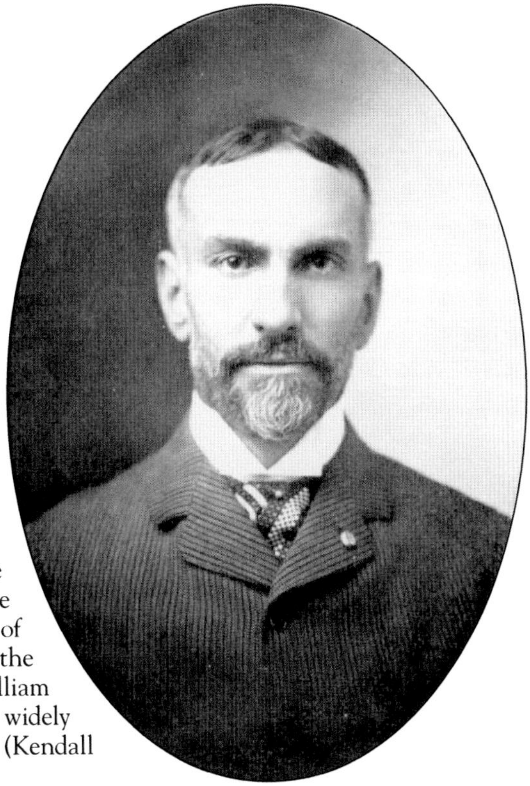

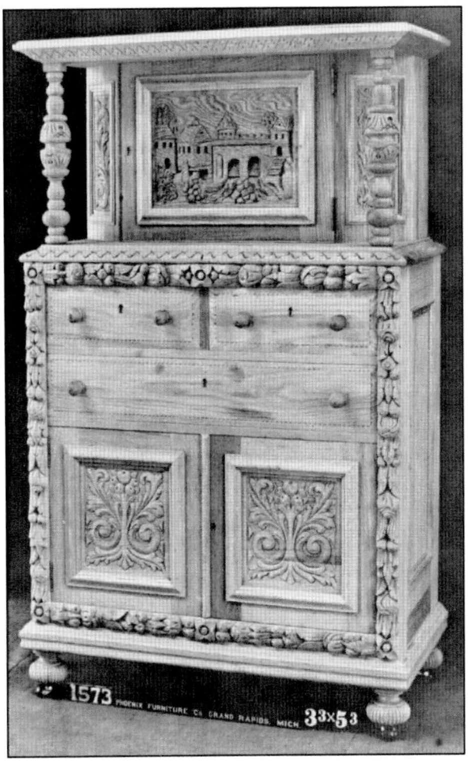

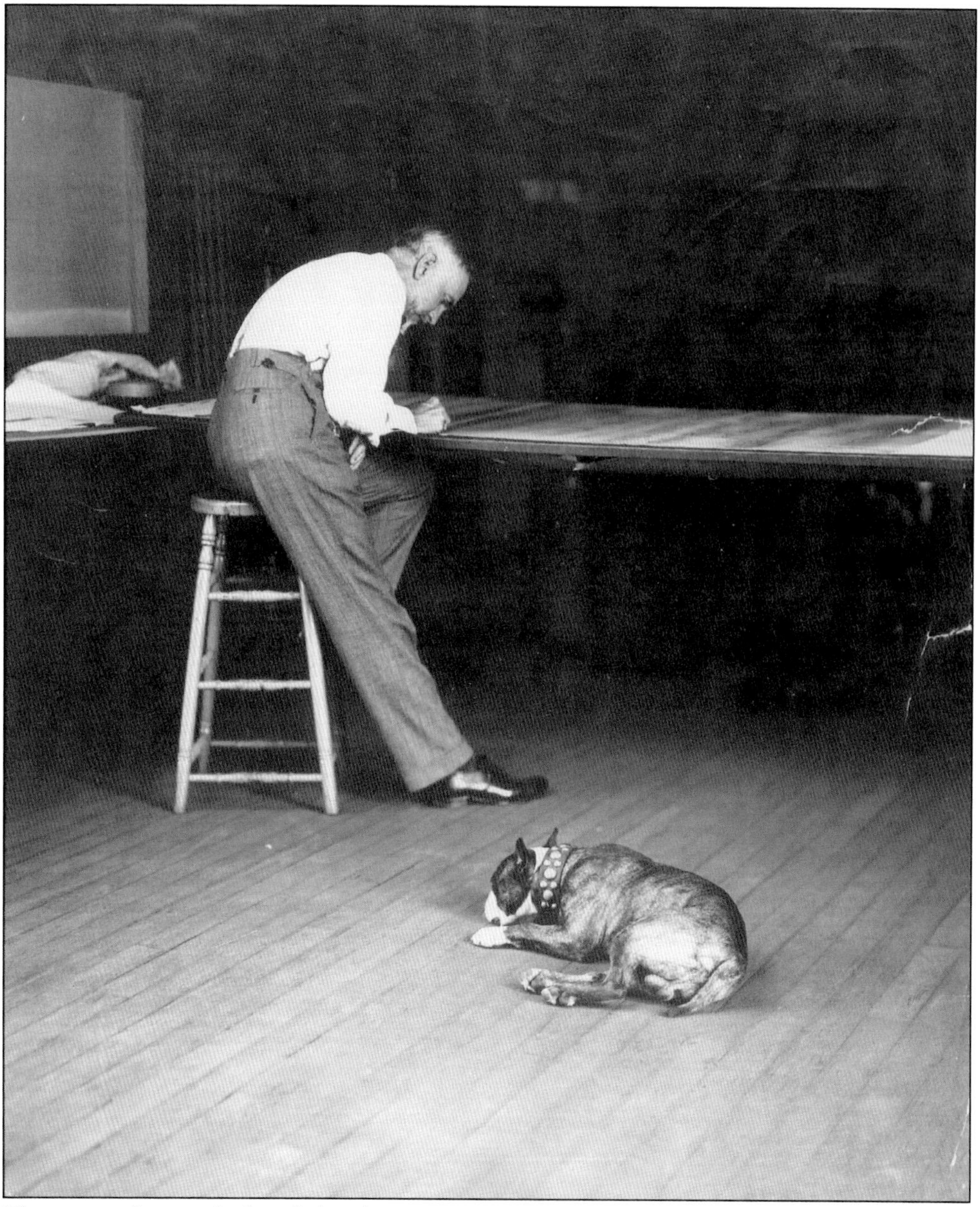

The artist often worked with his favorite companion snoozing at his feet—a Boston terrier named Toby. Ever the innovator, David Wolcott Kendall saw that tobacco juice highlighted the grain of the wooden floor. When he realized that depletion of the forests made fine hardwoods more difficult to find and more costly to buy, he devised a way to stain oak and ash so they were suitable for furniture. (Kendall Visual Resource Collection.)

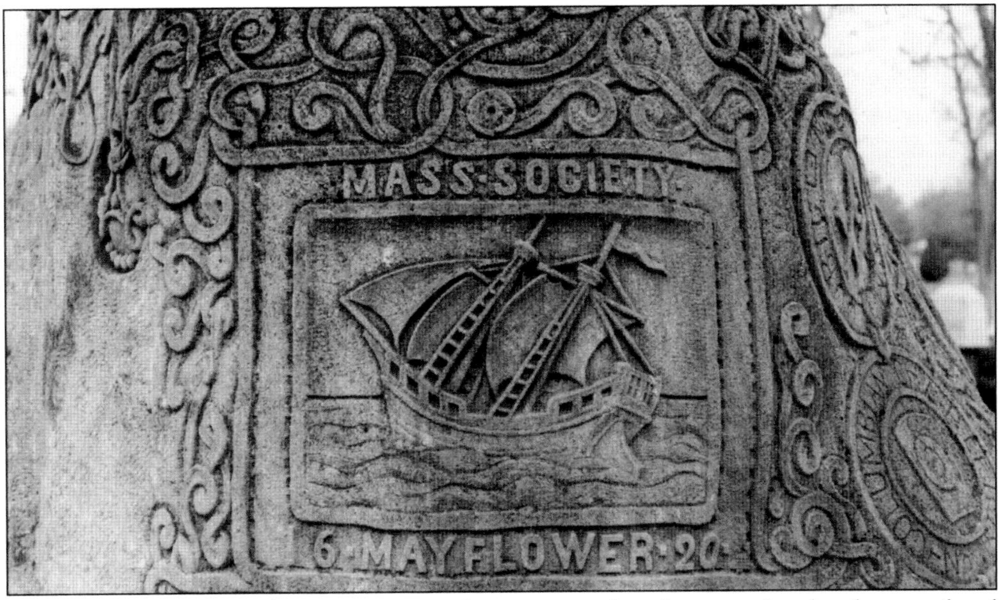

Although his furniture designs represent classic arts and crafts examples that have endured through time, some say Kendall's masterpiece is his memorial to his first wife, Delle Colby Kendall, who died in 1899. On the six-foot rock at the Oak Hill Cemetery on Hall Street, he honored her ancestry that goes back to the Mayflower and to John and Priscilla Alden. Among other carvings on the monument is one commemorating Kendall's involvement with the Benevolent Protective Order of Elks. (Norma Lewis.)

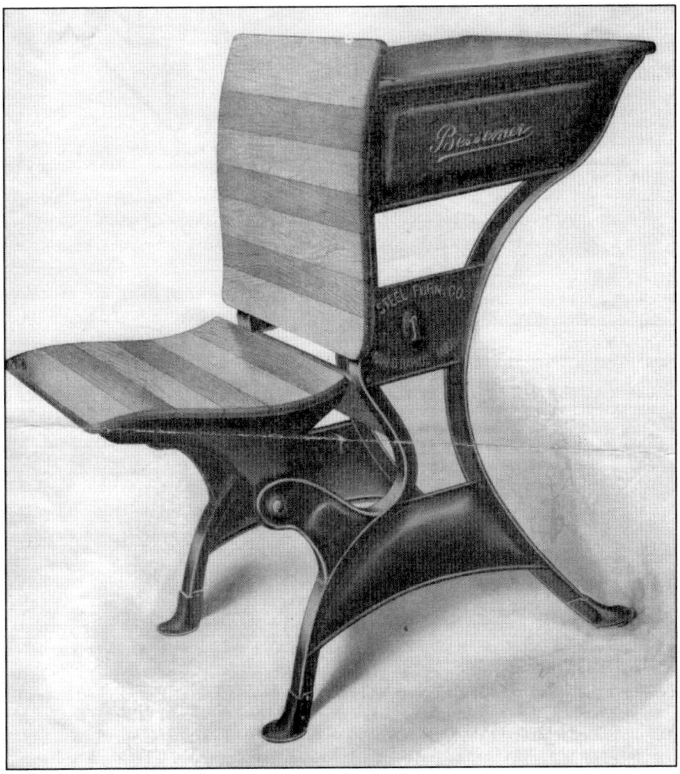

This is an early Steel Furniture Company school desk like those used by everyone over a certain age. The top has a pencil groove and a hole to hold a bottle of ink. Most such desks became ink-stained not long after installation. Did mischievous boys really dip the tips of the girls' braids into the inkwell, or is that just a rumor started by the girls? (Irwin Seating Company.)

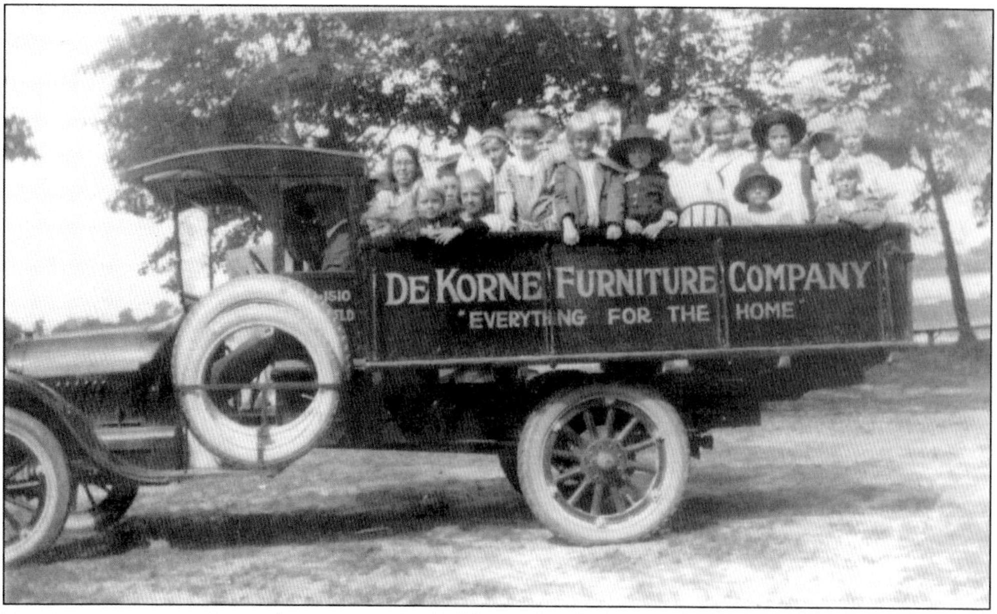

Furniture was more than a business to the DeKorne family. It was also being part of a community. Here the company's Federal Knight truck transports a load of children from the Broadway Avenue Christian Reformed Church to their annual Sunday school picnic at Myers Lake. Note the rounded back of a wooden child-size chair. Lewis DeKorne, son of Boudewyn DeKorne, is driving the truck. (Jack DeKorne.)

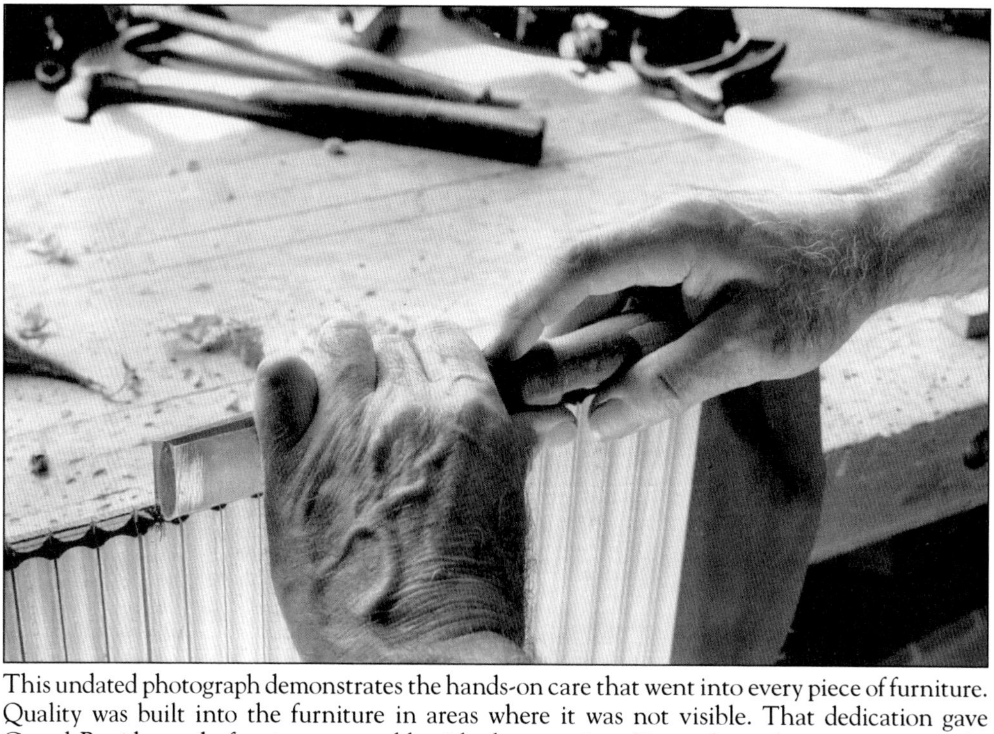

This undated photograph demonstrates the hands-on care that went into every piece of furniture. Quality was built into the furniture in areas where it was not visible. That dedication gave Grand Rapids–made furniture an unblemished reputation. Pieces from this city were sought after in earlier days and are still collected today. (Grand Rapids Public Library.)

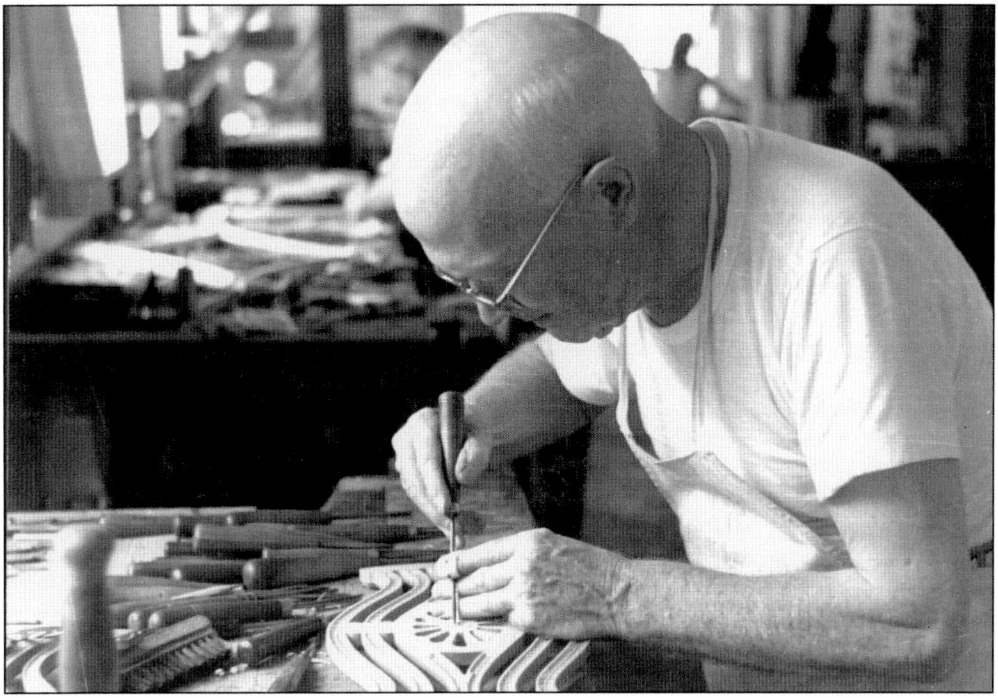

In the beginning, furniture making was all done by hand. Workers, many of whom acquired their skills in Europe, worked diligently at their tasks. Even after labor-saving machinery became routine, some steps still had to be done by hand. Craftsman like the one shown in the undated photograph above put the same pride and attention to detail into every piece. (Grand Rapids Public Library.)

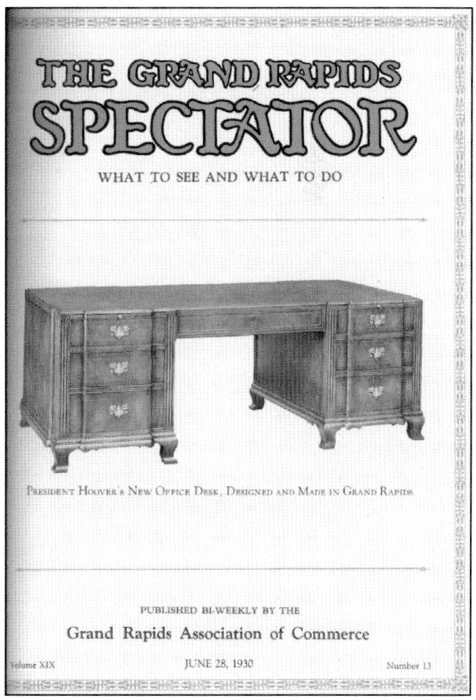

THE GRAND RAPIDS
SPECTATOR
WHAT TO SEE AND WHAT TO DO

President Hoover's New Office Desk, Designed and Made in Grand Rapids

PUBLISHED BI-WEEKLY BY THE
Grand Rapids Association of Commerce

Volume XIX JUNE 28, 1930 Number 13

The kind of attention to detail as shown by the unidentified worker above—and associated with the city's products—made Grand Rapids an obvious choice when Pres. Herbert Hoover needed an Oval Office desk. The desk was used in turn by Pres. Franklin D. Roosevelt and Pres. Harry S. Truman. Truman eventually presented it to Eleanor Roosevelt. (Grand Rapids Public Library.)

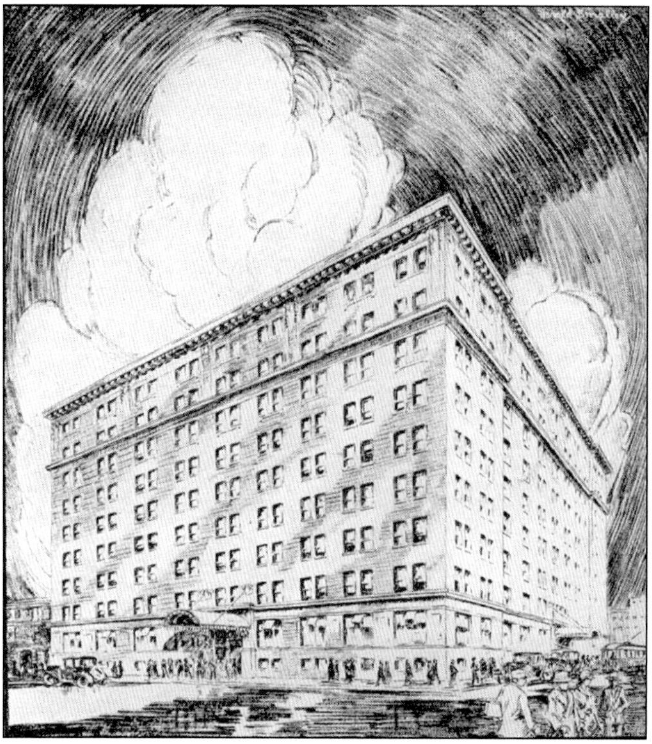

In the January 1929 issue of *Furniture Manufacturer*, local financier Dudley Waters announced the construction of a new nine-story furniture exhibition building to meet increasing demand for showroom space. The building, known as the Waters Building, was the second largest in the city. When completed, it was a separate building but connected with another showroom, the Furniture Temple. More than one-third of the space was leased before construction began. It would be the country's largest exhibit hall until Chicago's Merchandise Mart opened. (Grand Rapids Public Library.)

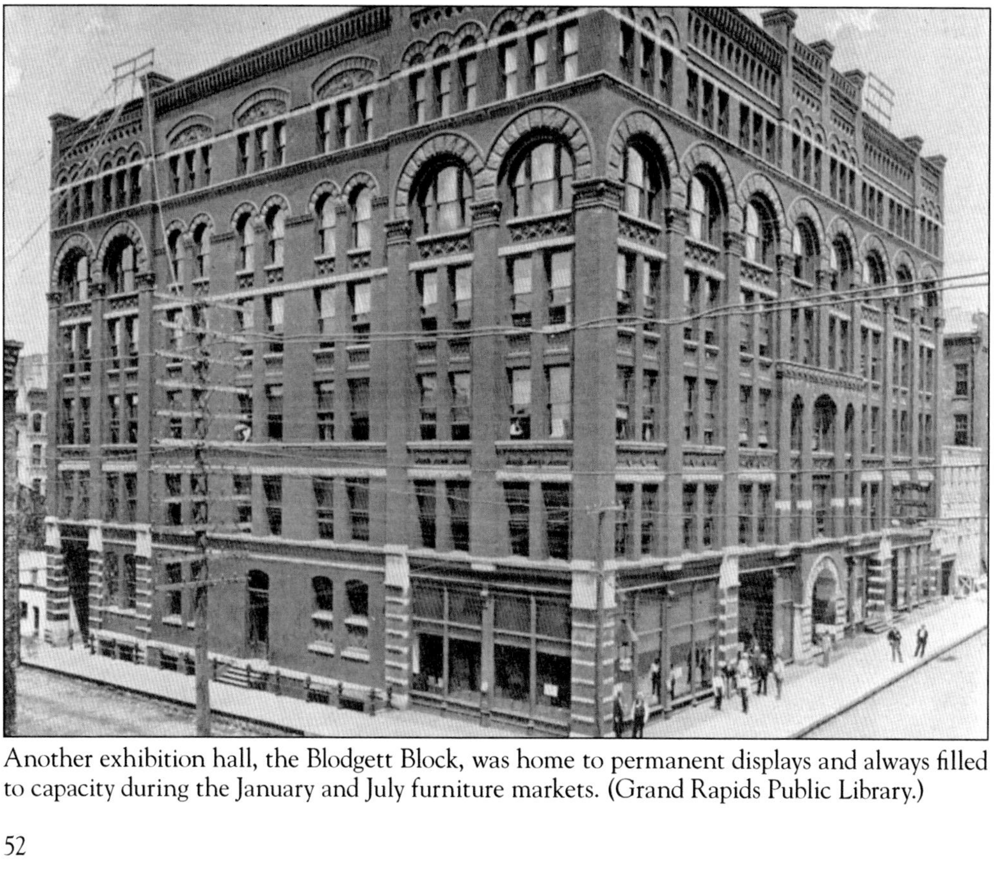

Another exhibition hall, the Blodgett Block, was home to permanent displays and always filled to capacity during the January and July furniture markets. (Grand Rapids Public Library.)

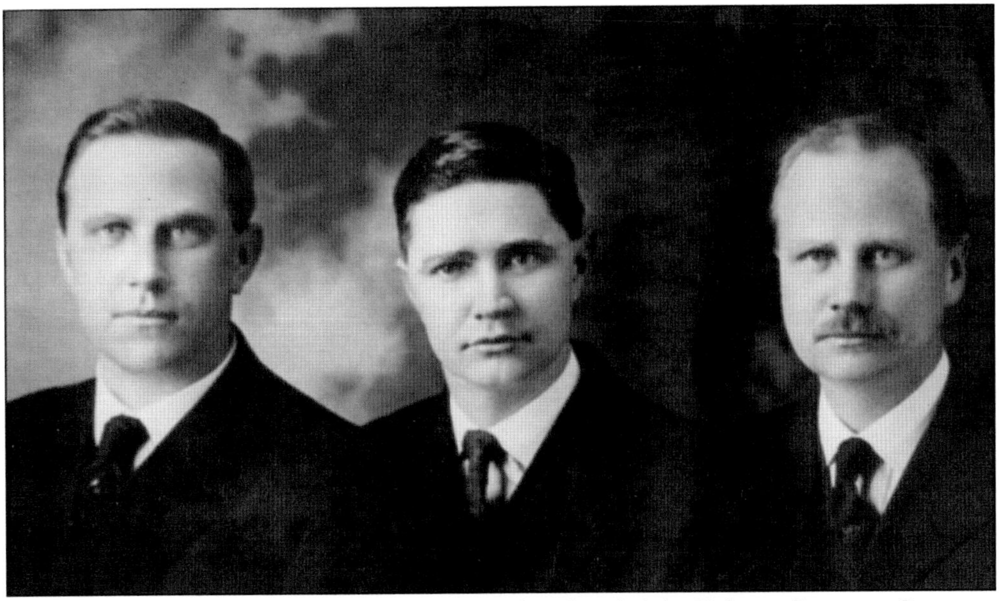

The Hekman brothers were photographed when they founded the Hekman Furniture Company in 1922; they are, from left to right, John, Jelle, and Henry. Sons of Dutch immigrants, they began business with a line of occasional tables, gradually adding living room pieces in several styles, including the English Yewwood Collection. During World War II, the company produced ammunition boxes and glider parts. (Charles Hekman.)

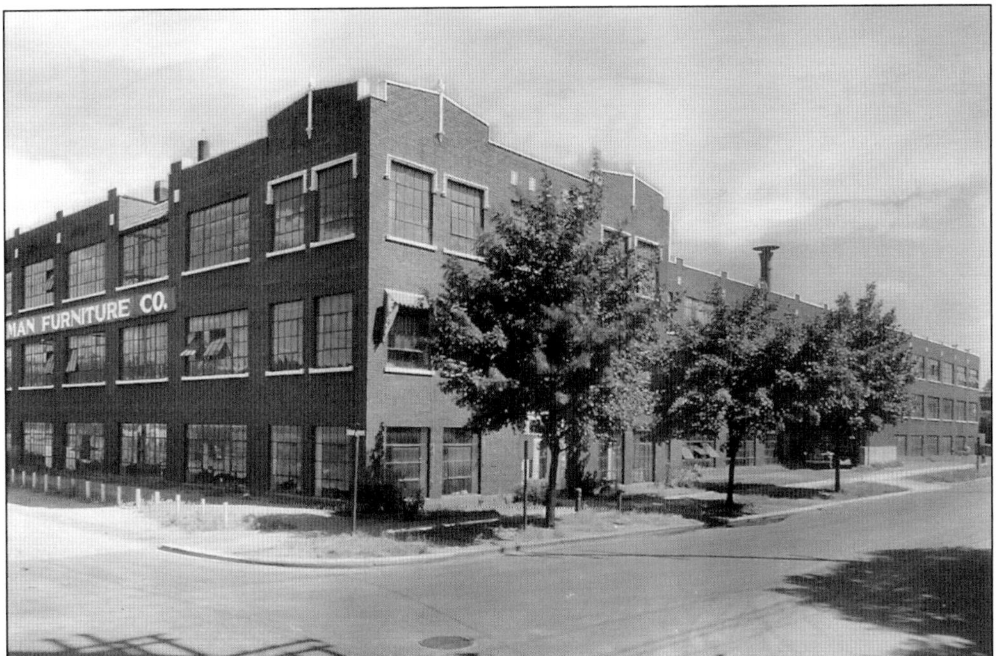

The Hekman factory, located on Buchanan Street in Grand Rapids, is seen here as it looked in 1950. In the 1960s, the company built a second factory in Lexington, North Carolina, followed by a third in High Point, North Carolina. (Charles Hekman.)

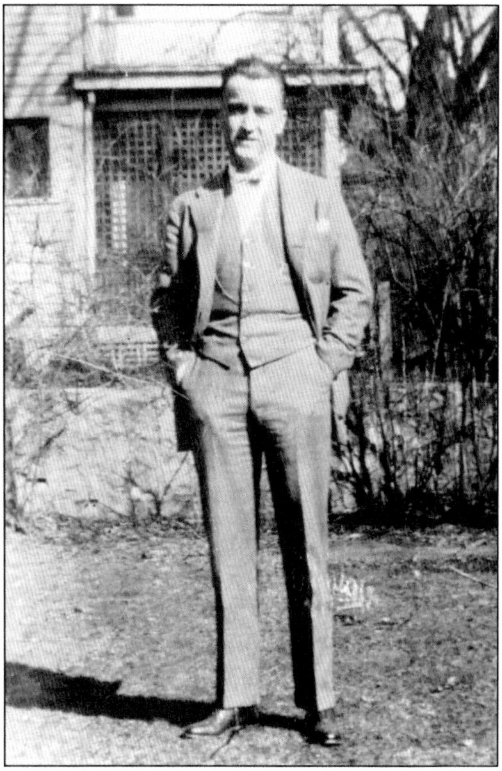

Walter Idema, Peter M. Wege Sr., and 10 investors founded Metal Office Furniture Company in 1912 to produce fireproof file cabinets and safes. Here Idema poses casually in what was probably a rare moment away from his office. (Steelcase, Inc.)

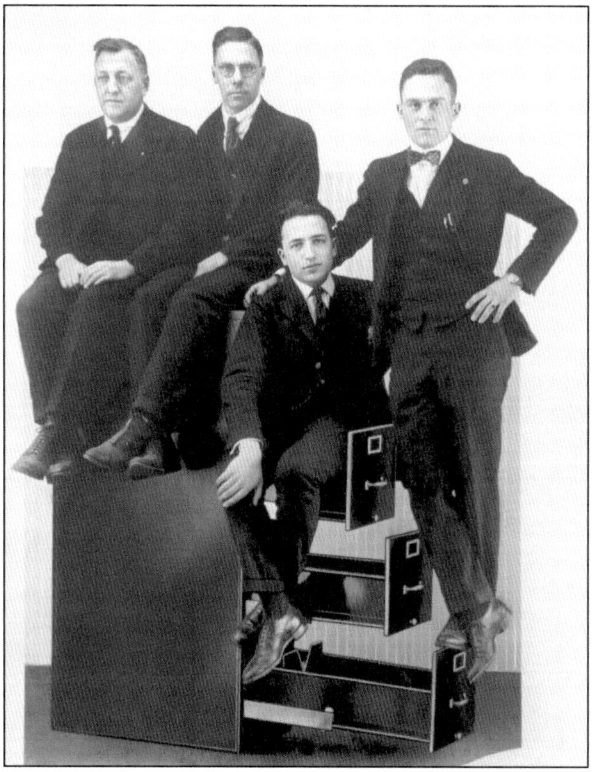

David D. Hunting's natural sales talent led Metal Office Furniture into the production of steel office desks. When the government needed 200 fireproof desks for the Boston Customs House, he bid. When the winning bidder's product did not meet the quality standard, the buyer asked Hunting for the address of his showroom so he could see a sample desk. There was no showroom because there was no desk. The company put together a prototype and the rest is history. Hunting, at the far right, and his staff demonstrate the strength of their steel file cabinets. (Steelcase, Inc.)

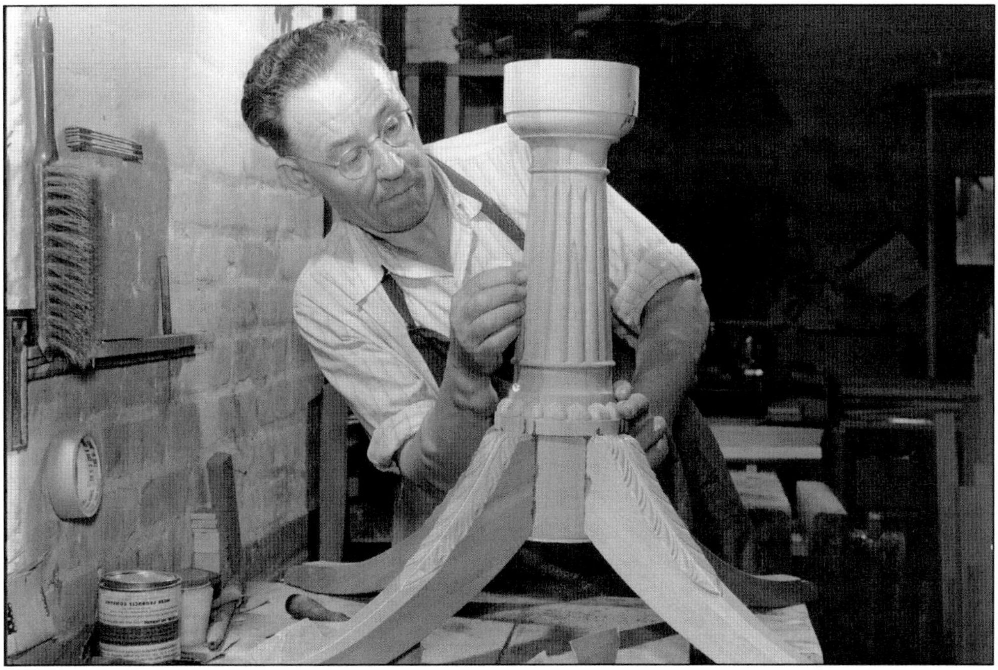

How many times did Jack Preston hand sand this pedestal table base before deeming it finished? Note the carving on the legs. Workers like Preston took immense pride in a job well done. His employer, Johnson Furniture Company, was established in 1908 by three brothers, Carl, Hjalmar, and Axel Johnson, all of whom were master cabinetmakers in their native Sweden. In 1963, the company merged with the Timber-Line Company but retained the Johnson name. (Collections of the Public Museum, Grand Rapids.)

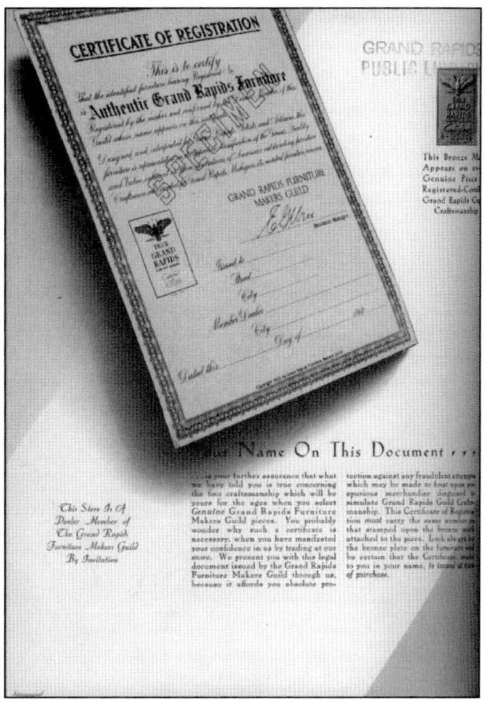

This advertisement, shown in a 1930s edition of the decorating magazine the *Stylist*, displays the certificate of authenticity customers were told to insist on when buying Grand Rapids furniture. Imposters tried passing off inferior pieces as Grand Rapids–made until they were sued and ordered to stop. (Grand Rapids Public Library.)

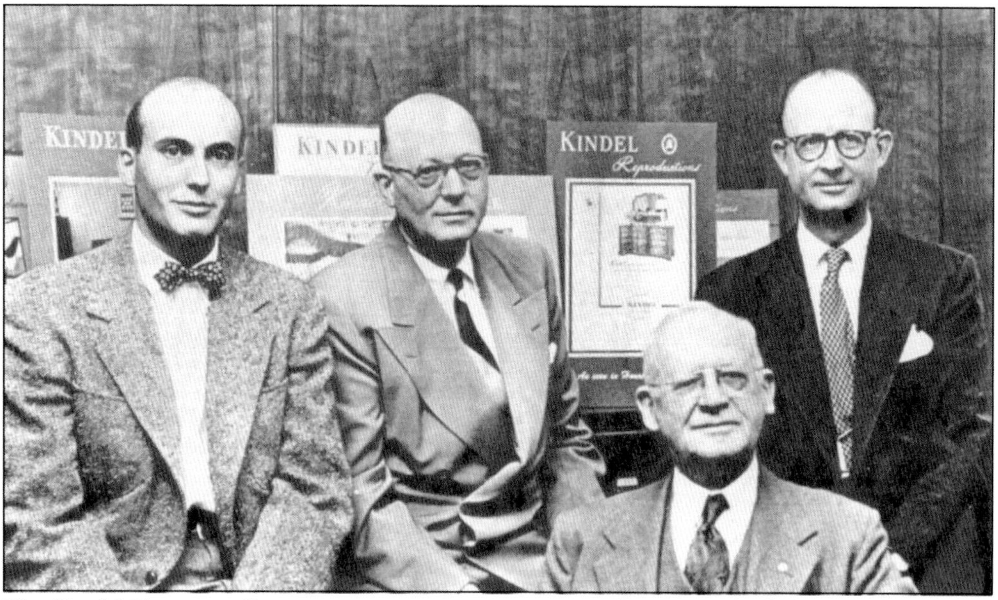

The Kindel Furniture Company management team in 1937 consisted of three generations of Kindels. From left to right are Ted Kindel, secretary in charge of quality control; Charles M. Kindel, vice president in charge of production; Charles J. Kindel, president and founder; and Tom Kindel, treasurer in charge of design and merchandising. (Kindel Furniture Company.)

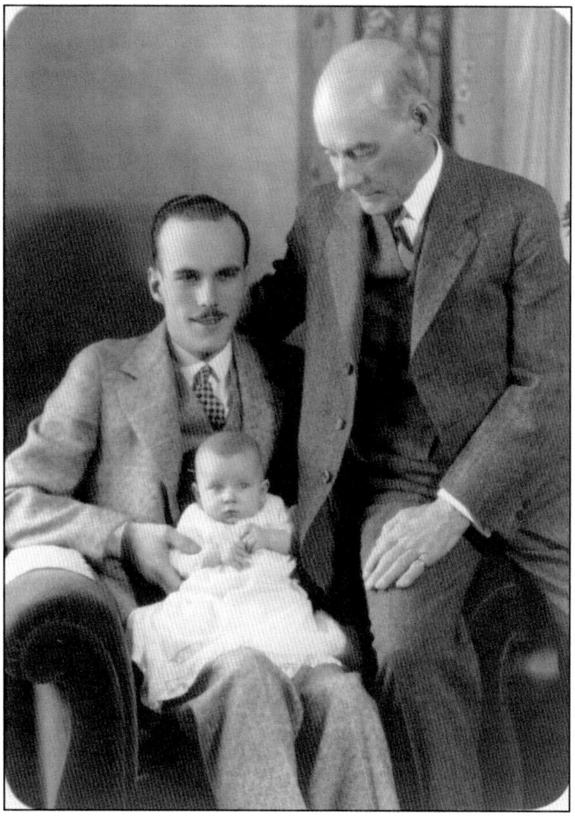

This is another company with a three-generation portrait, although unlike the Kindels above, the youngest Sligh is not yet a company officer. Posing in 1926 are Charles R. Sligh Jr. holding Charles R. Sligh III, while Charles R. Sligh Sr. admires his grandson. (Bentley Historical Library, University of Michigan.)

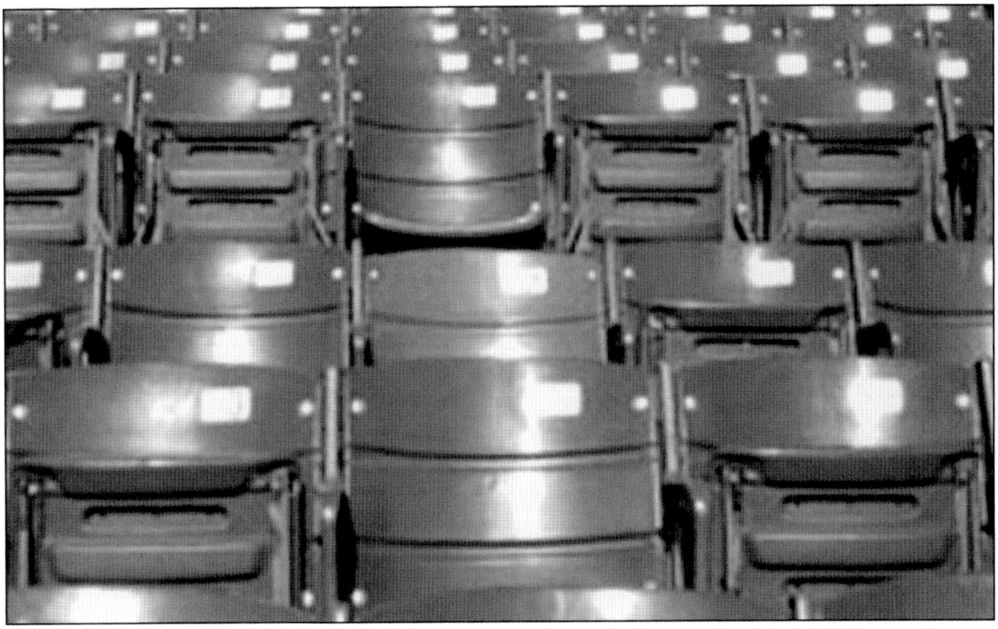

American Seating Company installed these seats at Boston's Fenway Park. Ted Williams, Boston Red Sox left fielder, played from April 1939 to September 1960, with two time-outs while he served as a Marine Corps pilot. He played his last game on September 28, 1960, and on his last at bat hit a home run. The ball hit the seat shown above (second row, center), and the club painted it red in Williams's honor. It has been considered a lucky seat ever since. (American Seating Company.)

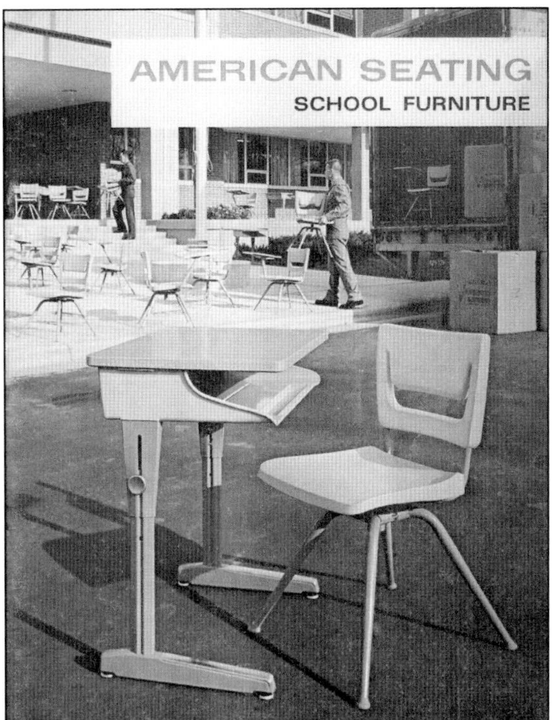

American Seating Company started out as Grand Rapids School Furniture Company in 1886. The desk at right, slightly modified over the years, has endured as a classroom staple. (American Seating Company.)

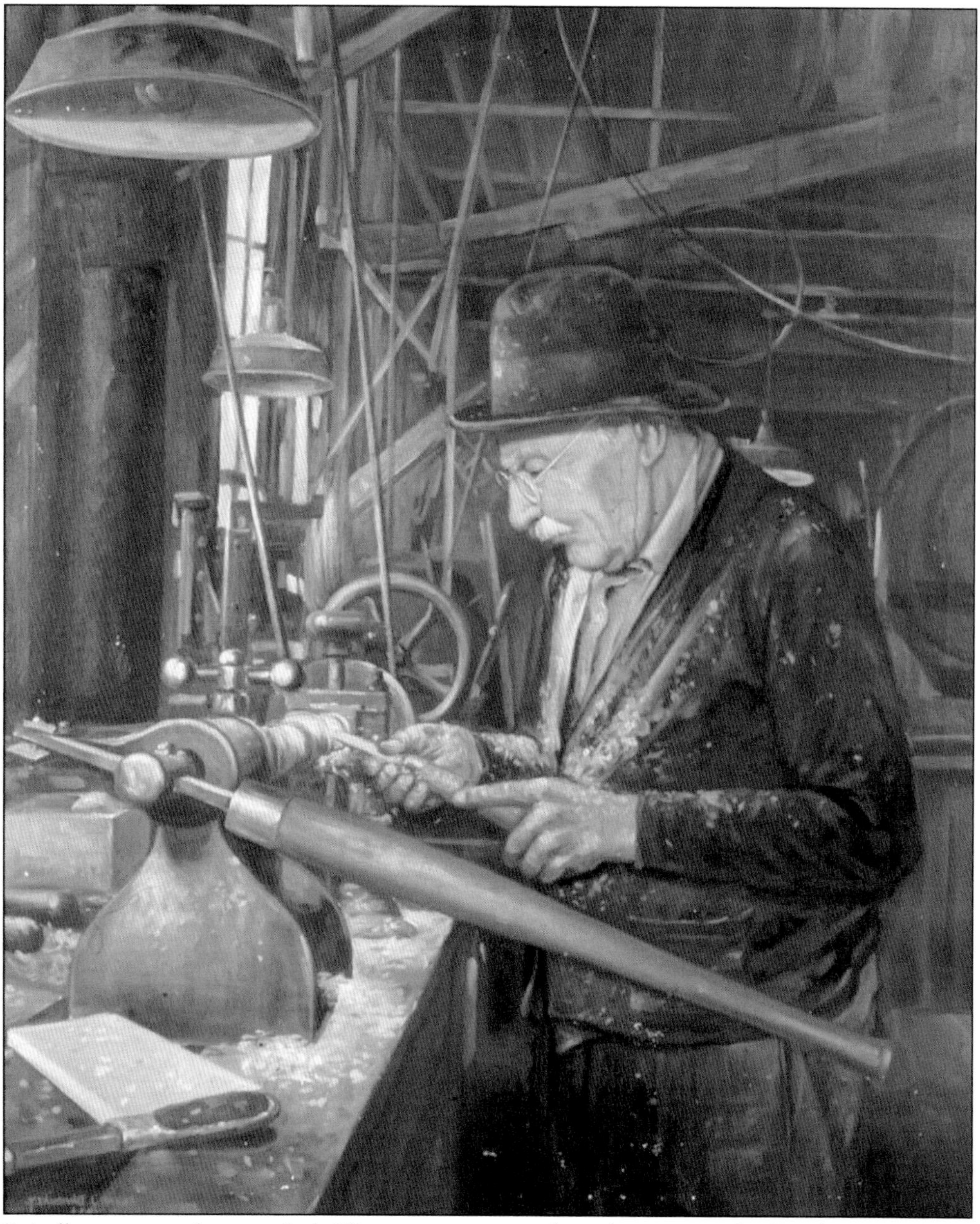

Spindle carver and turner Jack Weaver was captured in this portrait by Frank J. Davidhazy in 1934. Weaver worked for one company, the Phoenix Furniture Company, an unmatched 66.5 years. Phoenix Furniture did not last that long, but Weaver remained on the job when it was bought by the Robert W. Irwin Company. Davidhazy, brought to Grand Rapids to head the decorative design department at Robert W. Irwin, once had 36 artists under his supervision, all reproducing his designs on fine wood cabinets. He worked for several employers before opening his own studio in 1956 with his son, Frank S. Davidhazy. He spent a total of 68 years in the Grand Rapids furniture industry. (Collections of the Public Museum, Grand Rapids.)

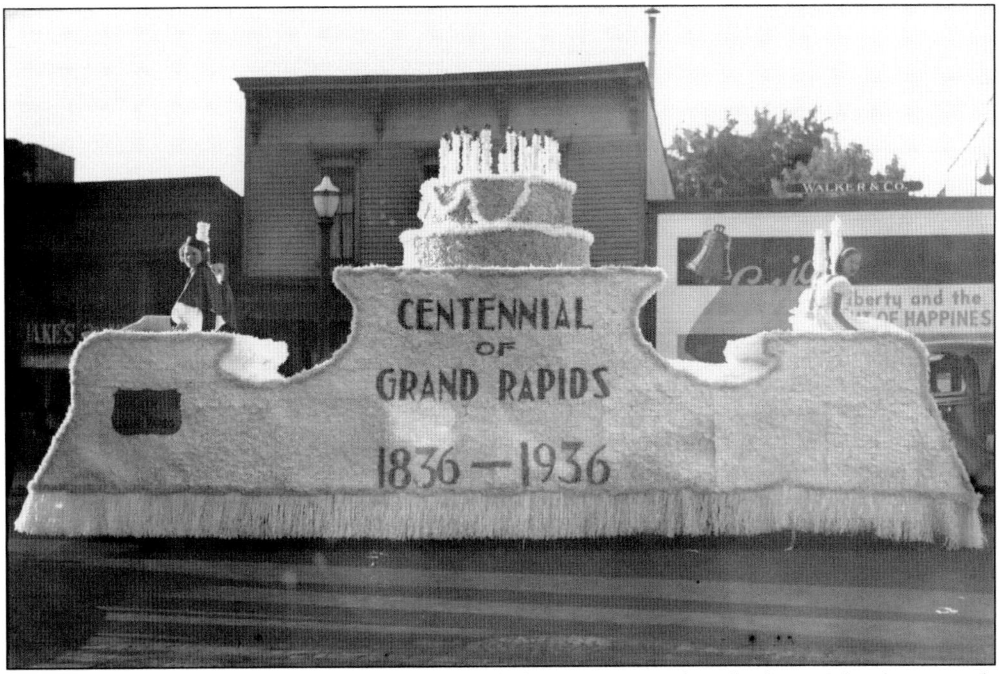

The year 1936 marked a century of Grand Rapids furniture—one hundred years that began with William "Deacon" Haldane's hoop-back Windsor chair and ended with an oversize chair atop a float, a throne for the young women chosen to ride in the July 7 parade. Thousands visited Grand Rapids for the celebration's major attraction: a 72,000-piece furniture display spread over 25 acres. (Grand Rapids Public Library.)

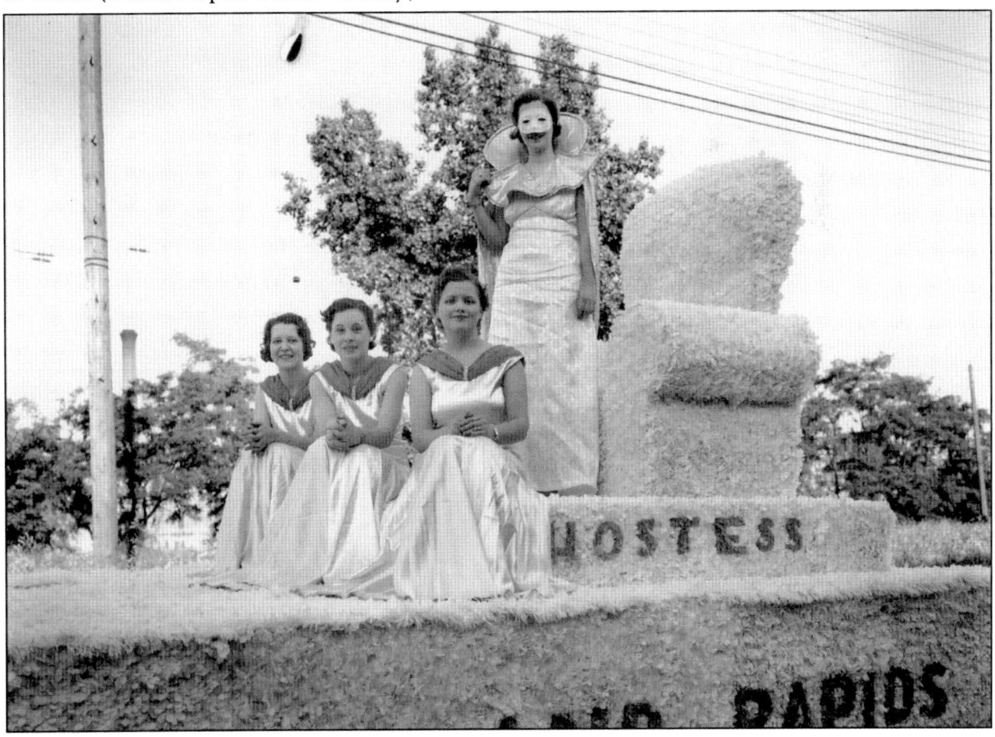

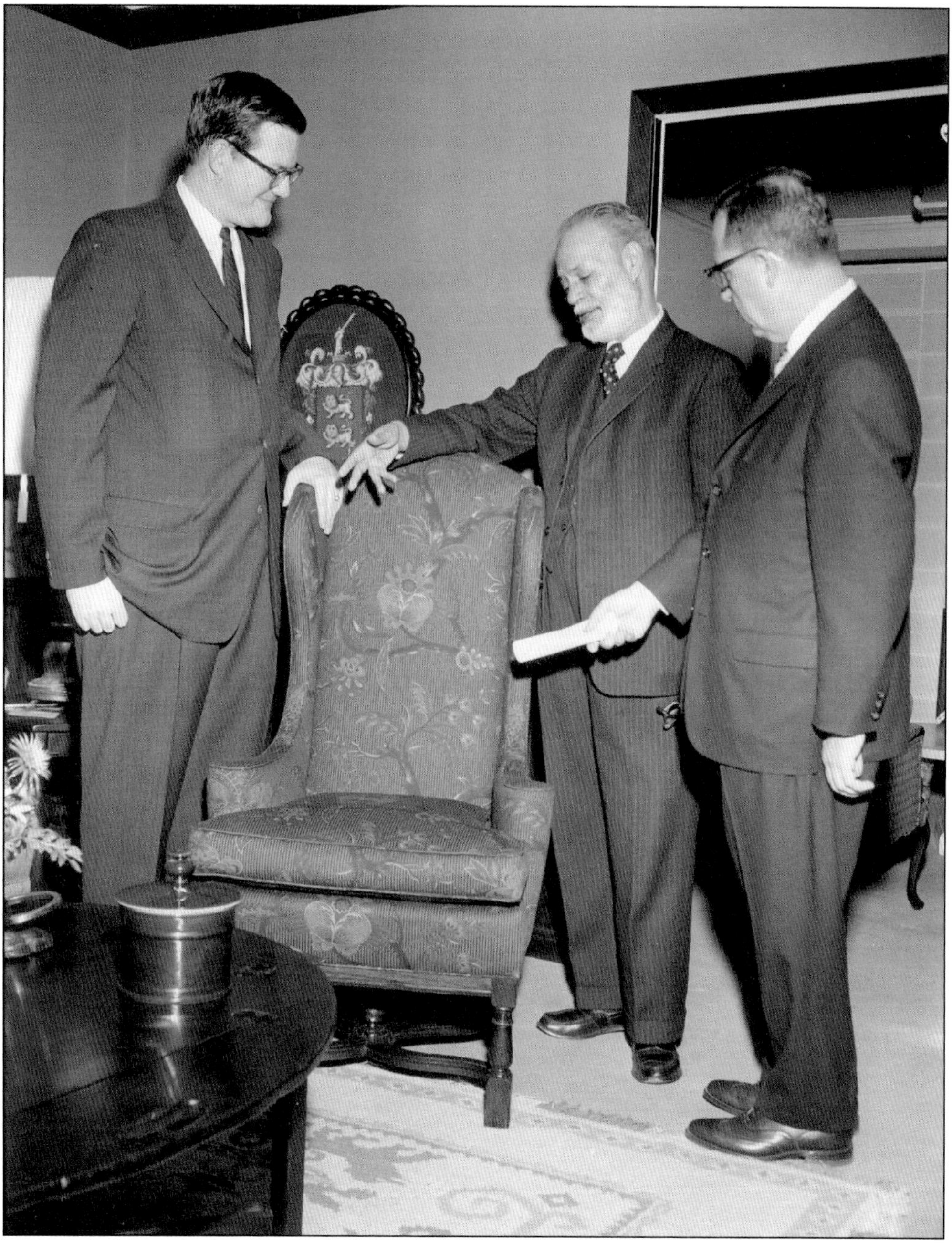

Furniture buyers from around the country descended upon Grand Rapids for the semiannual furniture market in July 1941. From left to right are Earl Johnson, president of Johnson Furniture Company; S. Bartley Cannell Jr.; and S. Bartley Cannell III. The Cannells are viewing pieces from Johnson's Forward Trend Group at the factory showrooms. The Cannells are continuing the tradition began by father and grandfather, S. Bartley Cannell Sr., in shopping Grand Rapids for their Los Angeles home furnishings store, Cannell and Chaffin. (Grand Rapids Public Library.)

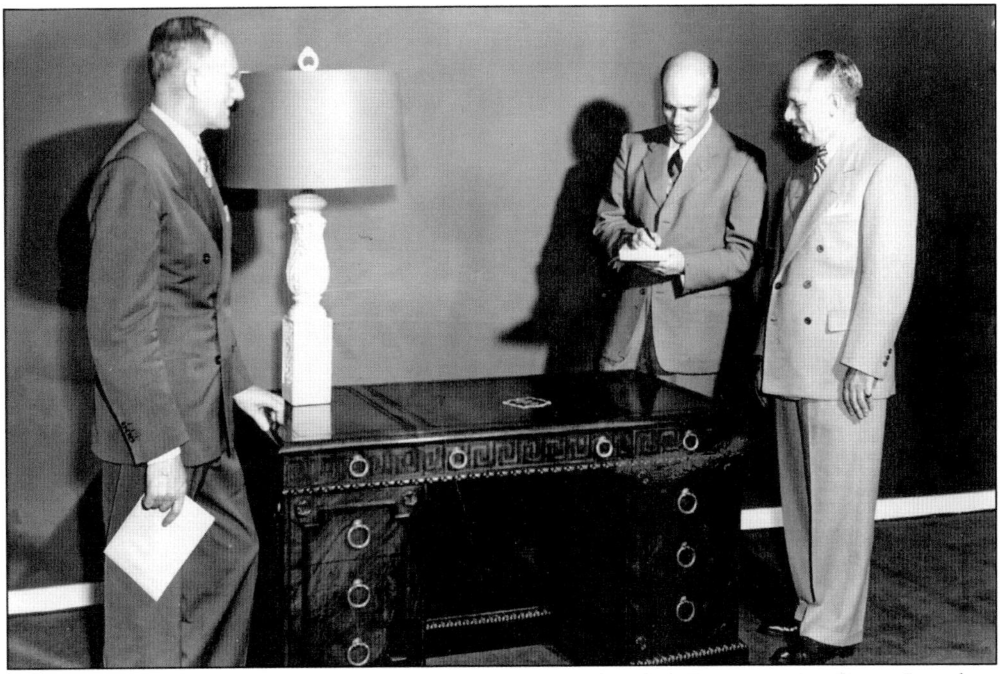

The furniture market appears to have been successful for the Sligh Furniture Company. President Charles R. Sligh Jr., center, is writing an order for the Higbee Company buyers from Cleveland, Ohio. Frank Tongue, left, is the assistant buyer, and Earl W. Coyne is the company's division merchandise manager. In 1941, desks were only a small part of the company's offerings. Today the company specializes in home office and entertainment storage products. The company headquarters are in Holland, Michigan, but manufacturing is done in Asia. (Grand Rapids Public Library.)

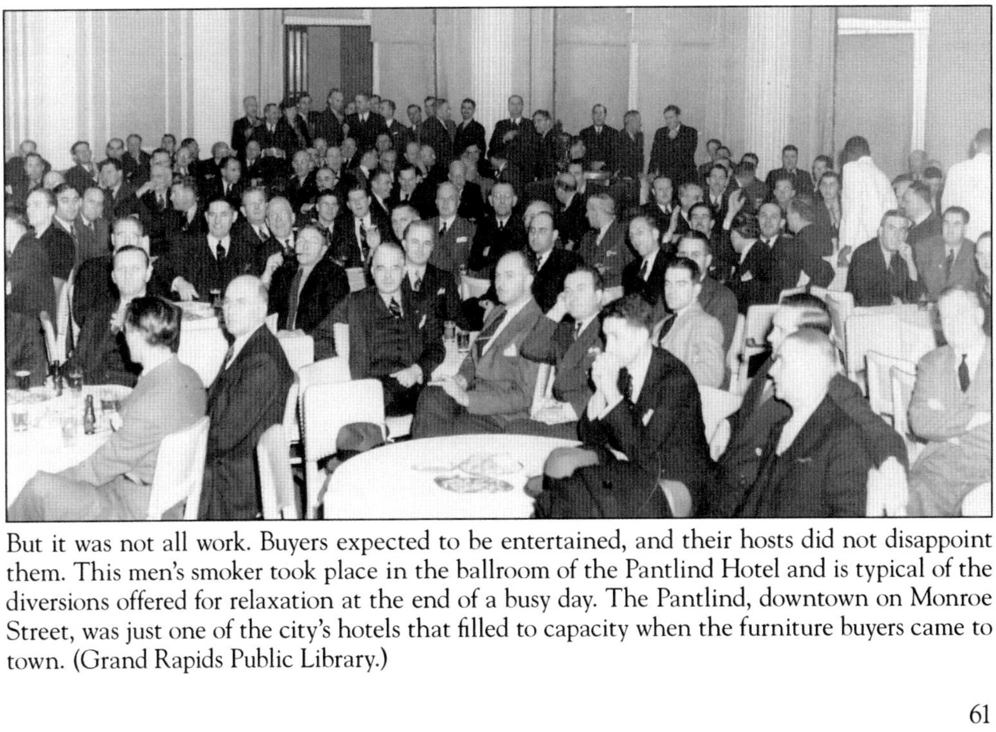

But it was not all work. Buyers expected to be entertained, and their hosts did not disappoint them. This men's smoker took place in the ballroom of the Pantlind Hotel and is typical of the diversions offered for relaxation at the end of a busy day. The Pantlind, downtown on Monroe Street, was just one of the city's hotels that filled to capacity when the furniture buyers came to town. (Grand Rapids Public Library.)

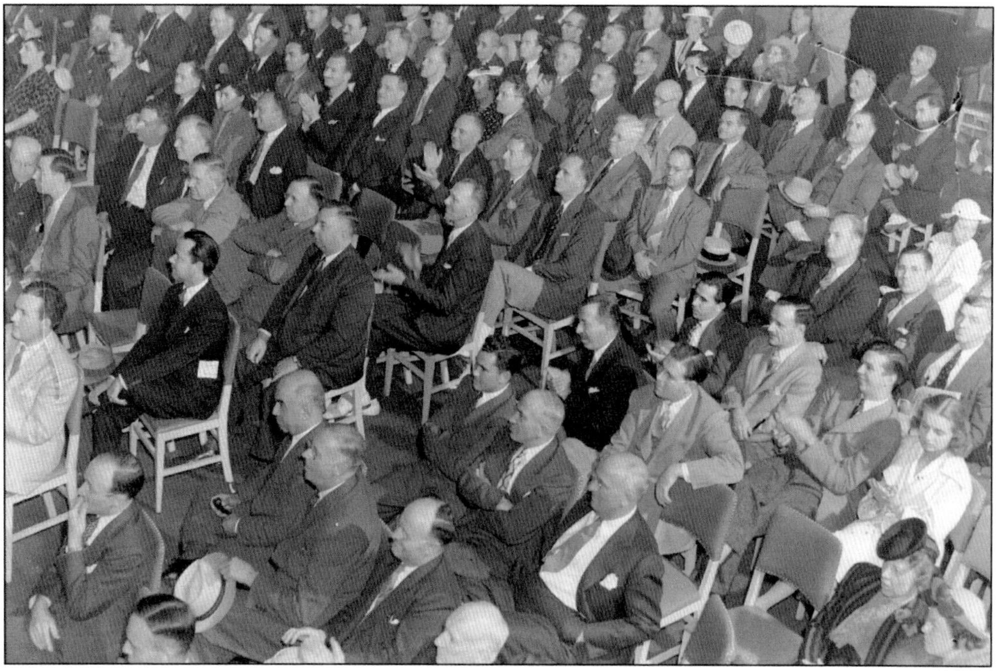

Factory owners and the Furniture Manufacturers Association planned enough entertainment to keep buyers coming back year after year. This group is enjoying a vaudeville show. A few women are in attendance, but the furniture buyers are still predominately male. (Grand Rapids Public Library.)

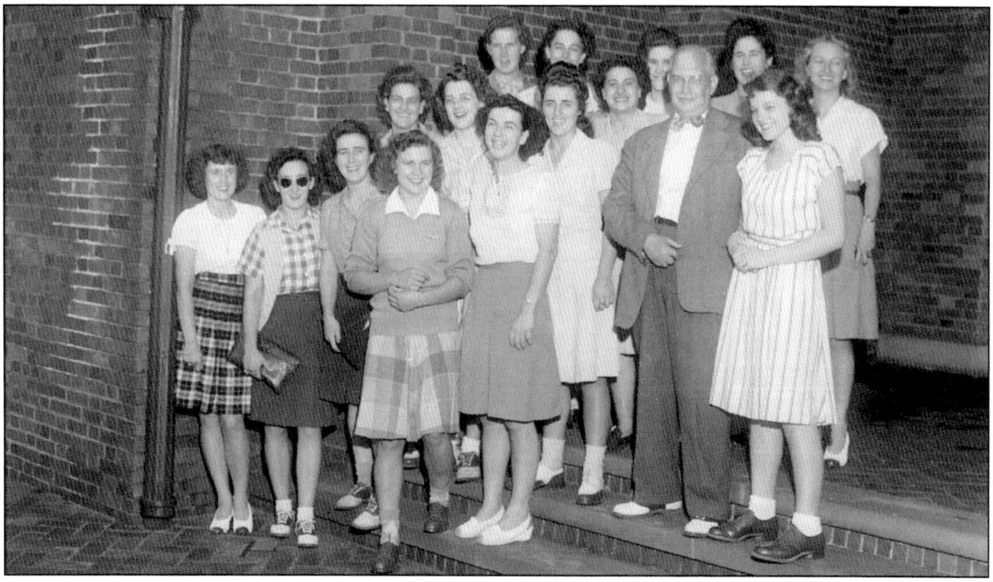

In 1939, the Grand Rapids Furniture Museum opened at 427 Fulton Street. Posing in front of the museum in August 1945 are the Grand Rapids Chicks. The team was part of the All-American Girls Professional Baseball League and existed for 10 years. Baseball fans could, and did, "root, root, root for the home team." The league, founded by Philip Wrigley in 1943, was immortalized in the 1992 film *A League of Their Own*. The Chicks brought home championships in 1947 and 1953. (Grand Rapids Public Library.)

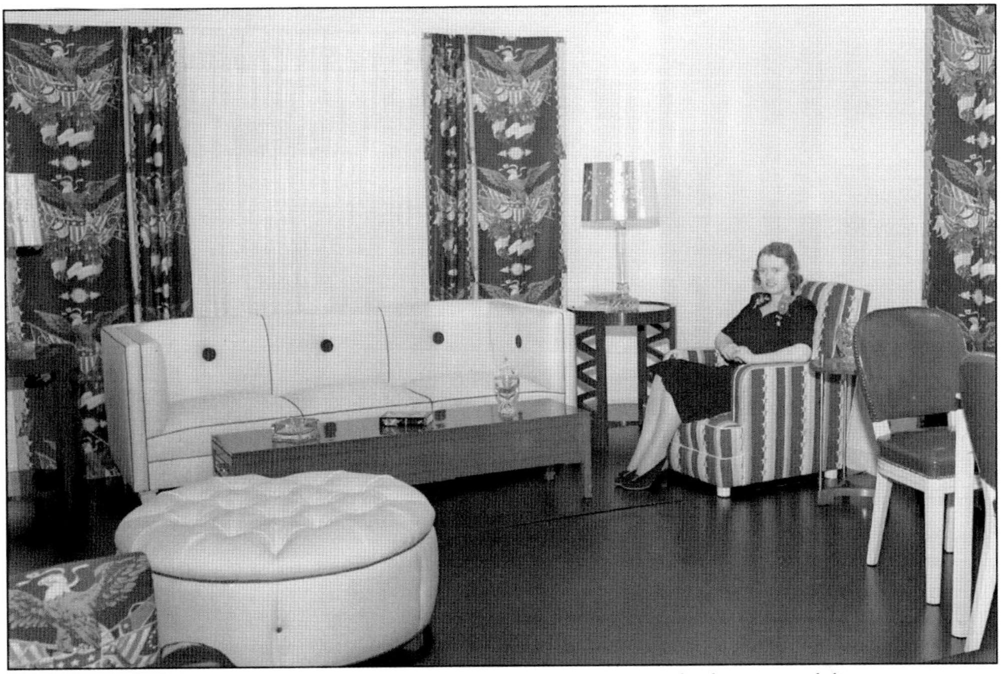

Furniture museum exhibits changed periodically. Here a new bedroom and living room are displayed. By 1959, the collection had been moved to the East Building of the Public Museum, Grand Rapids. Today it has grown into the renowned Furniture City exhibit at the museum's new Pearl Street building in downtown Grand Rapids. (Grand Rapids Public Library.)

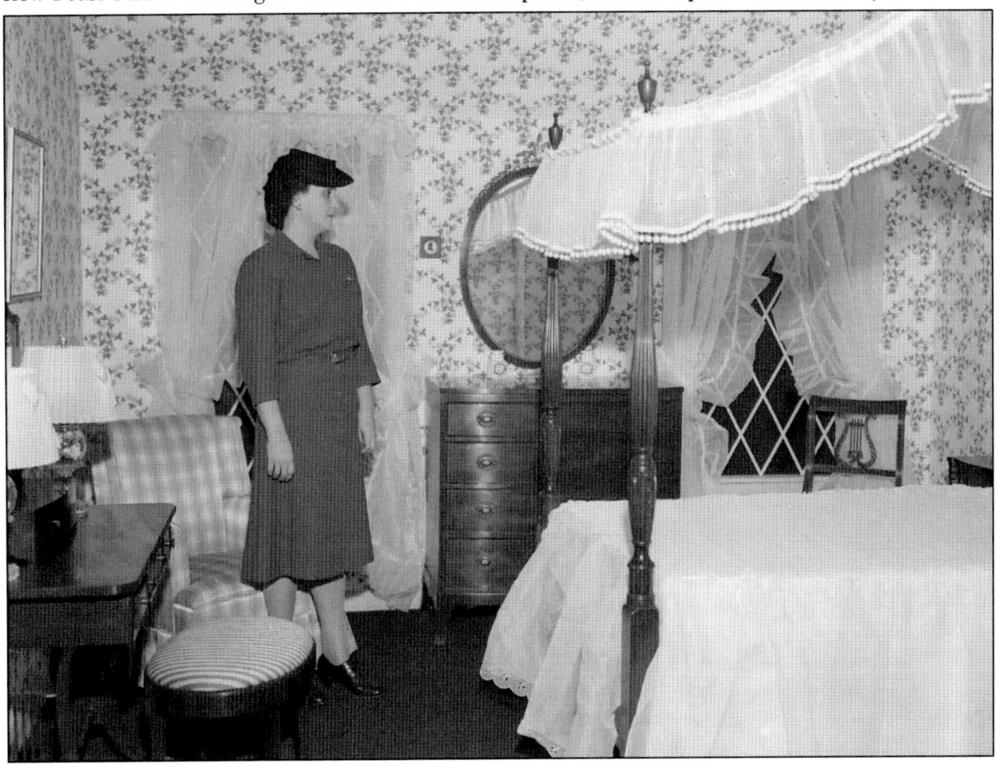

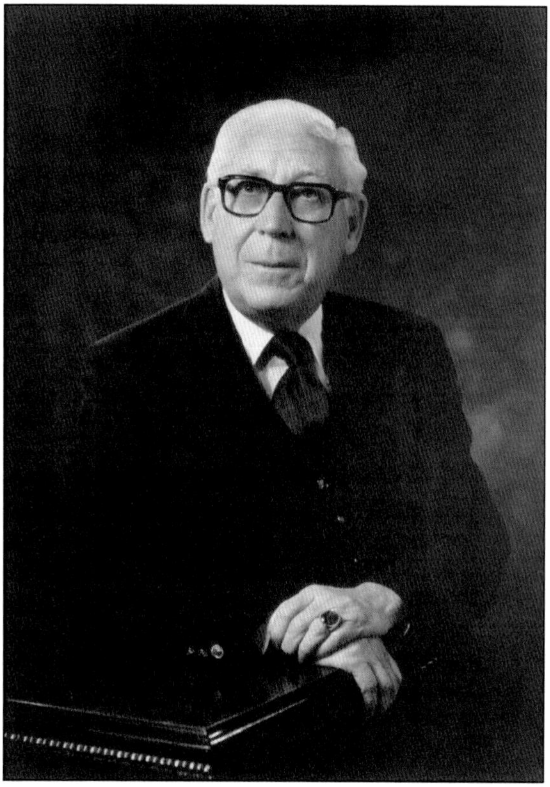

Howard Miller, founder of Howard Miller Clock Company and son of Herman Miller, was born in Grand Rapids in 1905 and died on September 21, 1995, at age 90. The company started as the Herman Miller Clock Company but changed the name in 1937. Located in Zeeland, less than 20 miles from Grand Rapids, it continues to produce high-quality clocks, including grandfather clocks destined to become heirlooms. (Howard Miller Clock Company.)

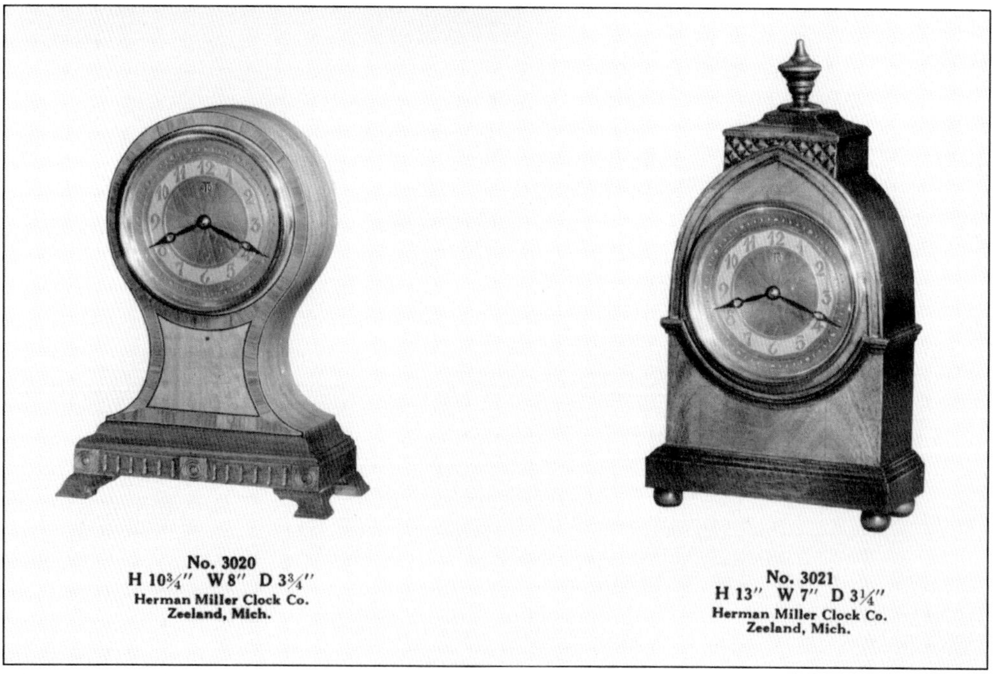

These two clocks are representative of those made by the Howard Miller company—and the ageless designs produced prior to 1937, as they appear in that year's catalog. (Howard Miller Clock Company.)

The Trend Clock Company, also in Zeeland, began in 1937 and became a Sligh subsidiary in 1968. In the early days, the company specialized in table clocks, like the classic example shown here, and other small wooden home accessories. Joining Sligh allowed the company to expand its line to include grandfather and mantel clocks. (Grand Rapids Public Library.)

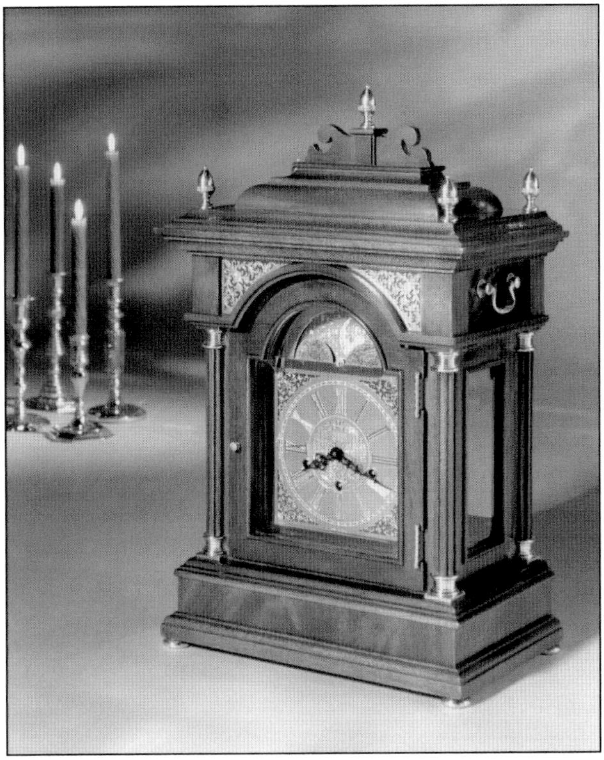

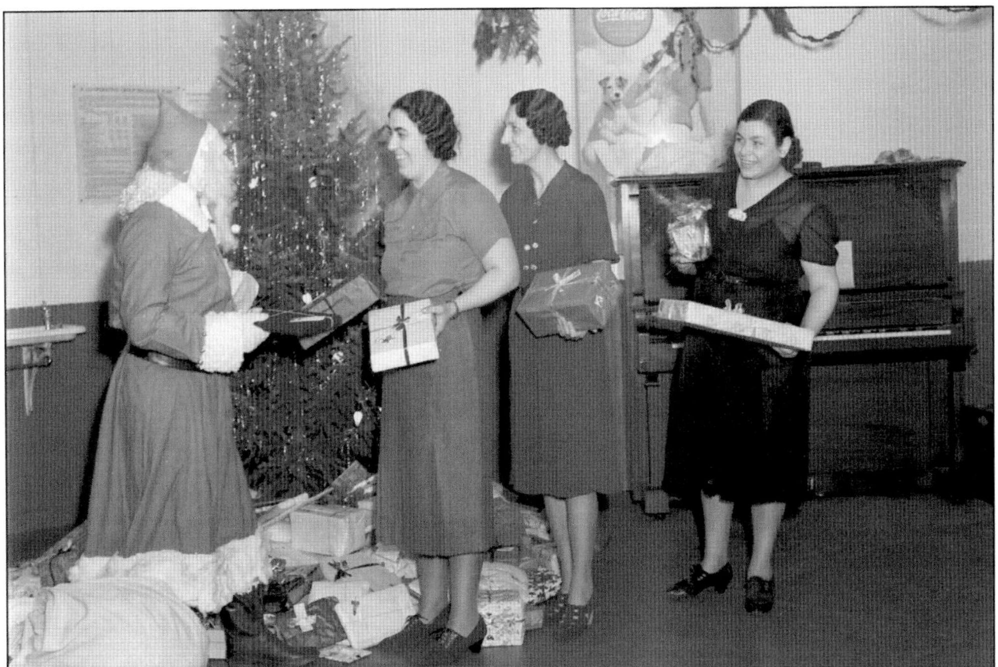

Women from McInerny Spring and Wire Company take time out to enjoy a Christmas party in 1938. The company supplied springs for mattresses and upholstered pieces to all the major furniture makers. McInerny also supplied the automotive industry. (Grand Rapids Public Library.)

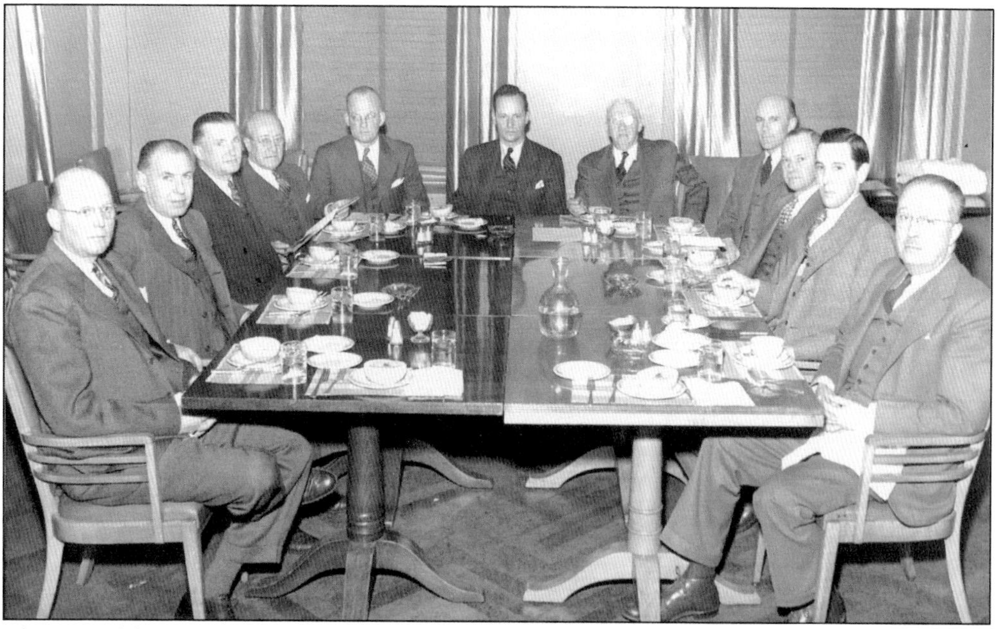

The powerful Furniture Manufacturers Association was essentially governed by the city's largest companies, not surprising since they employed 85 percent of the workforce. Directors attending this February 1945 meeting are, from left to right, Charles Kindel, Philip Cornelius, Fritz Mueller Sr., Clarence Dexter, Rodney Schopps, Steven Dunn, Stuart Foote, Charles Sligh, Earl Johnson, Joseph Griswold, and Charles Brower. (Grand Rapids Public Library.)

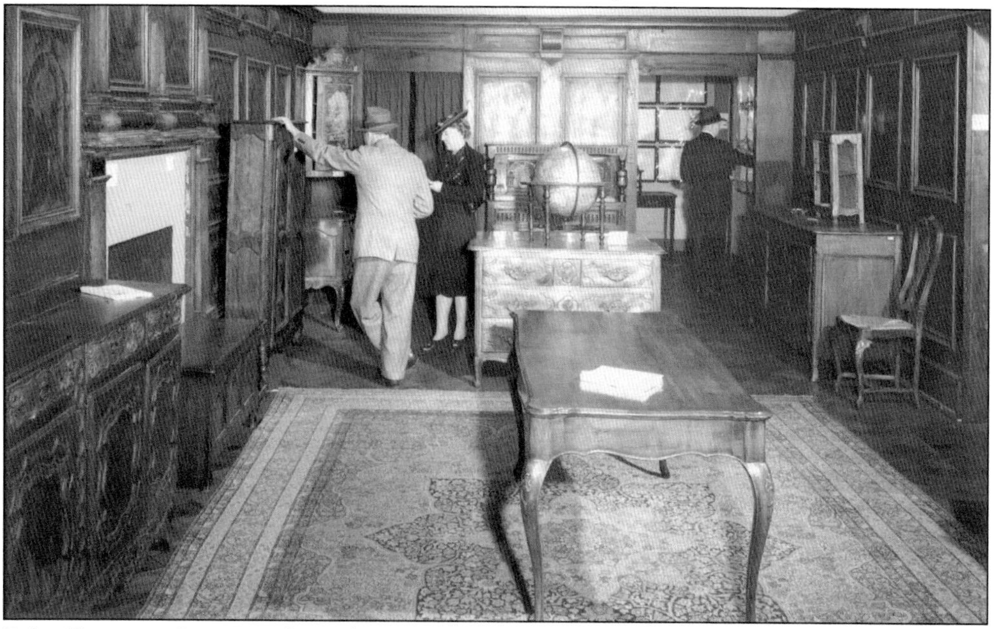

Baker Furniture Company, formed in 1903, became a major presence in both Grand Rapids and nearby Holland where it was headquartered. The company specialized in period reproductions from 18th-century Federal American, British, and French design. The Baker Museum for Furniture Research opened in Holland in 1941 and remained in operation until the mid-1990s. Here museum patrons enjoy one of the lavishly decorated rooms. (Grand Rapids Public Library.)

G. W. Haworth founded Modern Products Company in Holland, Michigan, in 1948 to produce retail fixtures like the one shown at right, which is a grocer's stand for packaged snack cakes. The catalog drawing below is of a necktie display rack. Haworth knew that innovation and flexibility were the keys to staying competitive and by the 1950s sensed the company's future lay in office furnishings. By 1975, the company had changed its name to Haworth and is, along with Steelcase, Inc., and Herman Miller, Inc., one of three industry giants. (Haworth, Inc.)

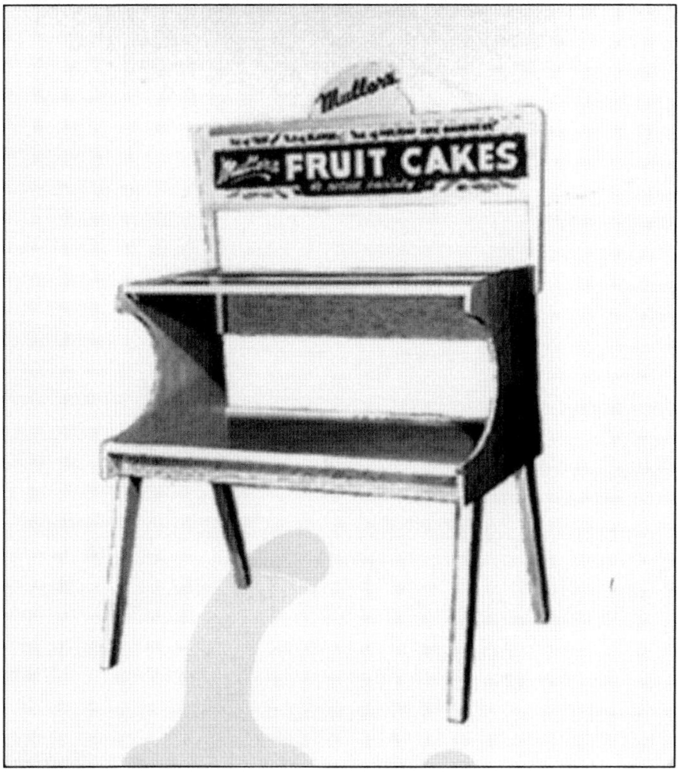

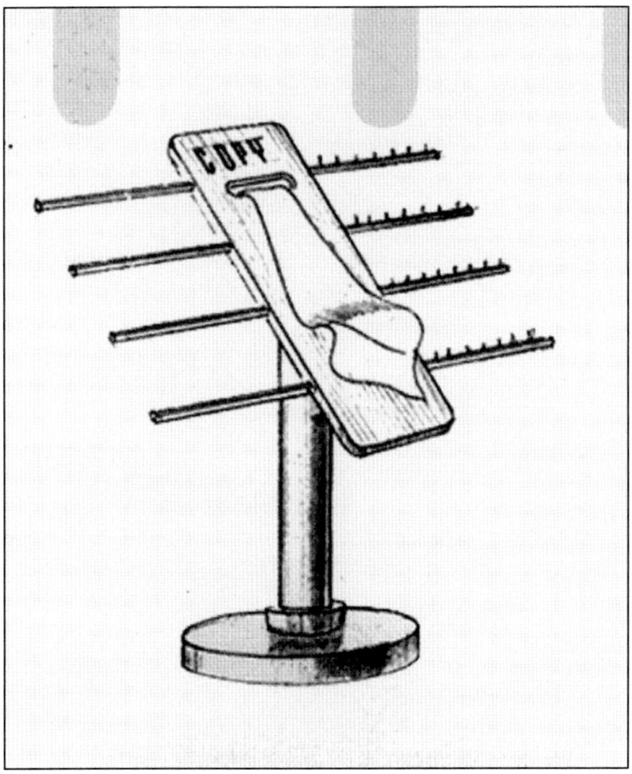

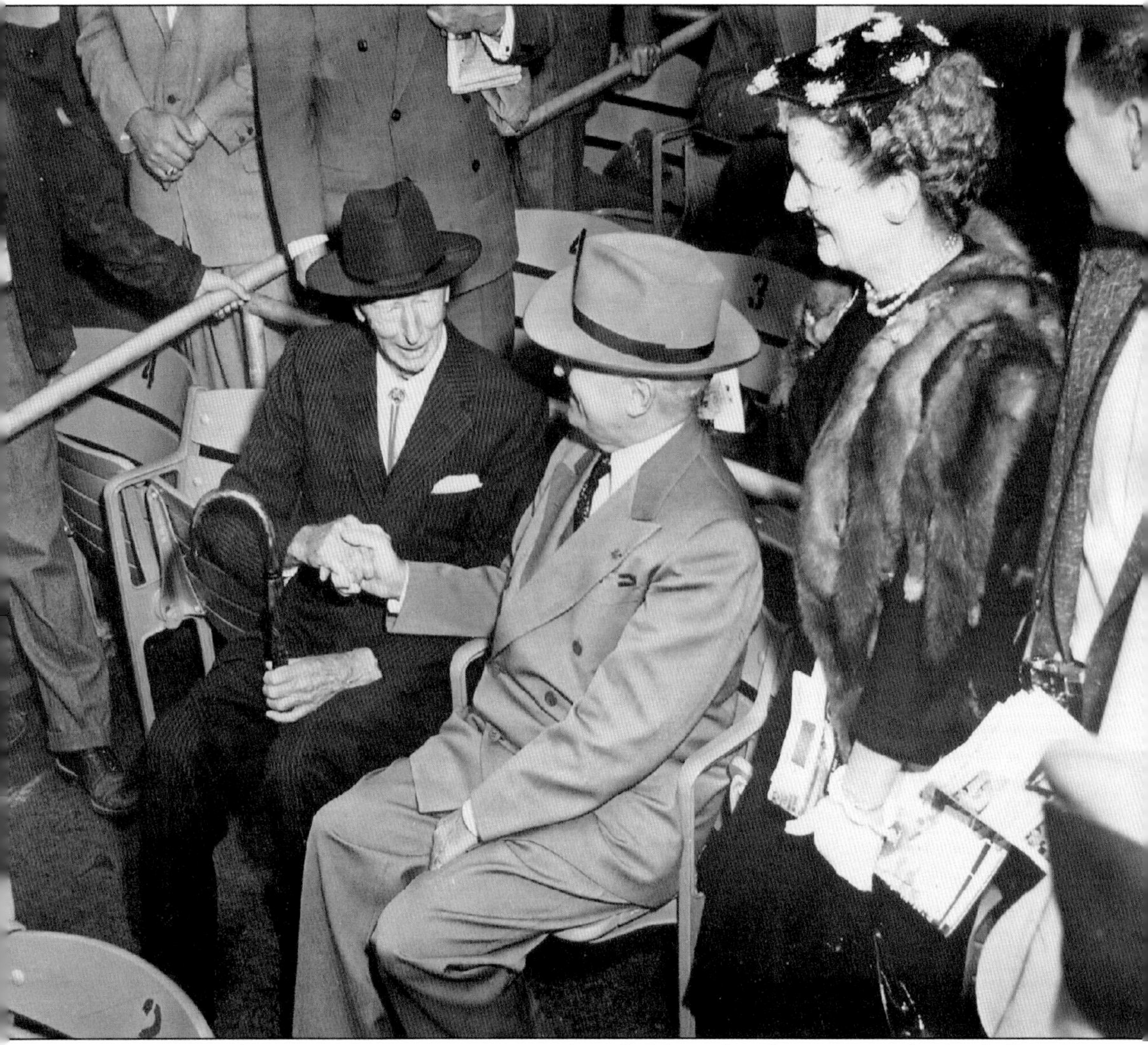

Former president Harry S. Truman greets unidentified fans after throwing out the first ball at the Kansas City (Missouri) Athletics opening game against the Detroit Tigers on April 12, 1955. He came back for the second game of the series on April 13. This was three years after Dwight D. Eisenhower replaced him in the White House. The seats at the Kansas City stadium were made by American Seating Company. (American Seating Company)

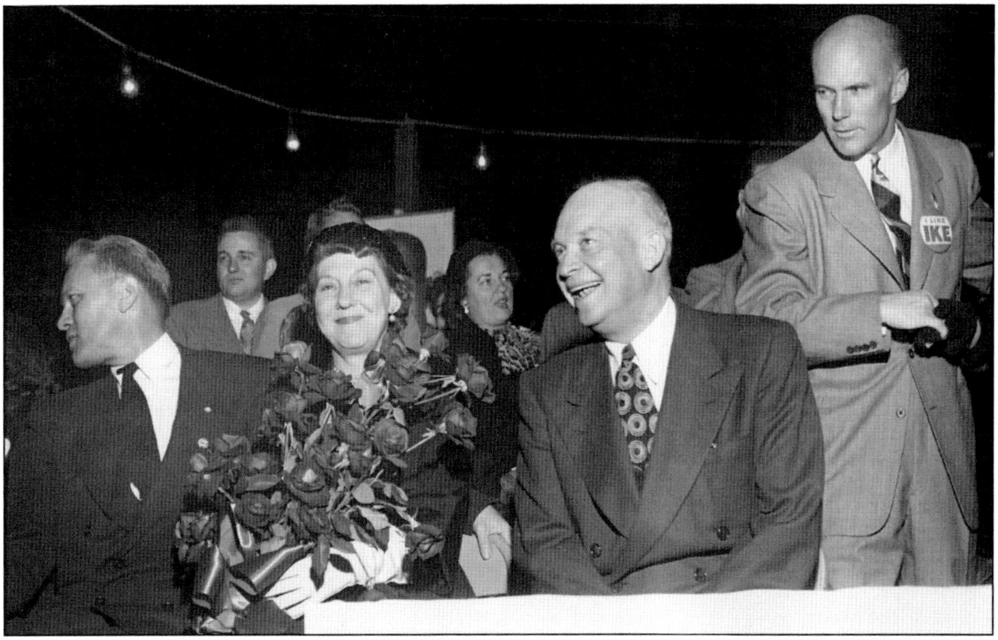

Grand Rapids liked Ike in 1952. One of Sligh Furniture Company's Nottingham desks was given to presidential candidate Gen. Dwight D. Eisenhower and his wife, Mamie, during a campaign stop in Grand Rapids. After the presentation, the Eisenhowers smiled for photographers. At far left is young congressman and future president Gerald R. Ford. To Dwight's right is Charles R. Sligh Jr. Ford, Grand Rapids' favorite son, represented the area in Congress for 25 years before being thrust into the vice presidency and the presidency. (Bentley Historical Library, University of Michigan.)

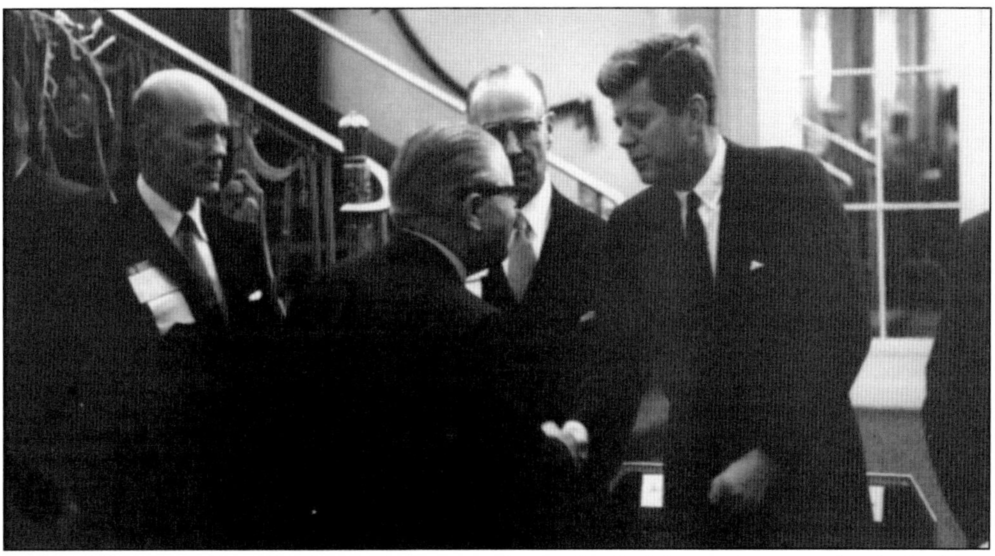

Although active in Kent County Republicans, Charles R. Sligh Jr. put business ahead of politics and, as a director of the Furniture Manufacturers Association, warmly greets Pres. John F. Kennedy in 1961. Sligh had the ability to present the manufacturer's point of view to presidents of both parties in a nonthreatening, nonpartisan manner. (Bentley Historical Library, University of Michigan.)

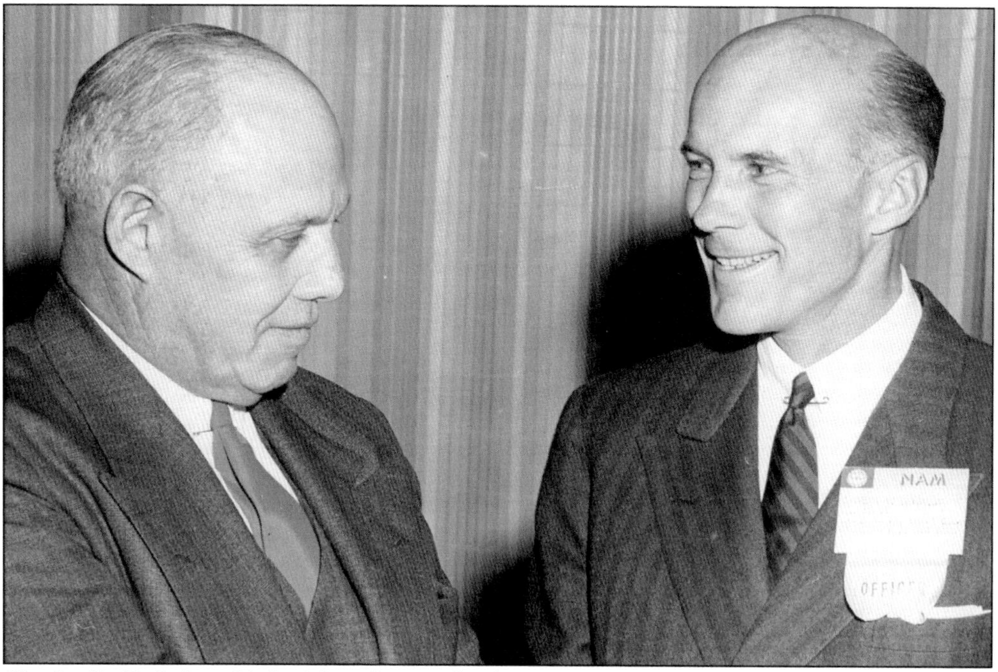

Charles R. Sligh Jr. publicly debated union leader George Meany, pictured at left above. Other televised debates on manufacturing issues were with Vice Pres. Hubert Humphrey, as well as labor leaders Walter Reuther and Leonard Woodcock. (Bentley Historical Library, University of Michigan.)

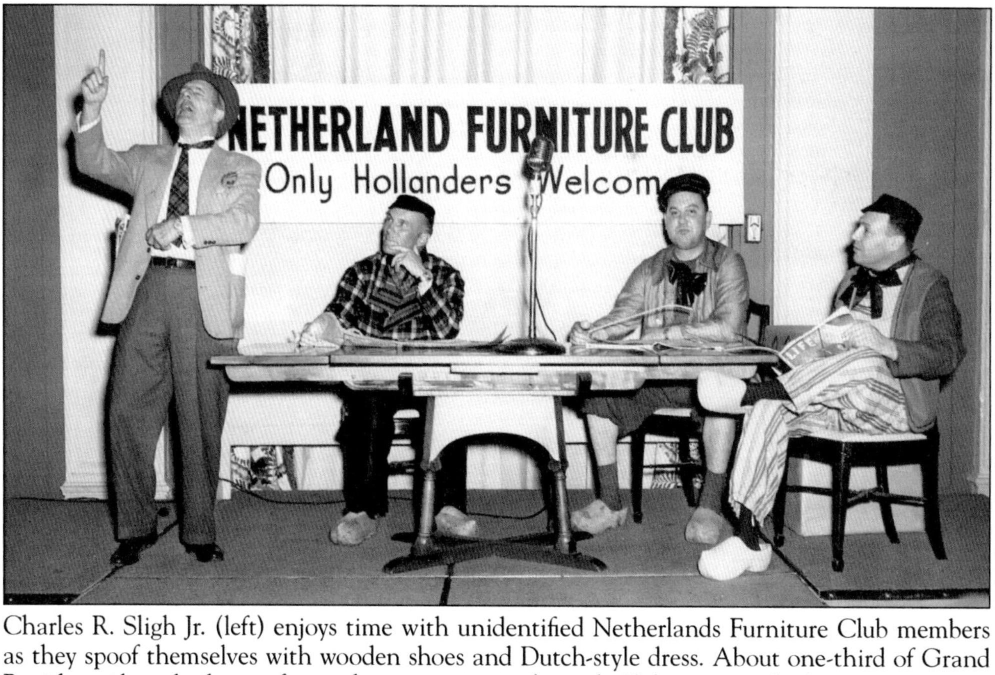

Charles R. Sligh Jr. (left) enjoys time with unidentified Netherlands Furniture Club members as they spoof themselves with wooden shoes and Dutch-style dress. About one-third of Grand Rapids residents had come from other countries in the early 19th century; the largest proportion was Dutch. That influence is still felt in the area today. (Bentley Historical Library, University of Michigan.)

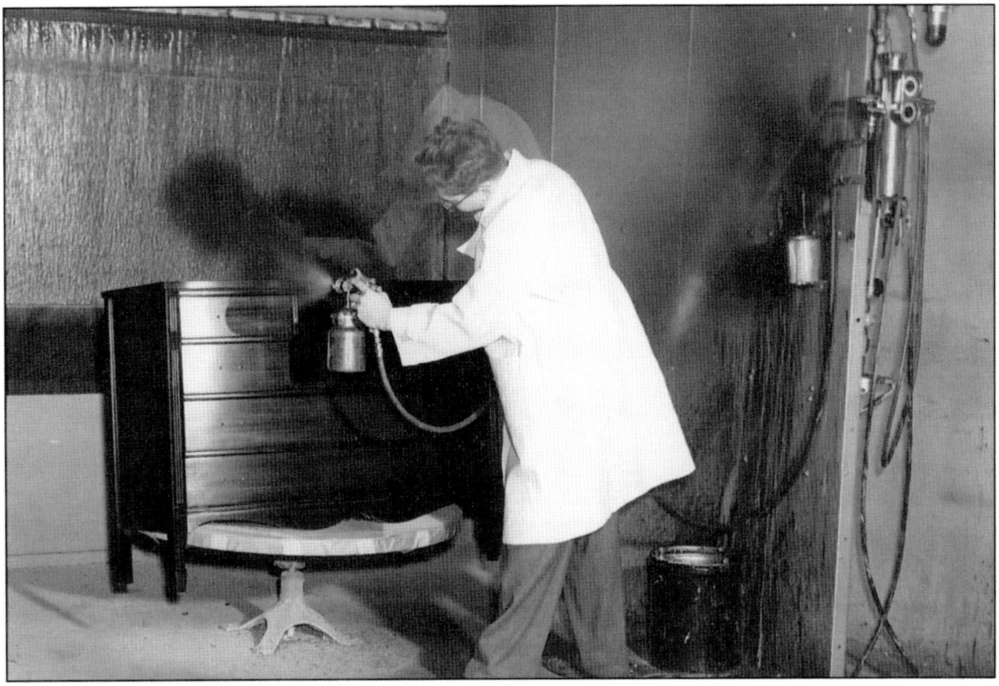

A furniture finisher applies a Guardsman coating to a piece in progress. The company has served the furniture industry since 1915 with varnish, coatings, and consumer furniture care products. The lower photograph shows the product being made. (Guardsman Products.)

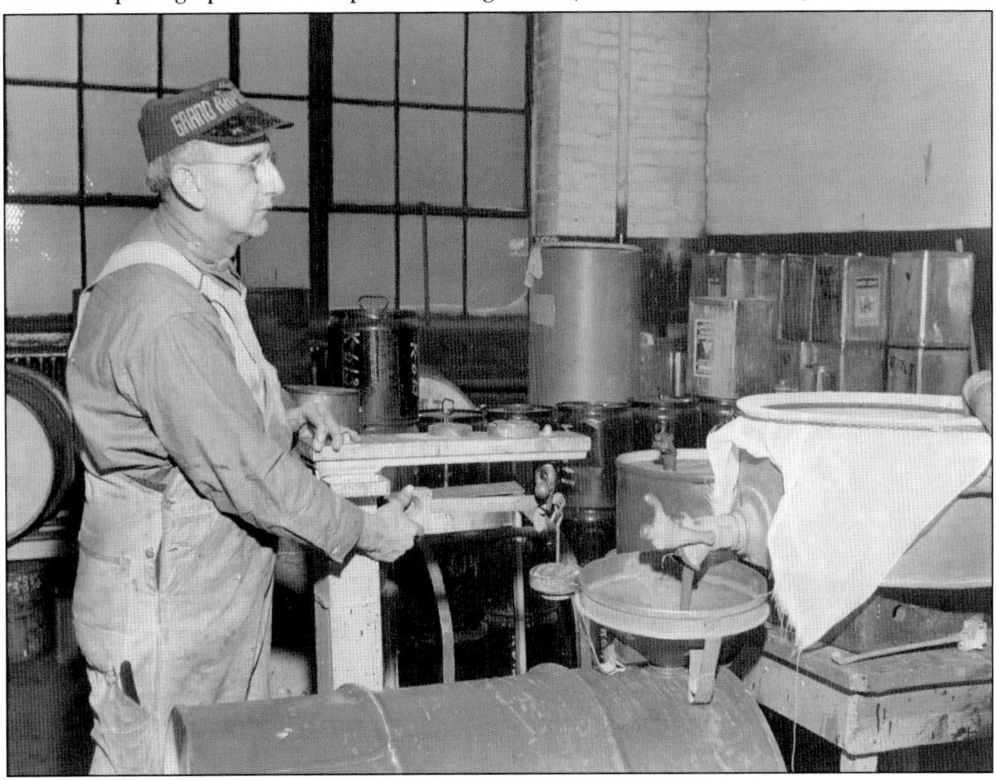

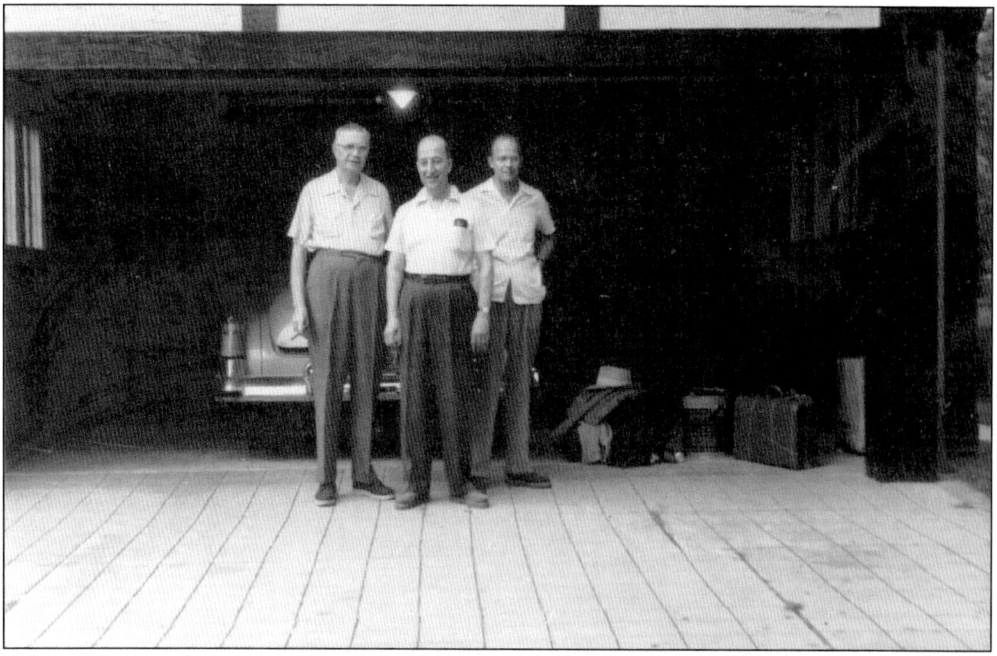

Hekman Furniture Company was founded in 1922 by brothers Henry, Jelle, and John Hekman. Henry Hekman served as the first president until 1952 when his brother Jelle took over. From left to right are Jelle, designer Carl Schmidt, and controller Ken Konondyk. (Charles Hekman.)

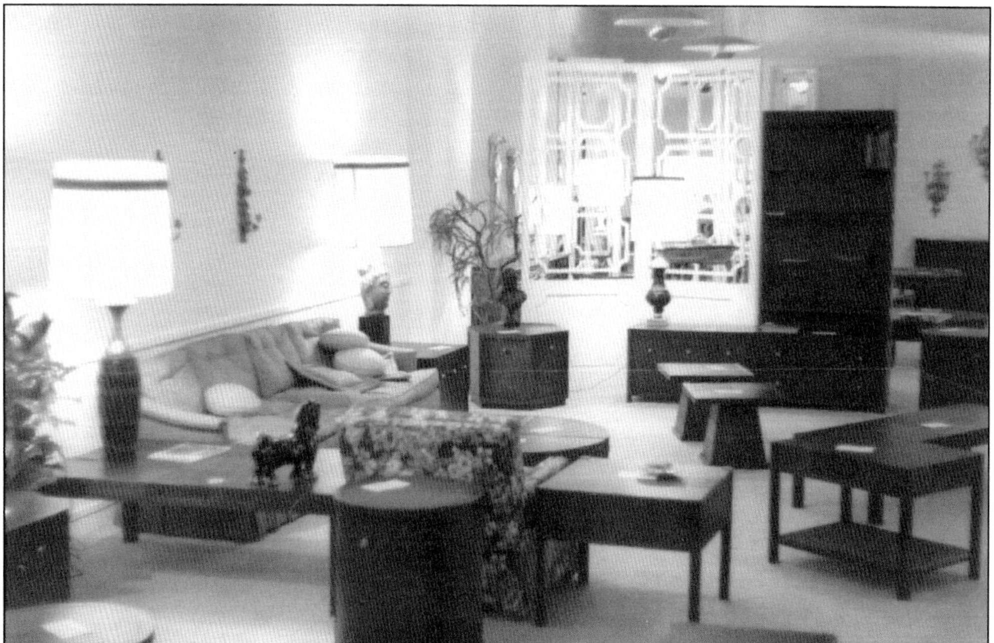

The Hekman Furniture Company displays its fine furniture at Marshall Field and Company in Chicago in the 1950s. By then the Hekman line had grown to offer complete lines of living room furniture after starting out with tables only. (Charles Hekman.)

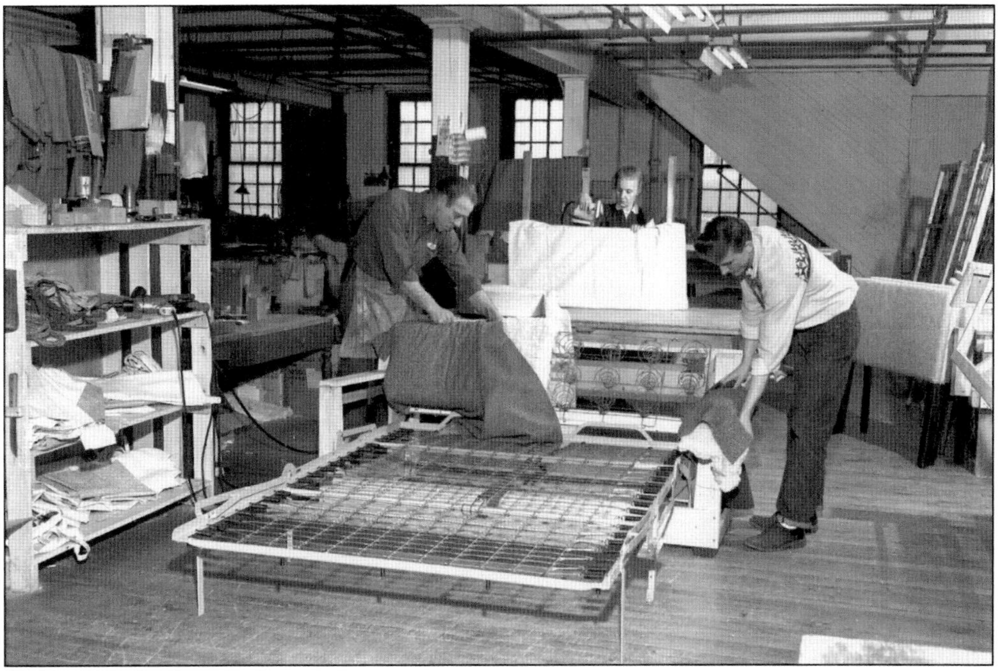

What began as the Hot Blast Feather Company in 1898 became Grand Rapids Bedding in 1914 and remained in business until 1970. From the beginning, its product line was mattresses, daybeds, and bedding. In the photograph above, workers prepare to add a mattress to a sofa bed frame. The image below shows one of the company's signature Spring Air mattress being tufted. The Spring Air line went into production in the 1930s and remained a consumer favorite. These images were taken in 1956. (Grand Rapids Public Library.)

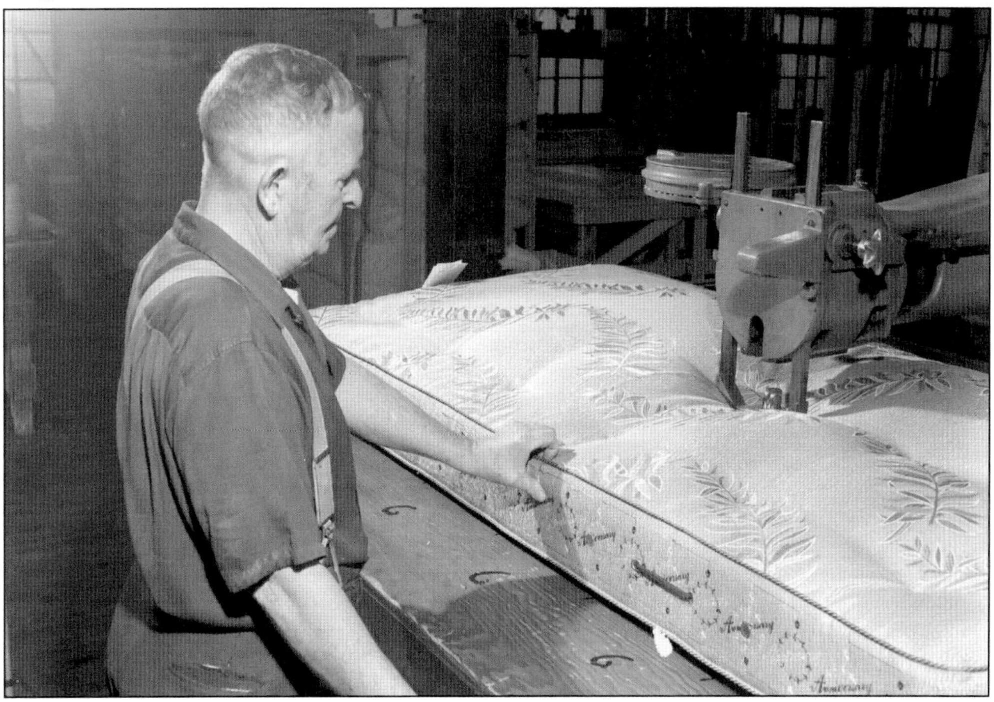

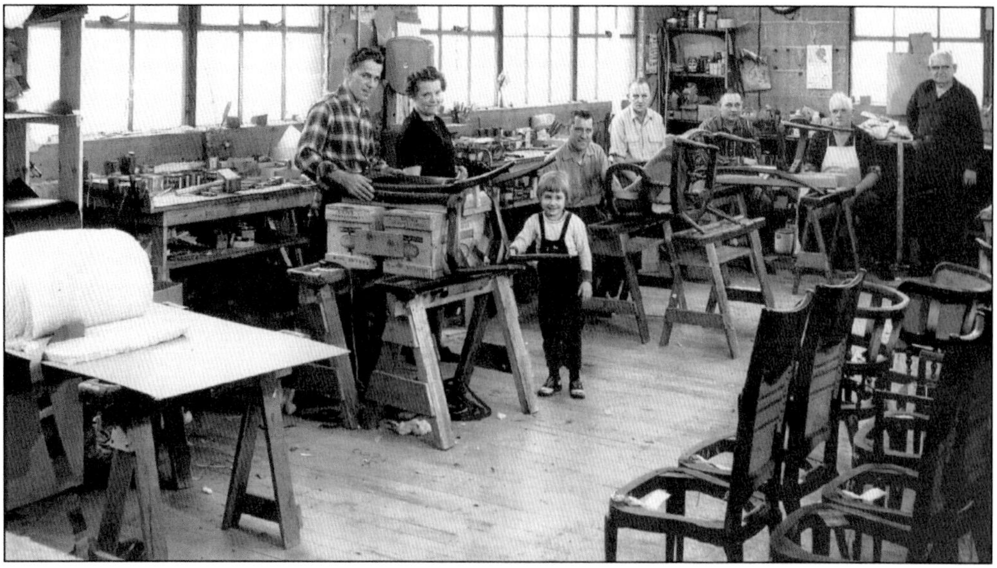

Ed Rosloniec and Walter Kulhawik operated R&K Upholstering at 440 Sixth Street in the northwest side of Grand Rapids. Pictured here in the 1950s are, from left right, Marion Rosloniec, Ed's wife Sonia Rosloniec, daughter Peggy Rosloniec, Walter Kulhawik, Burt Kielek, Ed Rosloniec, Louis Grezwatz, and John Bala. (Jacqueline Heynen and James Kulhawik.)

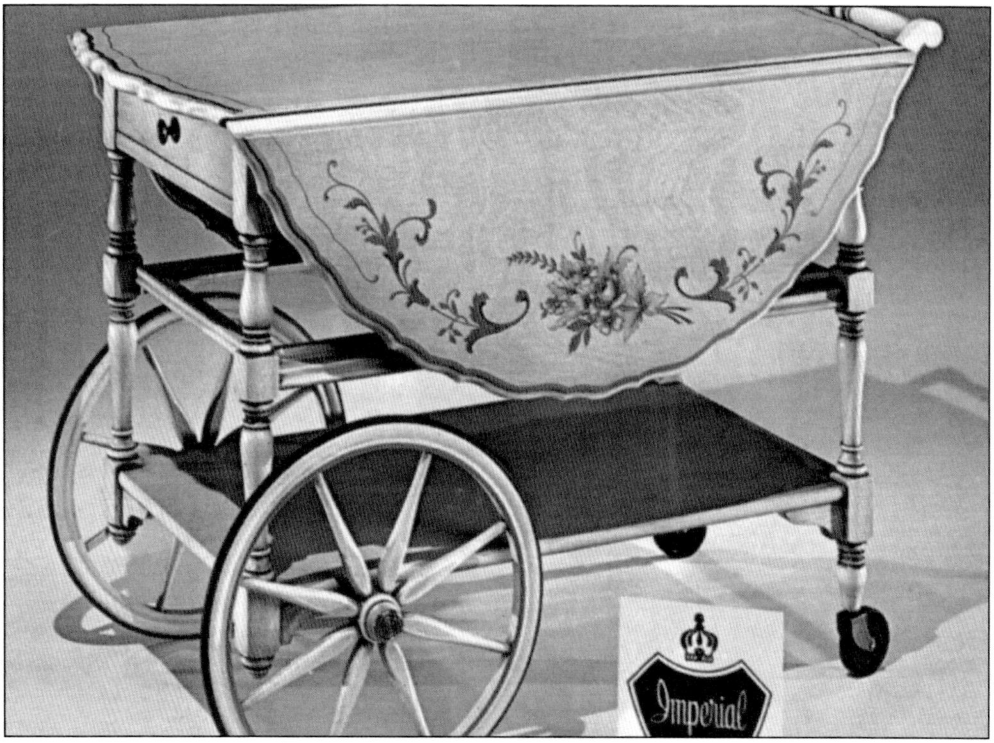

Companies sometimes used postcards to advertise their products at trade shows and furniture markets. This Imperial Furniture Company card dates from the 1960s. The company adopted the trademark shown on the bottom in 1962. The painted, gilt-trimmed tea cart could be used with many different decorating styles.

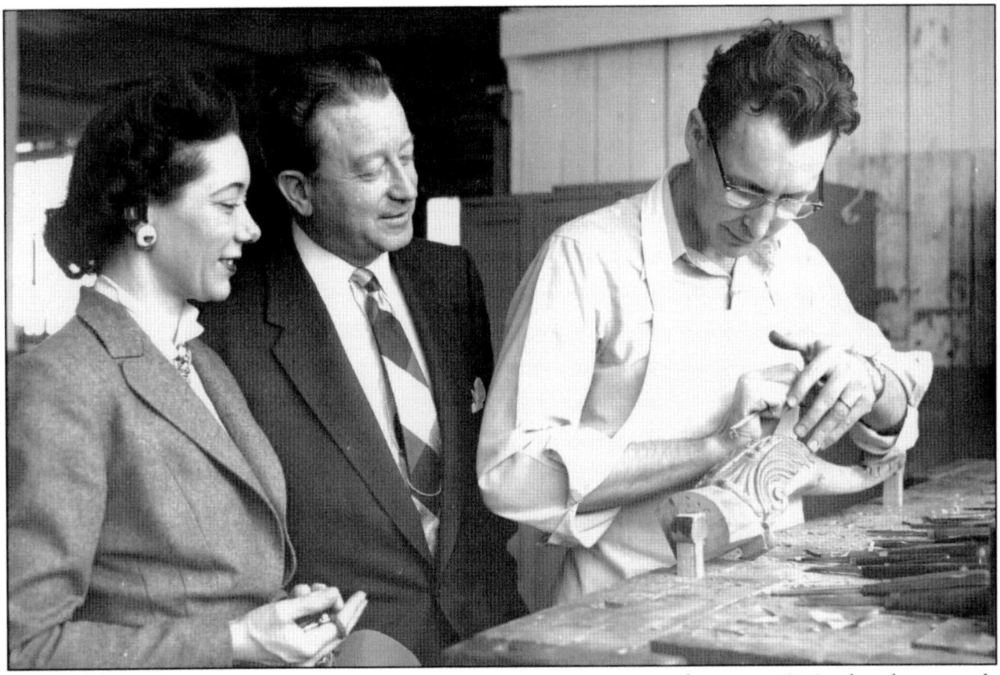

Grand Rapids furniture was featured on *The Arlene Francis Home Show* in 1957. In the photograph above, the television cameraman records a finisher adding the final touches to a table. Below, the show observes another craftsman at work. By then the migration of Michigan furniture makers to North Carolina was well underway, but the city's home furnishings sterling reputation was unblemished. While retailers might be attending the furniture markets in High Point, home viewers must have enjoyed watching craftsman work on pieces similar those in their own homes. (Grand Rapids Public Library.)

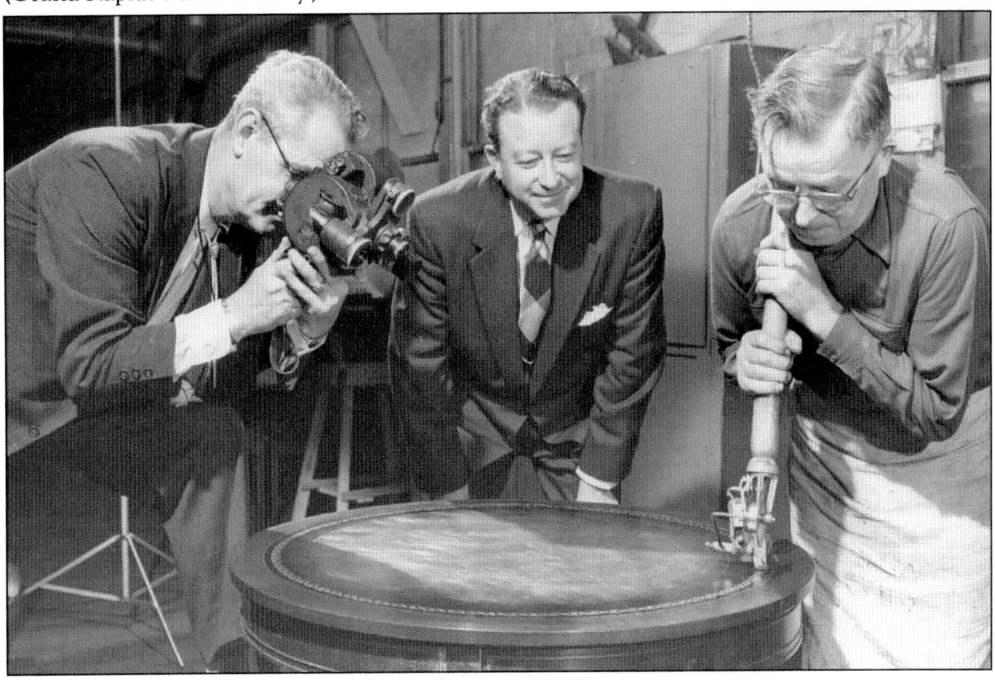

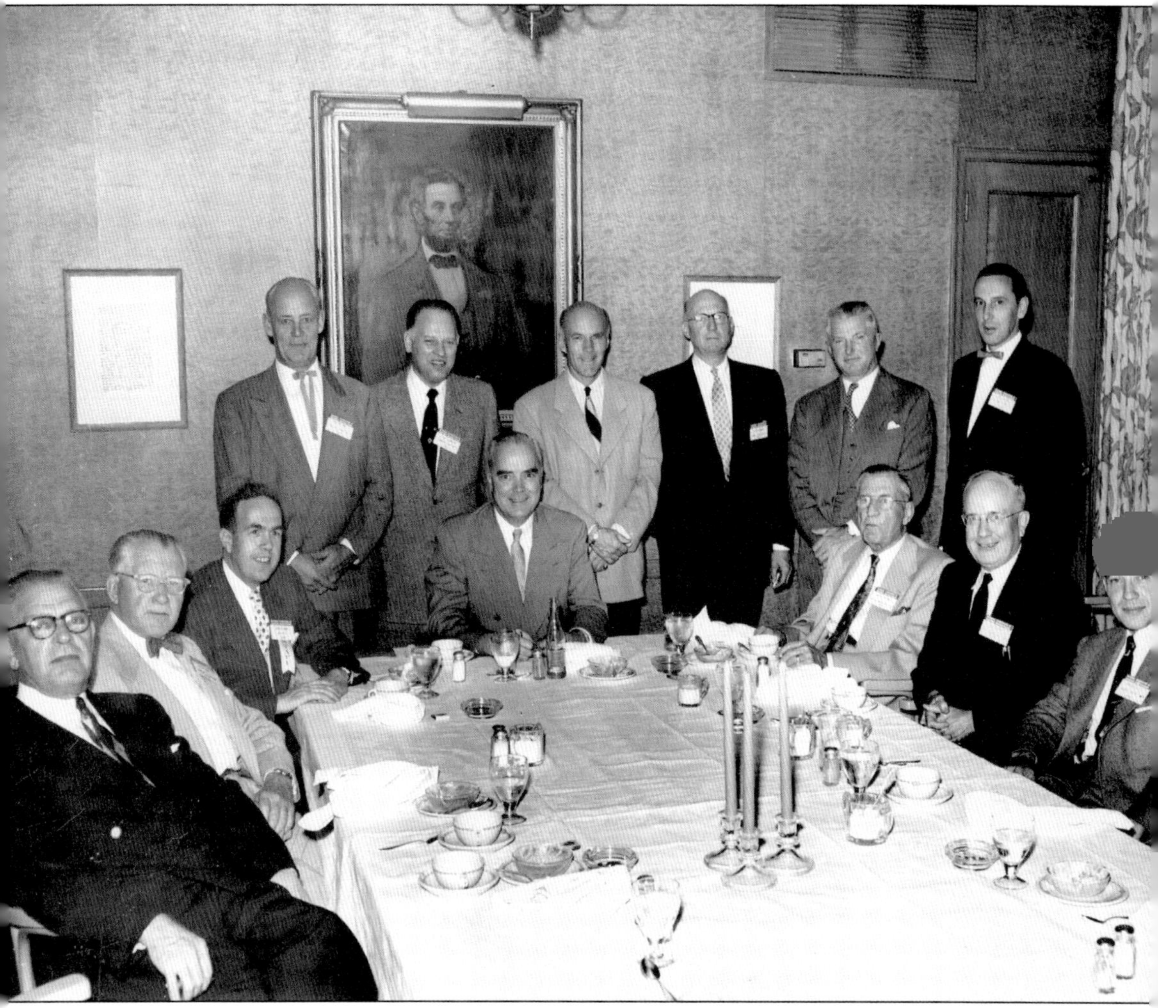

Along with the Furniture Manufacturers Association, Charles R. Sligh Jr. was active in the National Association of Furniture Manufacturers (NAFM) and in 1954 served on its advisory committee. Pictured are, from left to right, committee members C. E. Helgran, Kling Factories; Percy A. Tonk, Tonk Manufacturing Company; John M. Snow, NAFM executive secretary; A. N. Skinner, Fredick Couch Company; Clyne Crawford, Crawford Furniture Manufacturing Corporation; Walter S. Marder, La-Z-Boy Chair Company; Sligh; Charles M. Kindel, Kindel Furniture Company; F. H. Mueller, Mueller Furniture Company; Walter J. Mersman, Mersman Brothers Corporation; Joseph G. Griswold Jr., Widdicomb Furniture Company; Fred Batson, Kittinger Company; and Herman B. Hoopes, Brandt Cabinet Works. (Bentley Historical Library, University of Michigan.)

Three

The Challenges

Despite the phenomenal success of the furniture industry, outside forces threatened to cripple it. Individual companies suffered losses through floods and fires. In the earliest days, fire departments were all volunteer and amateur at best. Everything from logjams to melting snow and excessive rains caused the river to overflow, and most of the factories were in the path of the floodwaters.

World Wars I and II dramatically impacted American manufacturing. In both wars, the furniture industry rose above itself and served the country with distinction, producing everything from bombers to ammunition boxes to wooden M-1 rifle stocks. When the U.S. Navy asked for a more comfortable plywood leg splint, Herman Miller, Inc., and designer Charles Eames came through.

As if wars were not enough to contend with, depressions forced some companies into bankruptcy. In the late 1890s, the Sligh Furniture Company realized people did not have money for furniture and thought selling cheap transportation might keep it afloat during the troubled years. The Sligh bicycle was a colossal failure and almost closed the company.

Those who survived the lesser depressions and World War I found themselves again in peril when the Great Depression wreaked havoc on the economy. Steelcase, Inc., was one of the companies that kept employees on the payroll by reducing their hours. The company also looked for new products and found a winner with its Terrell Dew-Fresh produce display cases that periodically misted the contents. It succeeded because the attractive display sold more vegetables and, more importantly, was cost-effective to grocers because the unit reduced spoilage.

Perhaps the greatest threat was the strike of 1911. Many workers felt conflicted, believing union membership incompatible with church membership. Nevertheless, on April 19, 1911, 3,000 workers walked off the job, and production was limited to what the owners and management could turn out. Widdicomb was one of the companies hiring outside workers to cross the picket line. Strikers retaliated by breaking every window in Widdicomb's Fifth Street factory. The strike lasted four months and neither side was able to claim a decisive victory.

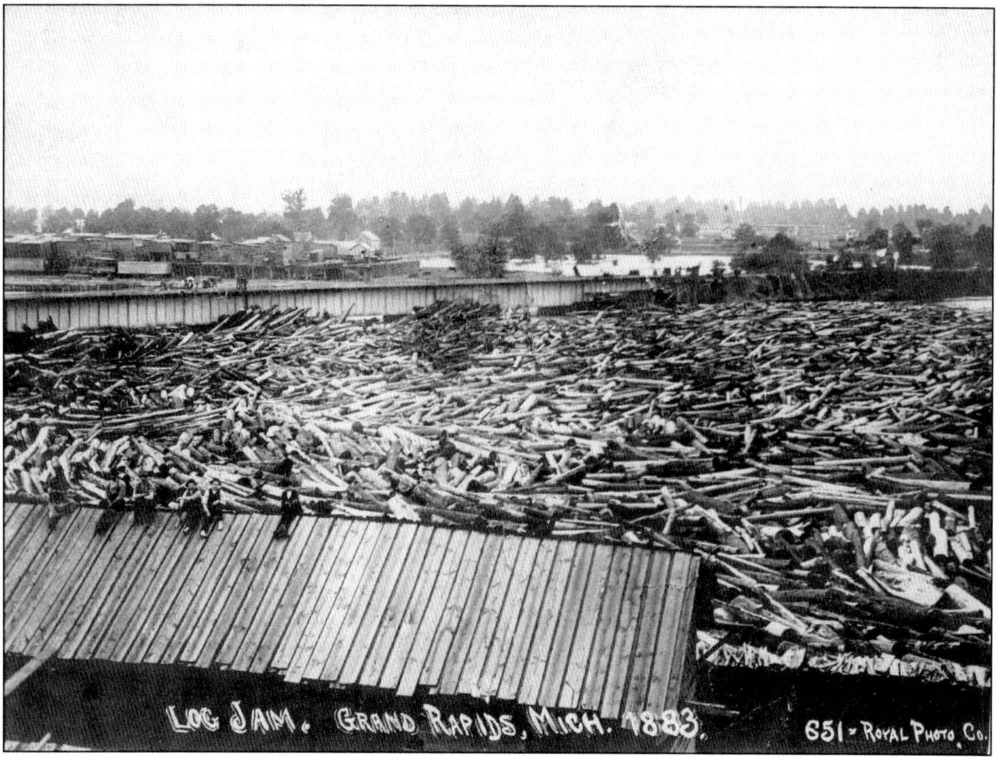

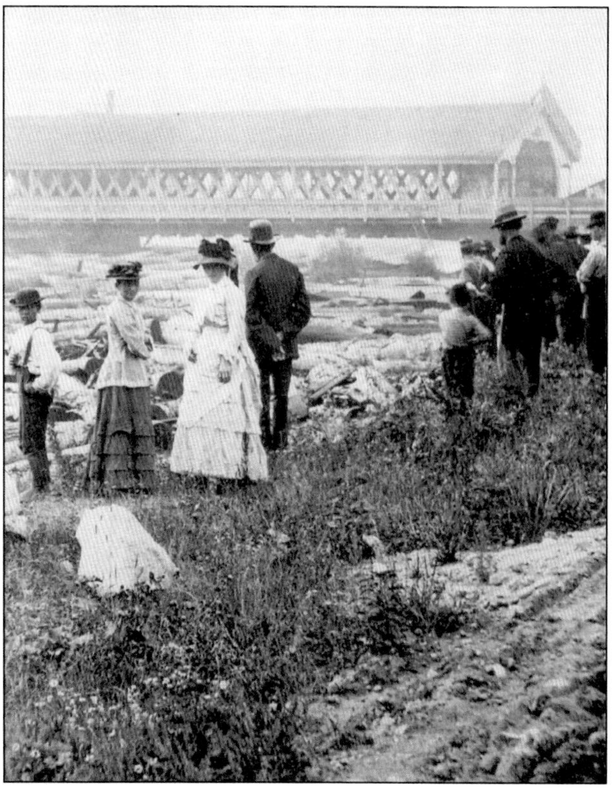

Although the forests would eventually be depleted, logs floating down the Grand River were still a common sight in July 1883. Unusually heavy summer rains caused one million feet of logs to break free. The resulting seven-mile, 30-feet-deep logjam is believed to be the biggest in American history. It was also the beginning of the end of logging on the Grand River. A small portion of the pileup is shown in the photograph above, while the image at left shows citizens gathering at the riverfront to see the phenomenon for themselves. (Grand Rapids Public Library.)

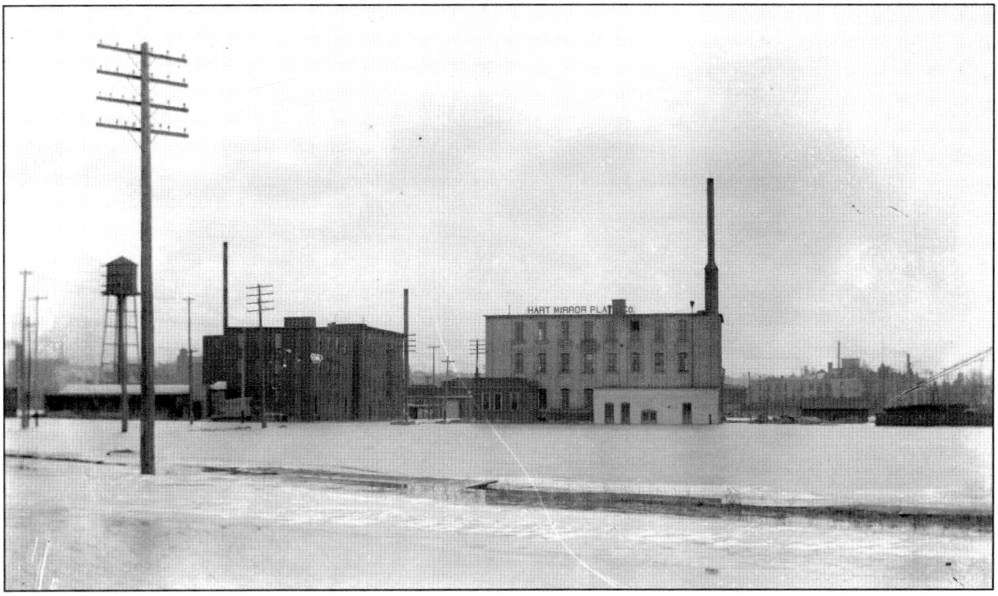

A major flood in March 1904 put 8,000 residents temporarily out of work, many of them furniture workers. Waters reached 24.5 feet at Pearl Street—5.5 feet over flood level. Here floodwaters approach the Hart Plate and Mirror Company. (Grand Rapids Public Library.)

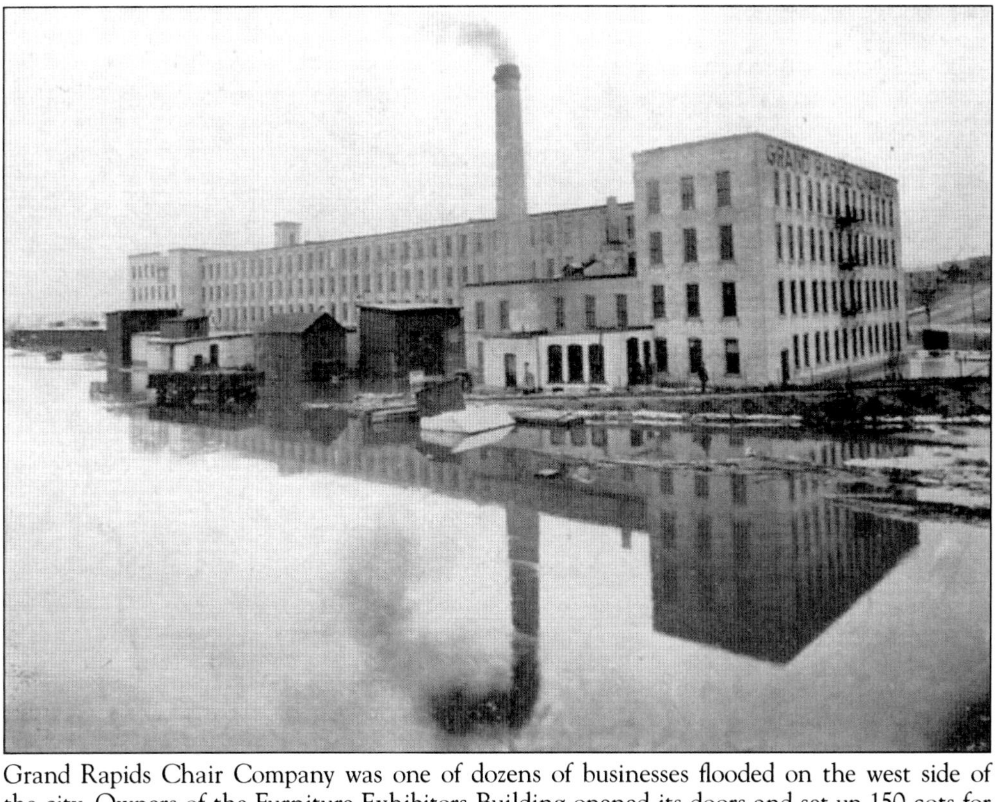

Grand Rapids Chair Company was one of dozens of businesses flooded on the west side of the city. Owners of the Furniture Exhibitors Building opened its doors and set up 150 cots for residents forced to flee their homes. (Grand Rapids Public Library.)

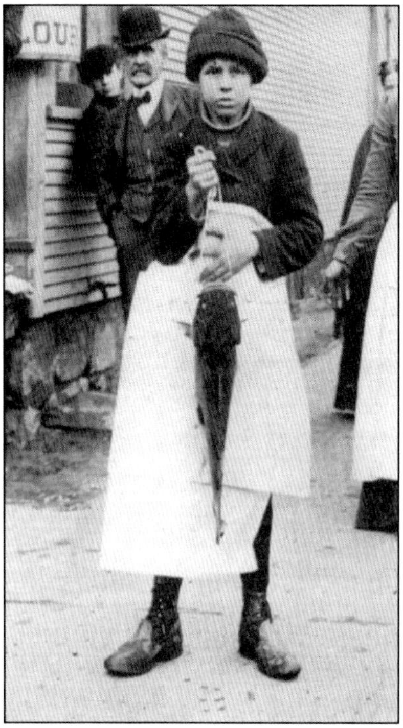

Anyone doubting the severity of the 1904 flood would have been convinced when this photograph appeared in the local newspapers. The boy displays a six-and-a-half-pound catfish he caught in his backyard on Turner Street, just blocks from the major factories. (Grand Rapids Public Library.)

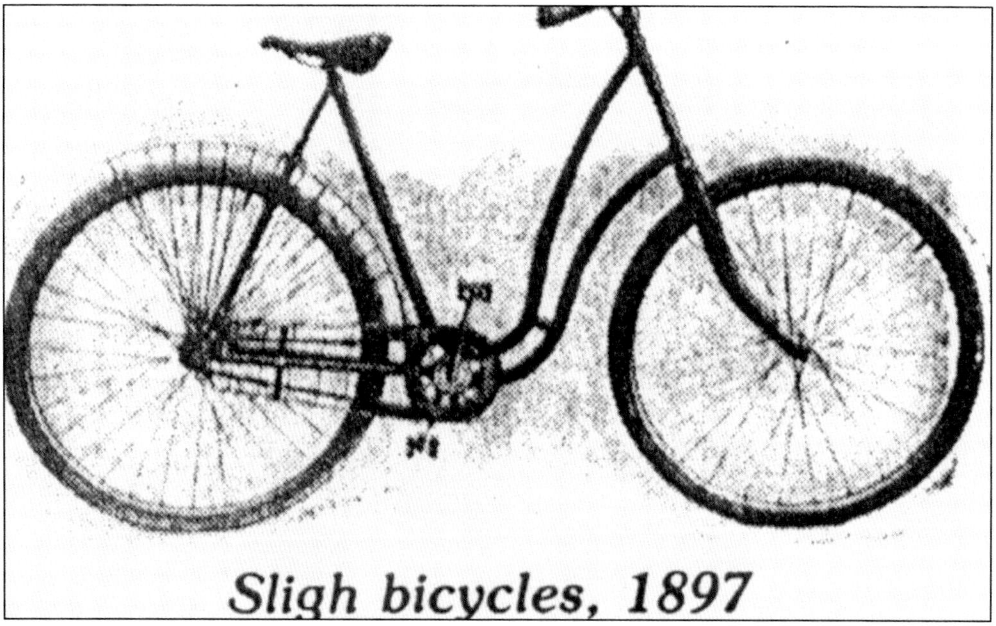

America was deep in the depression that began in 1893, which dramatically reduced furniture buying. When the Sligh Furniture Company saw sales drop 50 percent, it seemed prudent to introduce a depression-proof product. Inexpensive transportation looked like a good idea, so in 1895, Sligh began making bicycles. Far from being a good idea, the bicycle division folded and almost put the company out of business. Fortunately the economy rebounded, and Sligh went back to doing what it did best—manufacturing fine furniture. (Robert Sligh, Sligh Furniture Company.)

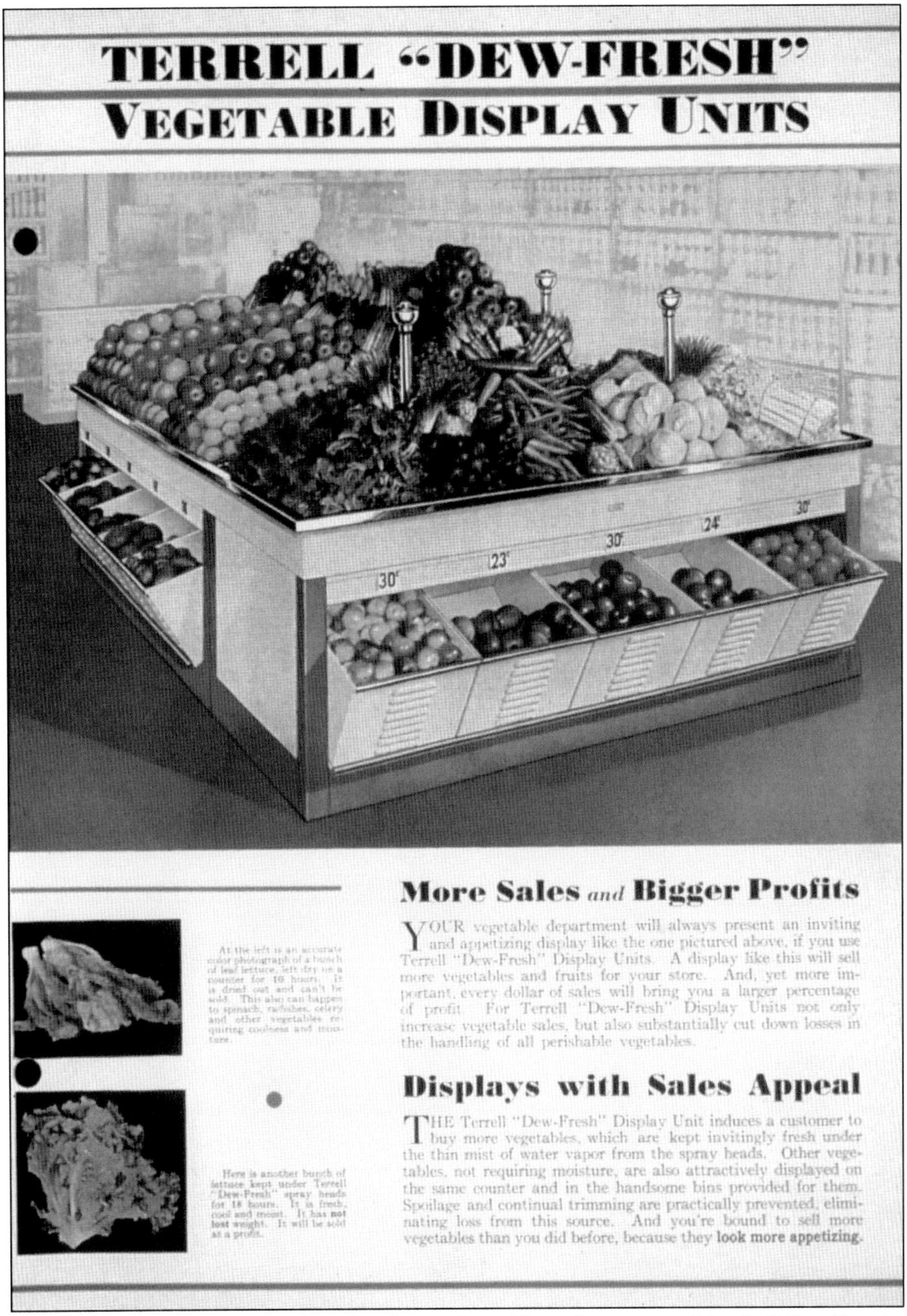

When the Great Depression hit, Steelcase, Inc. (then known as Metal Office Furniture Company), sought ways to ride out the storm. Employees worked part-time to avoid layoffs. One product that kept the factory open was the Dew-Fresh vegetable display unit shown above. Grocers found it displayed produce attractively and kept fruits and vegetables fresh longer by misting them. It was just one of the ways this company has managed to creatively stay ahead of the curve. (Steelcase, Inc.)

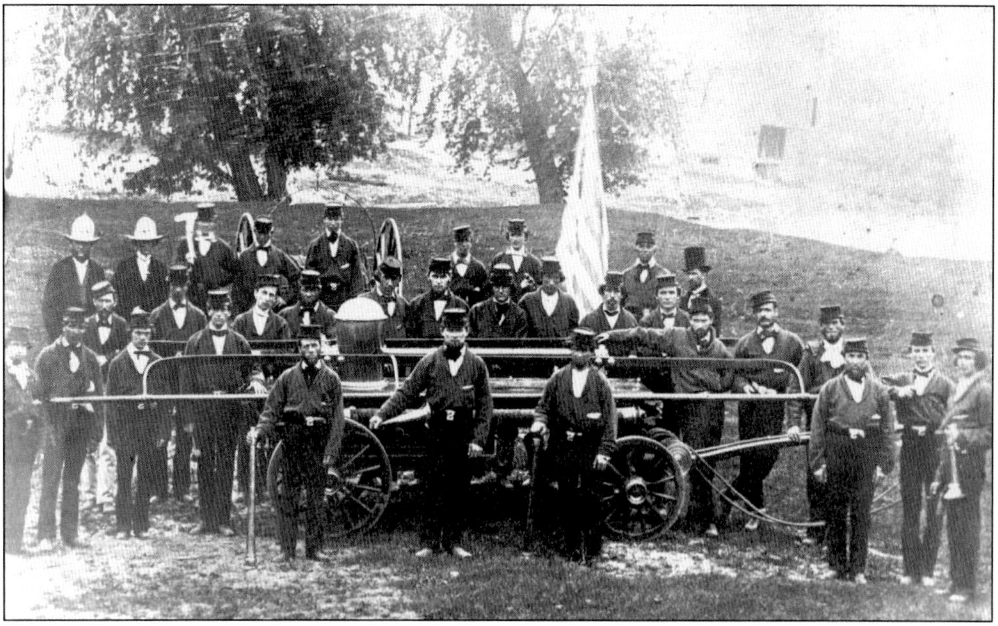

Fires were a hazard from the industry's infancy. By the early 1800s, the city boasted three volunteer fire departments. Above is the Kent unit. What the unit lacked in proper equipment and training, it made up for in enthusiasm. Not only were the firefighters unpaid, they were fined 50¢ if they missed a fire. (Grand Rapids Public Library.)

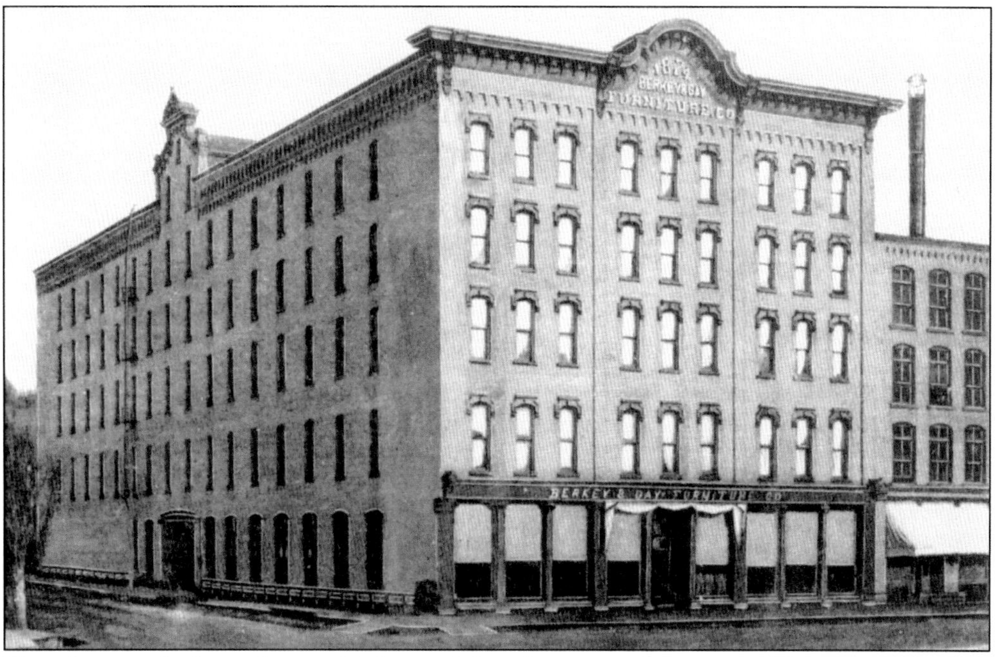

This photograph shows the new Berkey and Gay factory on the corner of Canal and Hastings Streets. It was erected in 1874 after the old building went up in flames in a fire that destroyed the entire area. The company suffered another fire in November 1943, resulting in at least one fatality. Grand Rapids fireman Louis Coleman Sr. died fighting the blaze. (Grand Rapids Public Library.)

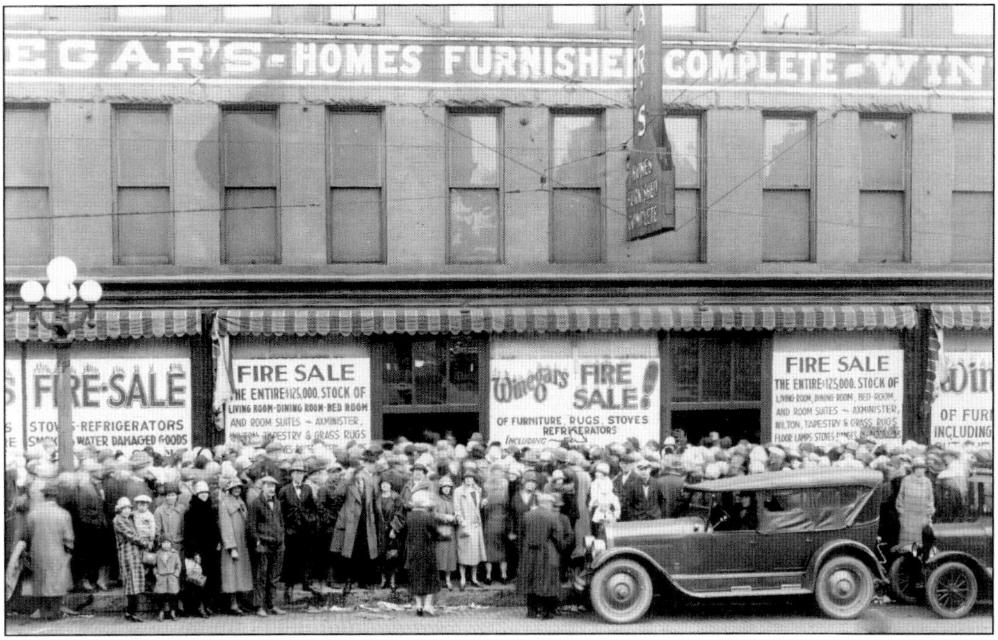

The Winegar Furniture Store on the corner of what is now Division Avenue and Cherry Street drew a large crowd on the day of its fire sale. Frequent fires created many such scenes. (Grand Rapids Public Library.)

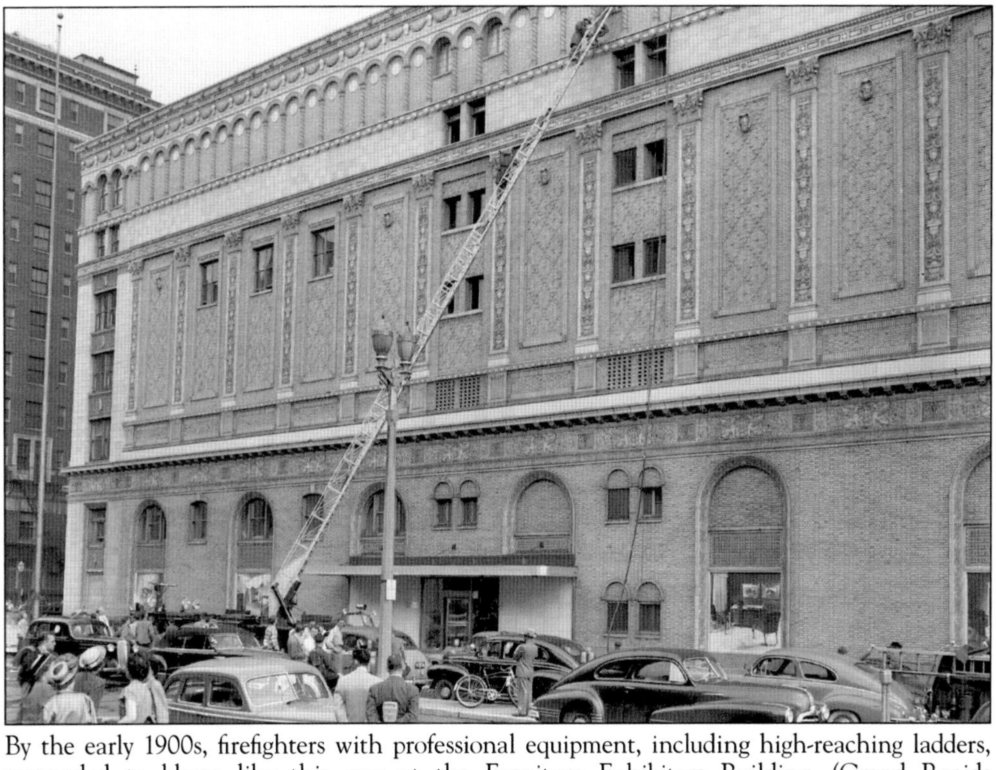

By the early 1900s, firefighters with professional equipment, including high-reaching ladders, responded to blazes like this one at the Furniture Exhibitors Building. (Grand Rapids Public Library.)

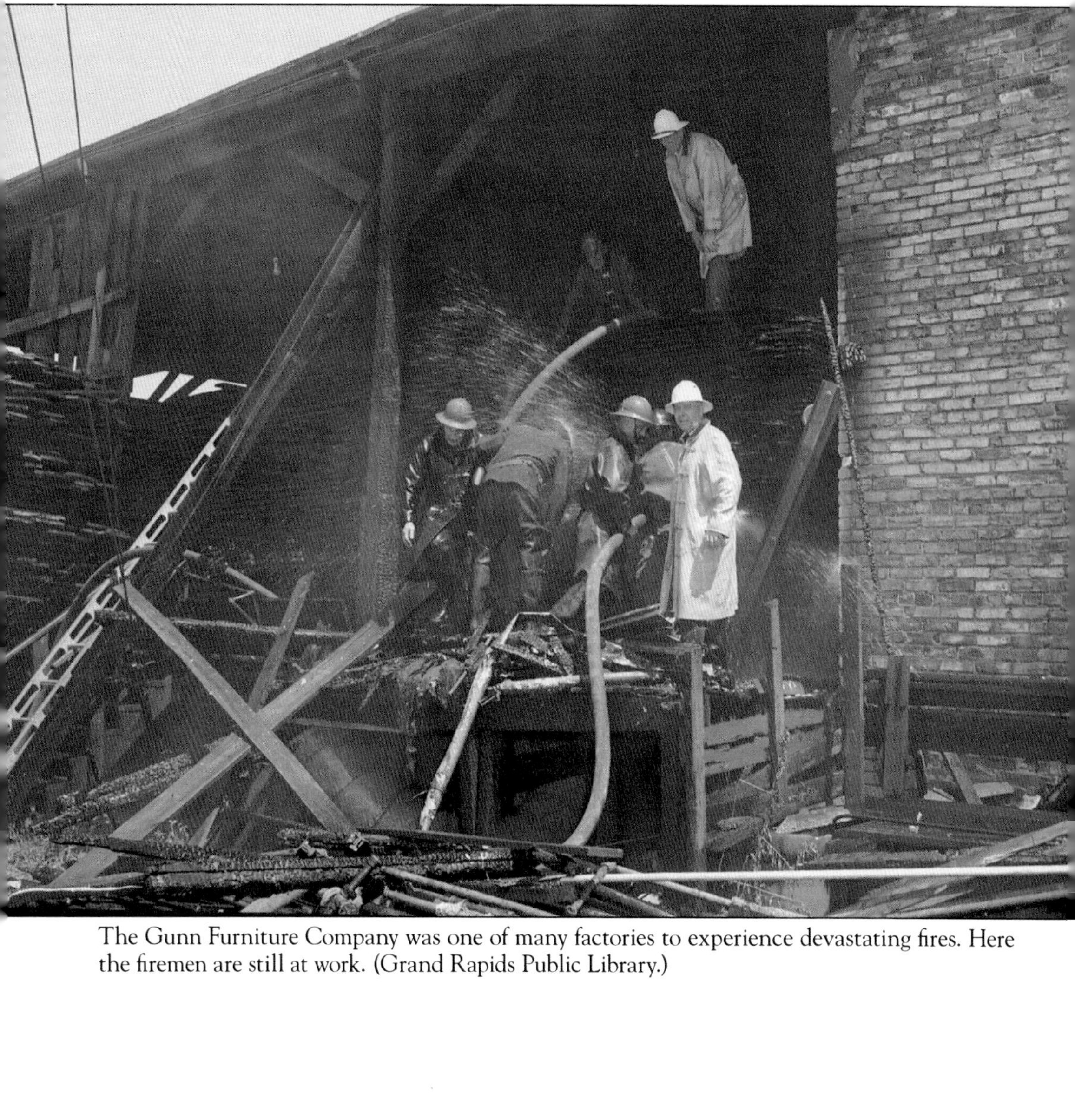

The Gunn Furniture Company was one of many factories to experience devastating fires. Here the firemen are still at work. (Grand Rapids Public Library.)

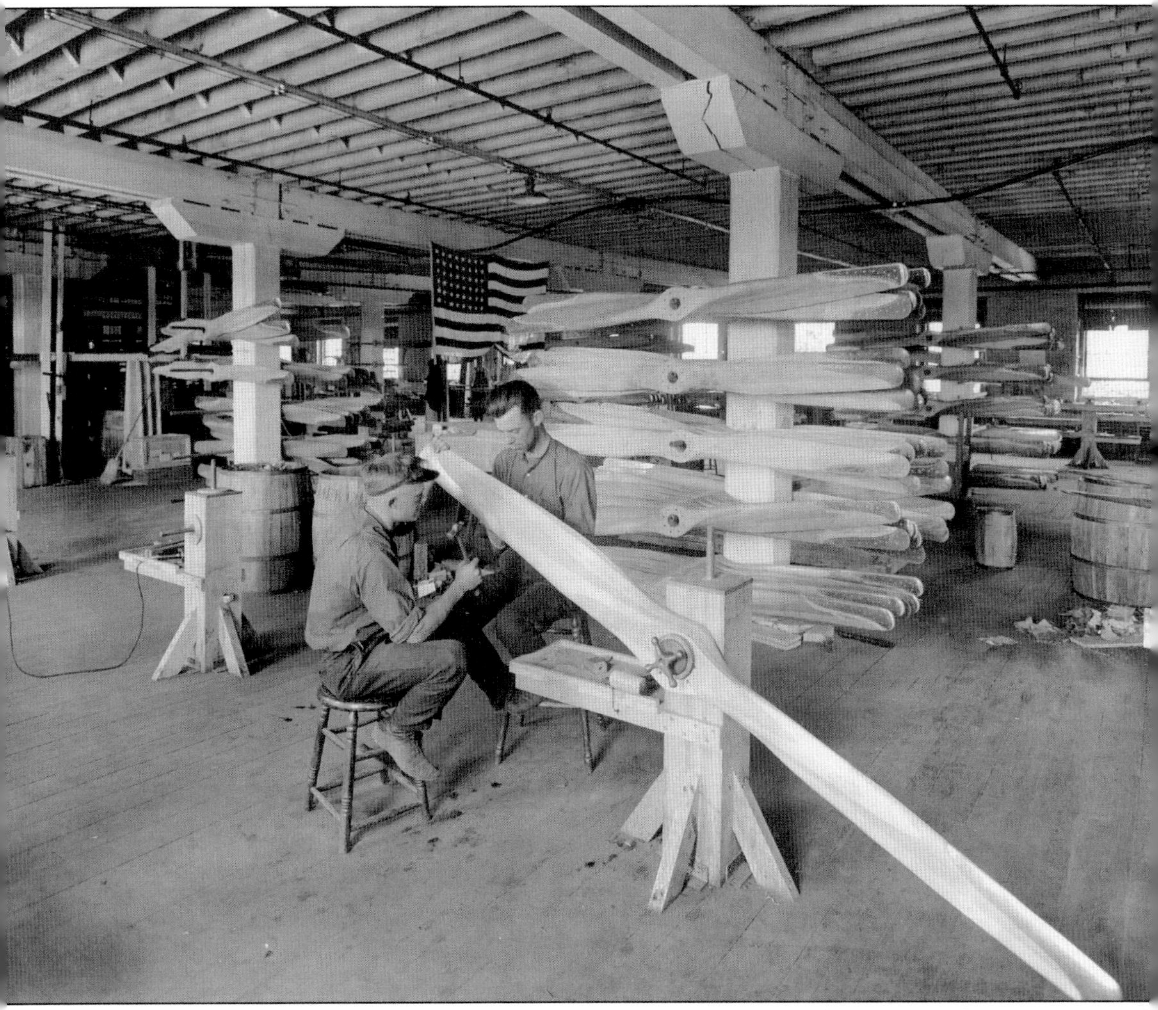

When the U.S. Army needed 1,000 Handley-Page bombers during World War I, 15 furniture companies formed the Grand Rapids Airplane Company and met the demand. The Berkey and Gay, Century, Grand Rapids Chair, Grand Rapids Furniture, Grand Rapids Showcase, Imperial, Johnson, Macey, Phoenix, Royal, Showcase, Sligh, Stickley, Widdicomb, and Wilmarth companies all dedicated one-third of their manufacturing facilities to the project. Except for the motors, the bombers were produced entirely by the Grand Rapids Airplane Company. This c. 1918 photograph shows the propeller production area within the Phoenix Furniture plant. (Grand Rapids Public Library.)

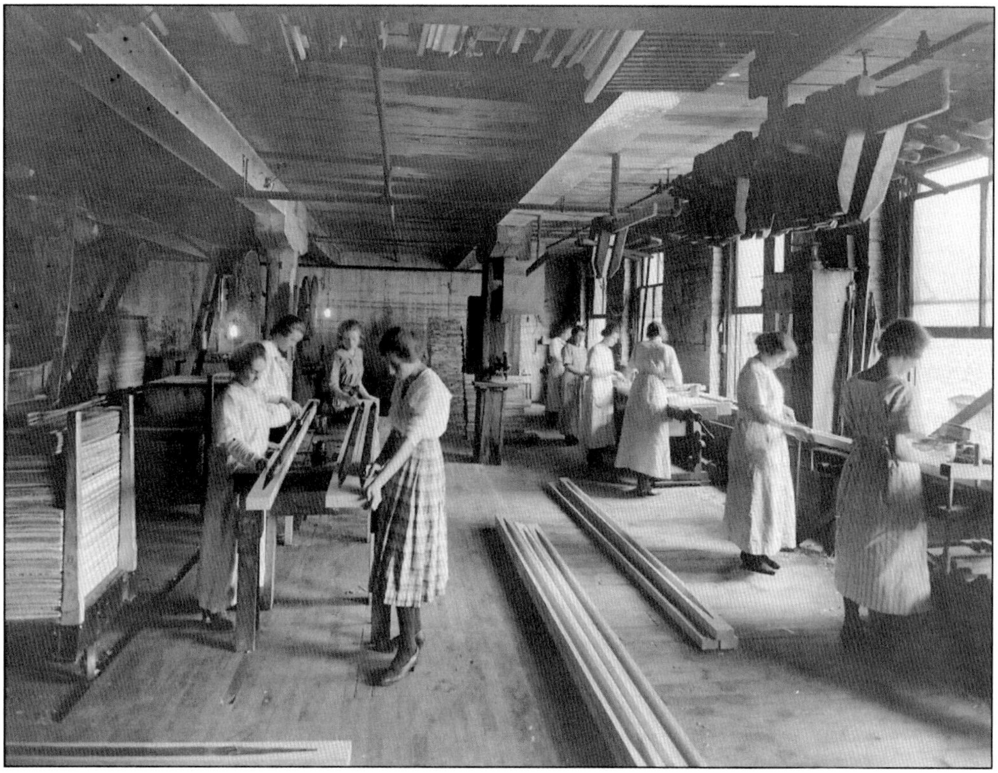

Women usually worked in the finishing or decorating departments. The ladies above were probably recruited to replace men at war and to meet the deadline for completion of the bombers. They are working on main plane ribs for the bombers. This photograph was taken at the Wilmarth Showcase factory in the area dedicated to the war effort. (Grand Rapids Public Library.)

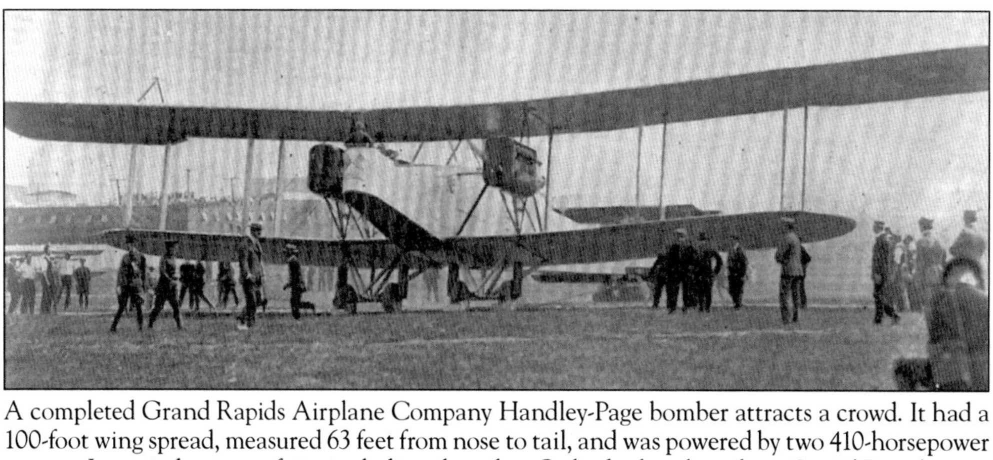

A completed Grand Rapids Airplane Company Handley-Page bomber attracts a crowd. It had a 100-foot wing spread, measured 63 feet from nose to tail, and was powered by two 410-horsepower motors. It carried a crew of six, including the pilot. Only the bombers from Grand Rapids were American-made, all others were produced in England. (Grand Rapids Public Library.)

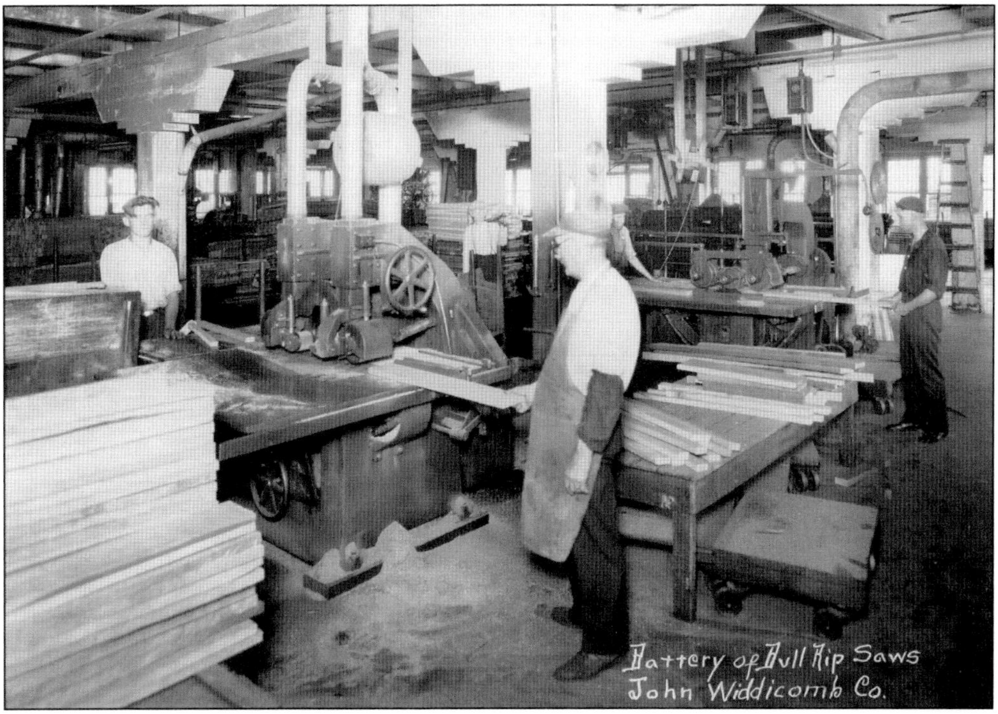

Strikes also posed a threat to the industry, and one of the laborers' concerns was unsafe working conditions. Ripsaws were unprotected in all the factories, not just the Widdicomb plant shown in the photograph above. Workers at the routing tables were also susceptible to injuries, as in the unidentified factory below. (Grand Rapids Public Library.)

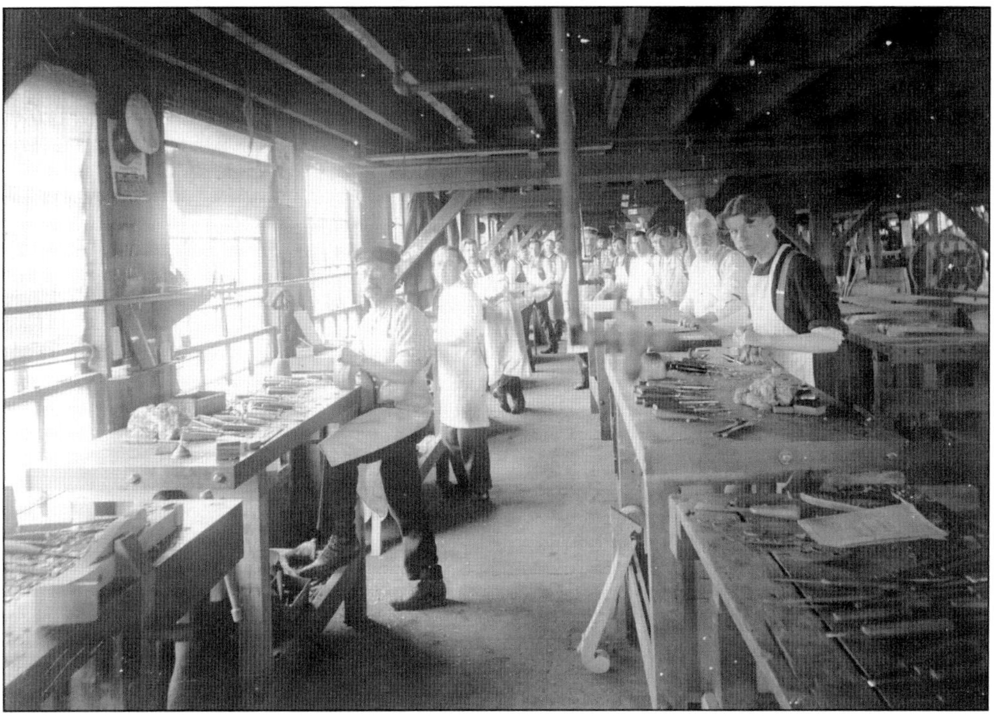

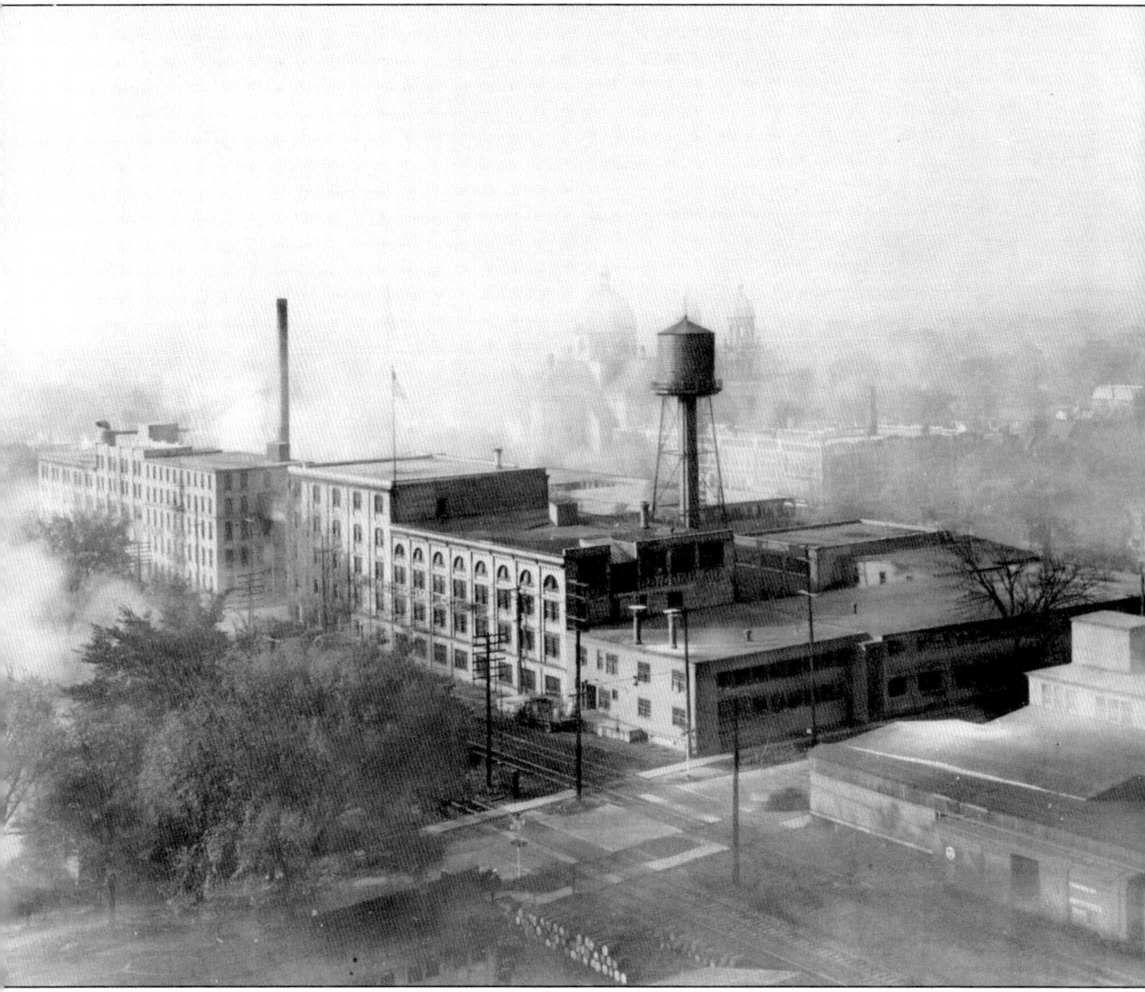

Widdicomb management angered strikers by bringing in workers from Chicago to replace those who walked off the job at the Fifth Street factory. They retaliated by breaking the factory's windows and stoning Harry Widdicomb's car. Like many factory owners, Widdicomb felt paternalistic toward his employees and was hurt that they turned on him by striking. (Grand Rapids Public Library.)

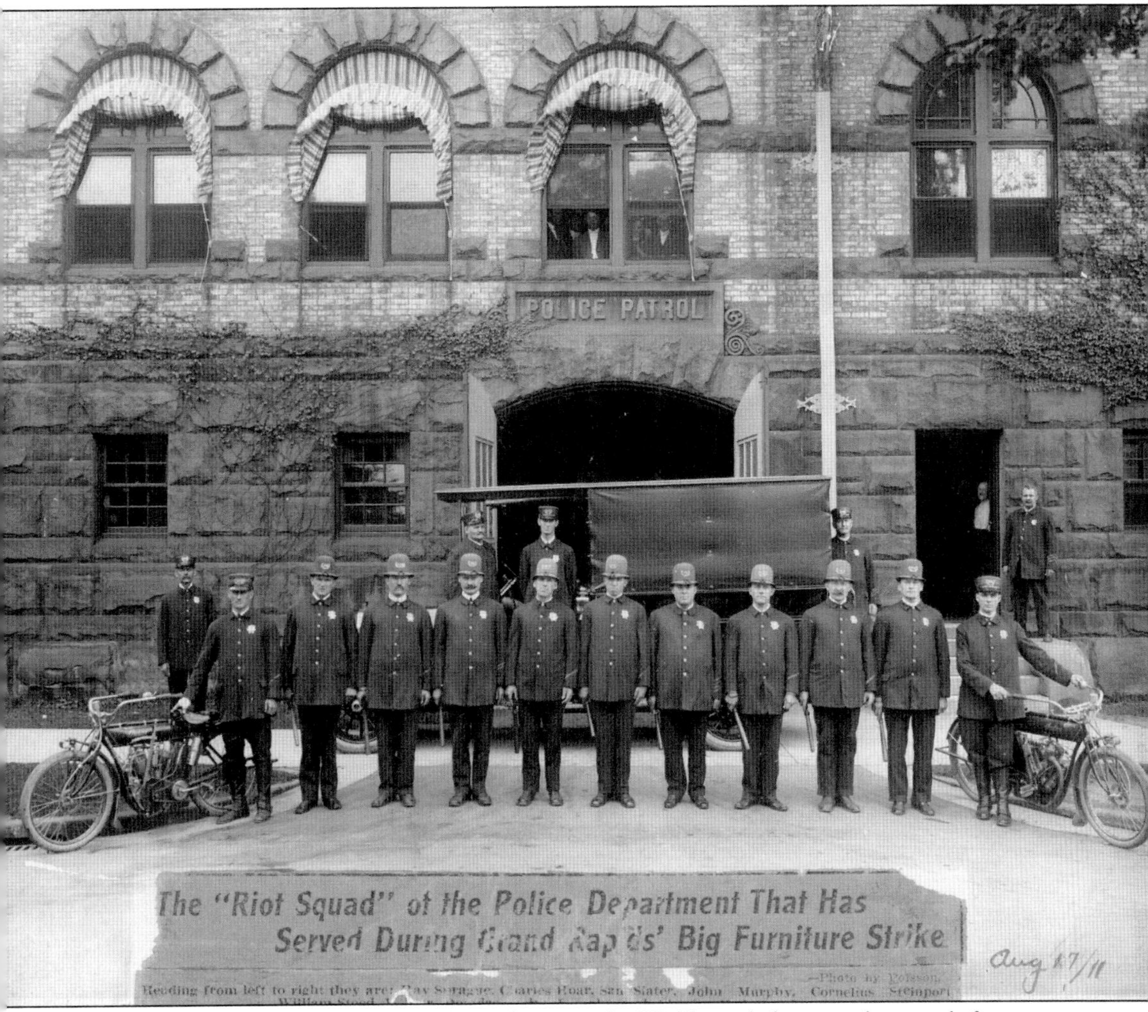

This police riot squad responded to the violence at the Widdicomb factory, along with fireman who turned their hoses on the rioters. Mayor George Ellis hired an extra 100 policemen, many of whom were out-of-work strikers and sided with their colleagues. To complicate things further, Sheriff William J. Hurley sympathized with the owners and hired non-striking employees as deputy sheriffs. (Grand Rapids Public Library.)

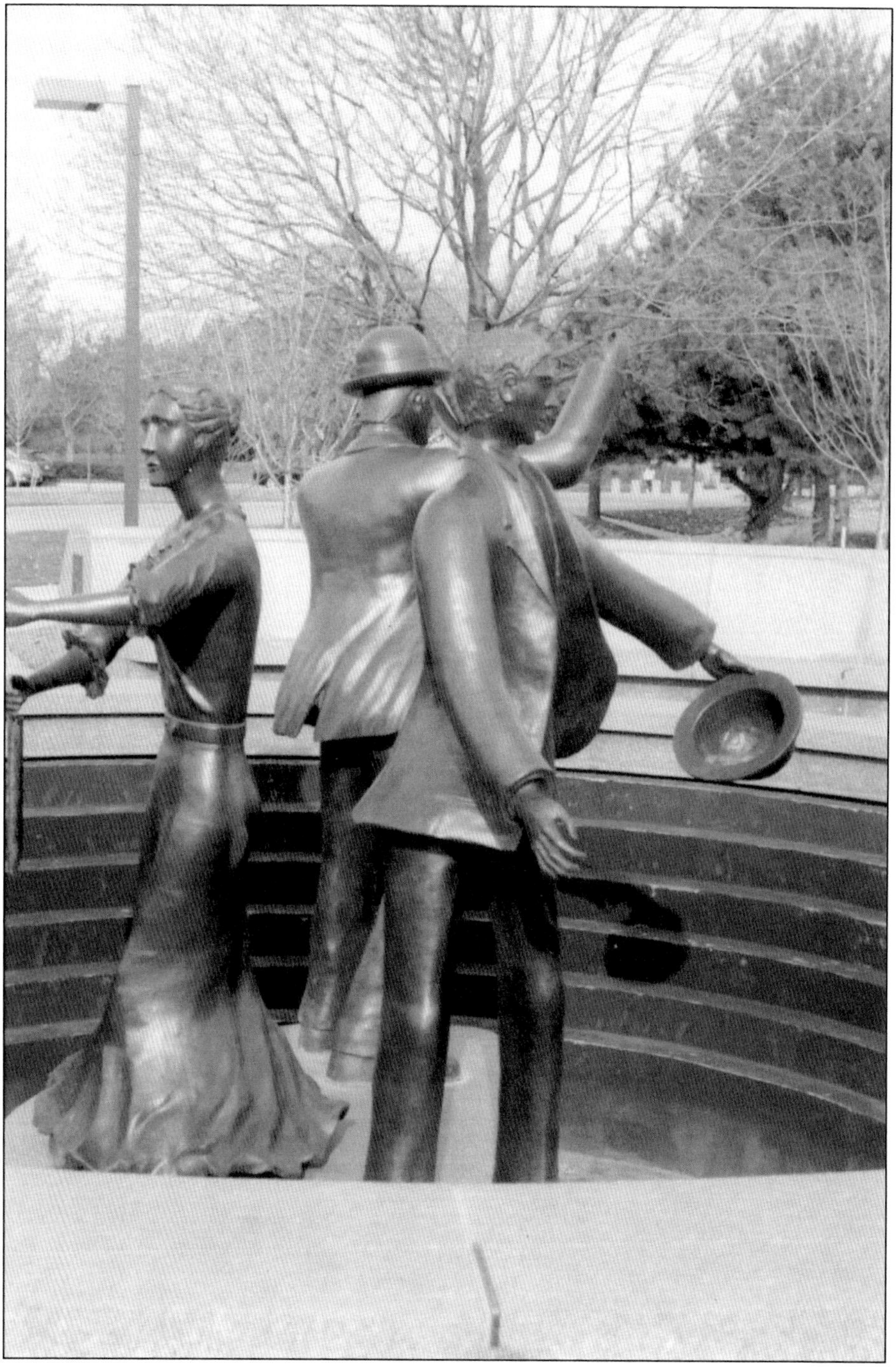

The *Spirit of Solidarity*, a statue executed by Roberto Chenlo and commemorating the furniture strike of 1911, was unveiled on the grounds of the Gerald R. Ford Presidential Museum on Pearl Street in April 2007. The $1.3 million granite sculpture and fountain features three figures, facing away from one another and representing the craftsmen, laborers, and families who found common ground. The woman looks innocent but has rocks hidden under her long skirt. (Norma Lewis.)

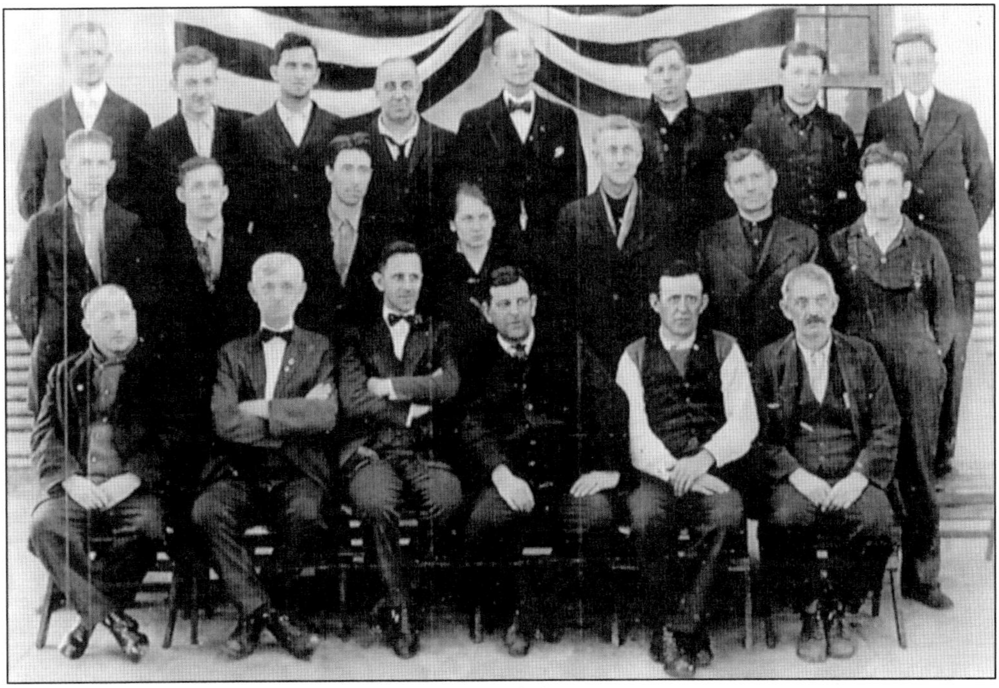

American Seating Company was way ahead of the times in initiating proactive programs. To improve relations between labor and management, in 1919 the company began a form of management that included input from employees' representatives. Based on the Unites States government, they instituted a cabinet, a senate, and a house of representatives. Above is the cabinet, made up of top management. Pictured below is the house with one member for every 40 employees. Employees elected their house representatives. (American Seating Company.)

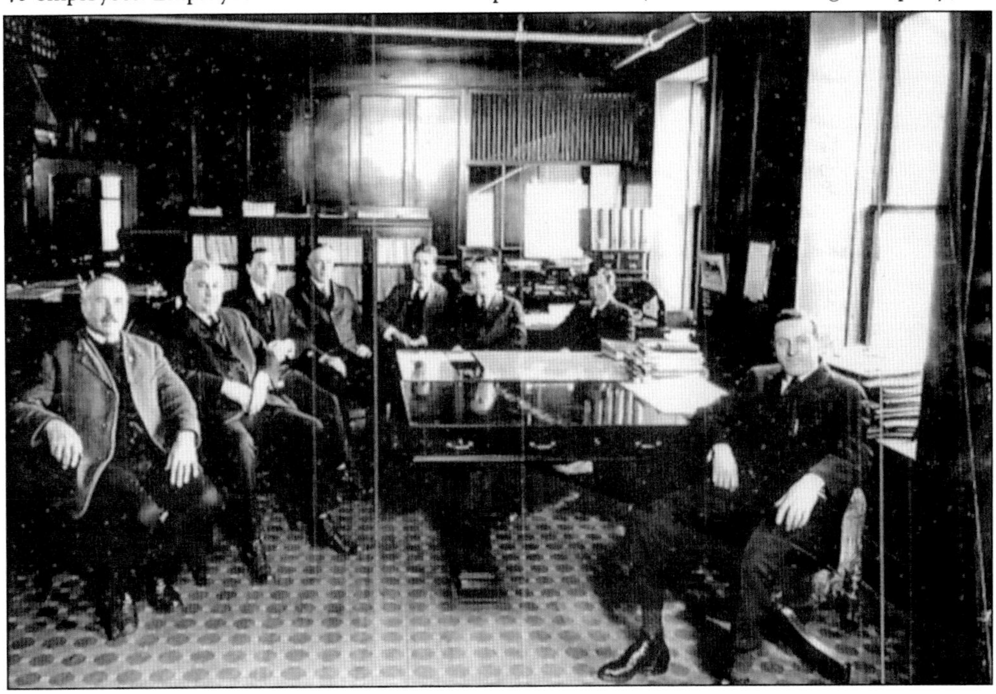

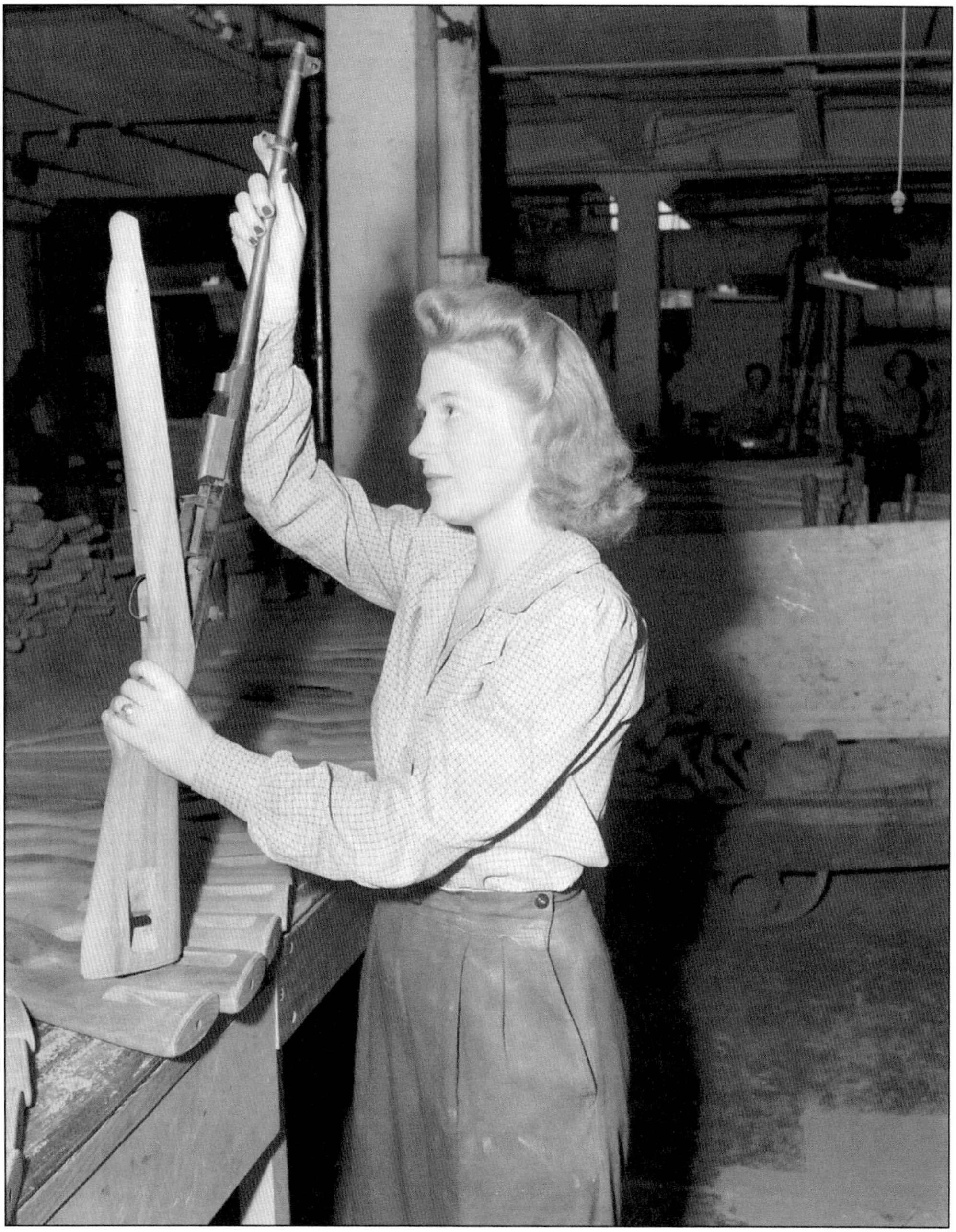

During World War II, the Robert W. Irwin Company made gunstocks for M-1 carbines. While Rosie riveted, Clara Bush inspected. Her job was to make sure the parts met strict quality standards. When lives were at stake, there was no margin for error. After this photograph was taken (August 30, 1943), she felt she could make a larger contribution to the war and decided to join the WACs even though her brother had been killed in the South Pacific. (Grand Rapids Public Library.)

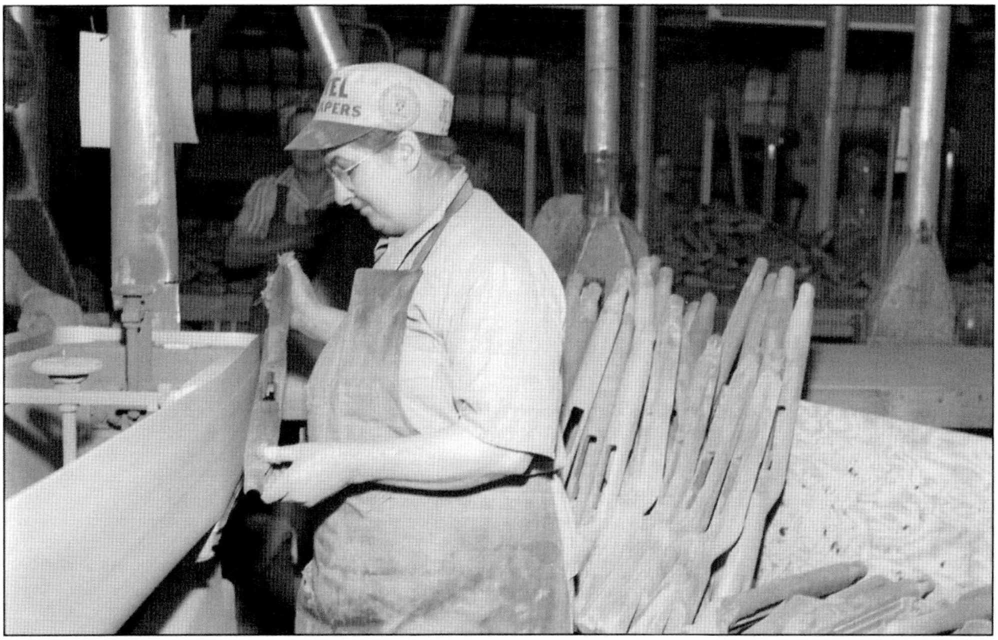

Robert W. Irwin employees sand the gunstocks before sending them to the Irwin-Pederson Company where the M-1s were assembled. The Irwin-Pederson Company later became the Saginaw Steering Gear Division of General Motors. An enthusiastic crowd watches on July 28, 1943, as packed carbines leave the factory for shipment overseas. Patriotism reached an all-time high after the Japanese attacked Pearl Harbor, so any war effort was considered heroic. (Grand Rapids Public Library.)

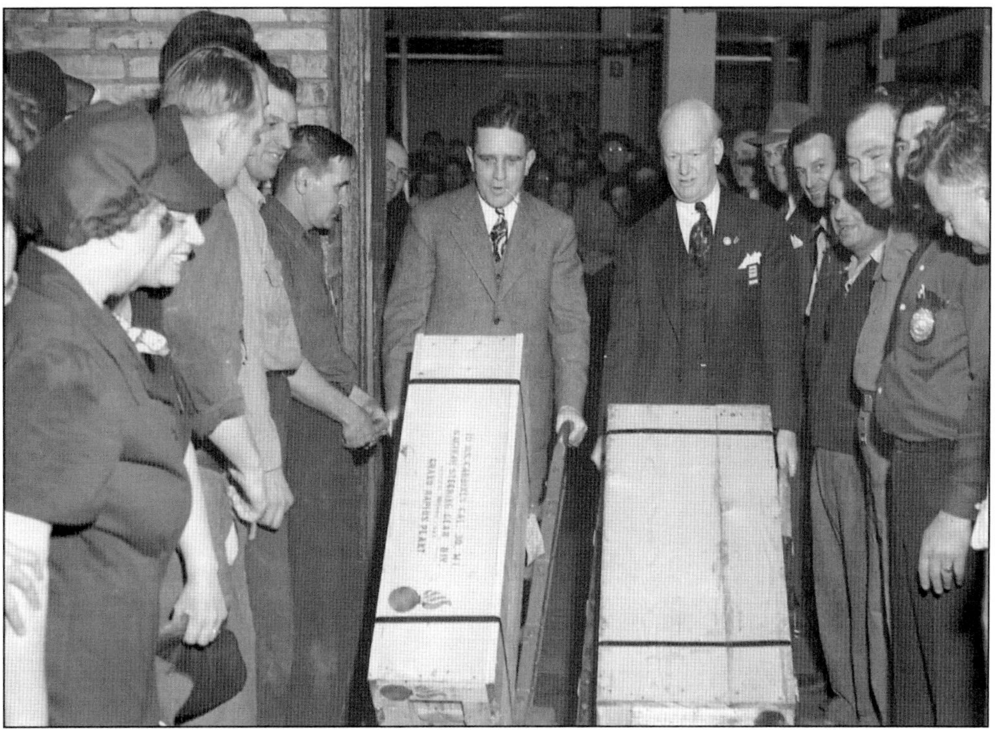

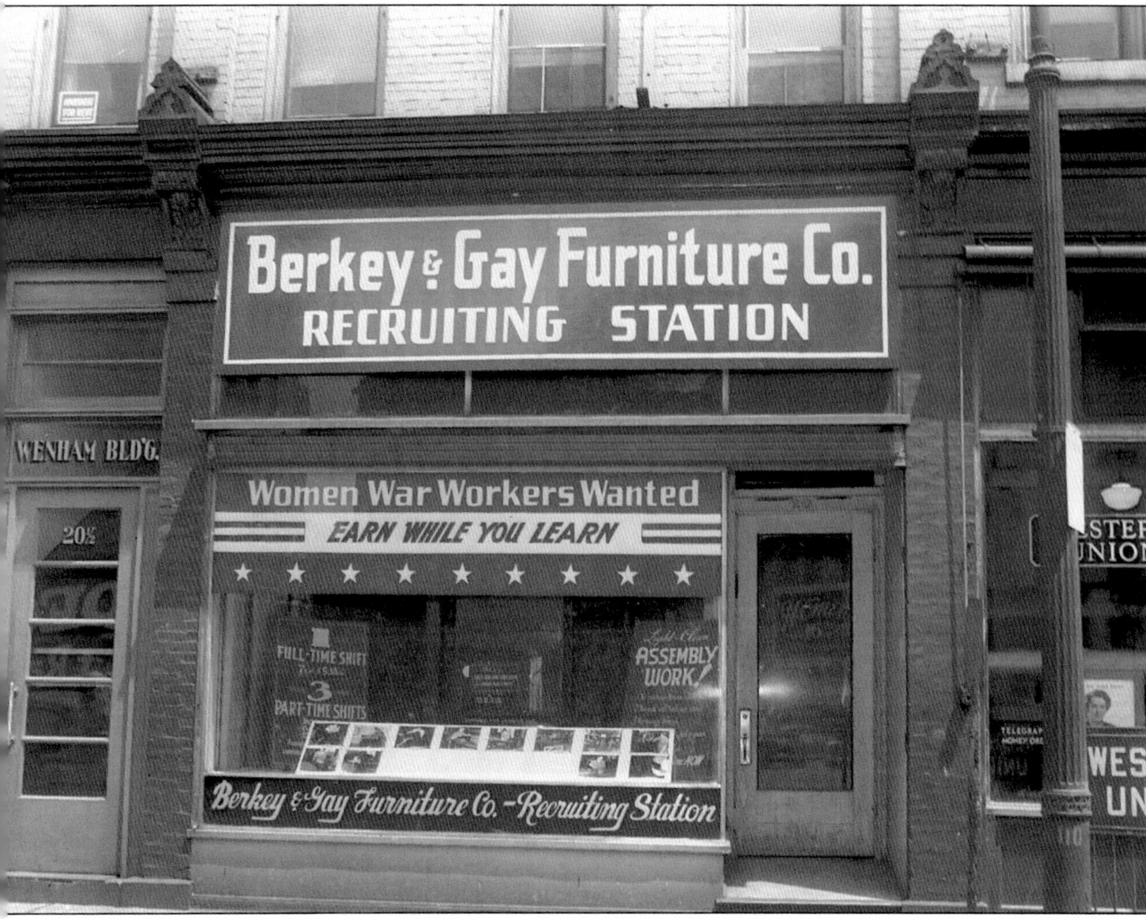

Factories across America needed help during the war. Although normal demand for their usual products was down, they had a larger responsibility: manufacturing for the military. With many of the men on active military duty, it fell to women to make up the shortfall. Berkey and Gay opened a recruiting office to entice them away from their home fires and into the factory. Women rose to the challenge, and their contributions were as important and as necessary as that of the troops. (Grand Rapids Public Library.)

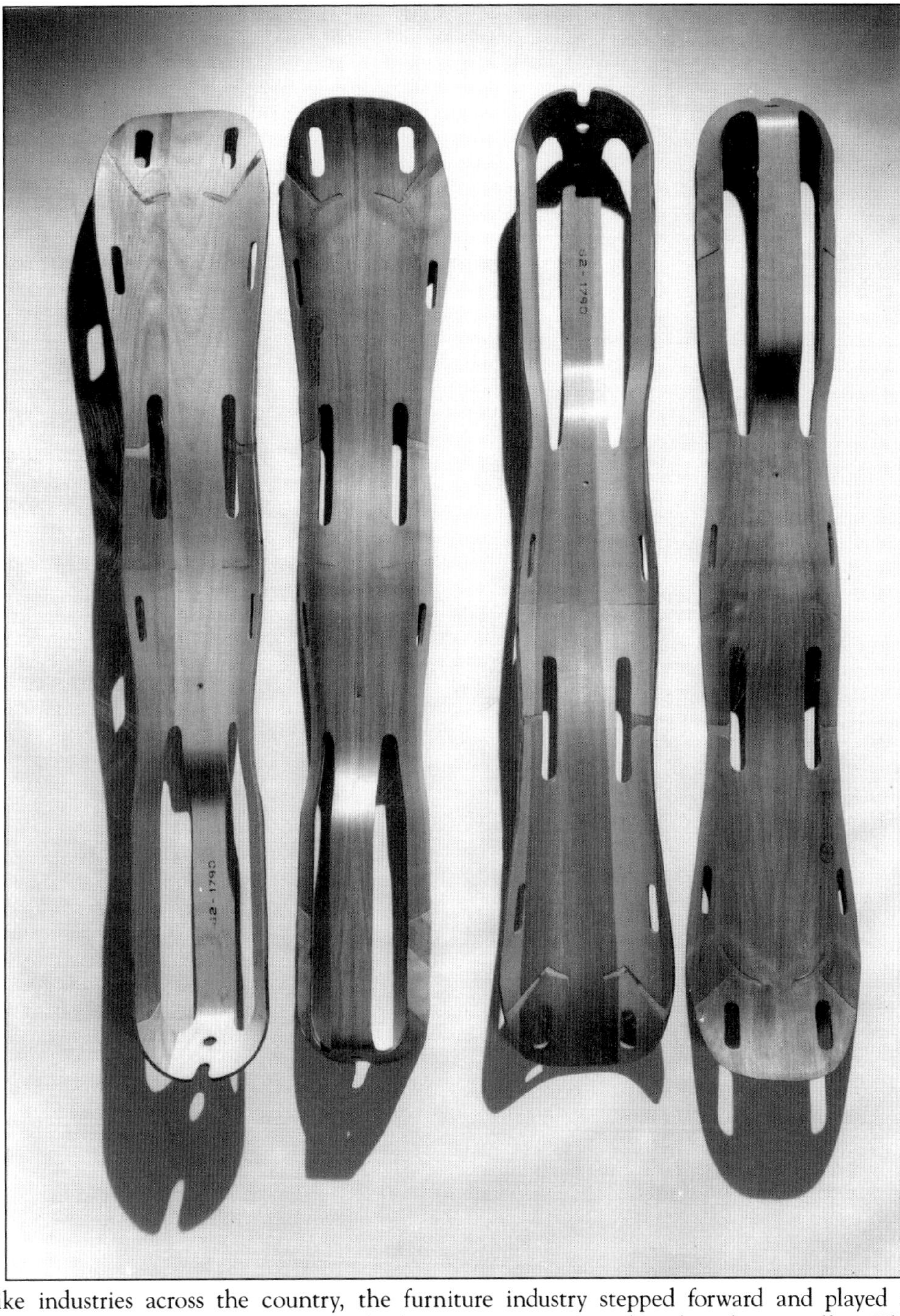

Like industries across the country, the furniture industry stepped forward and played an important role in World War II. All the large companies contributed to the war effort. They produced everything from submarine furnishings to aircraft parts to ammunition containers. When the United States Navy commissioned Herman Miller, Inc., to design a better splint for leg injuries, Charles Eames met the challenge with this one made of molded plywood. It was so beautifully proportioned and finely executed that today some collectors consider them wall art. (Herman Miller, Inc.)

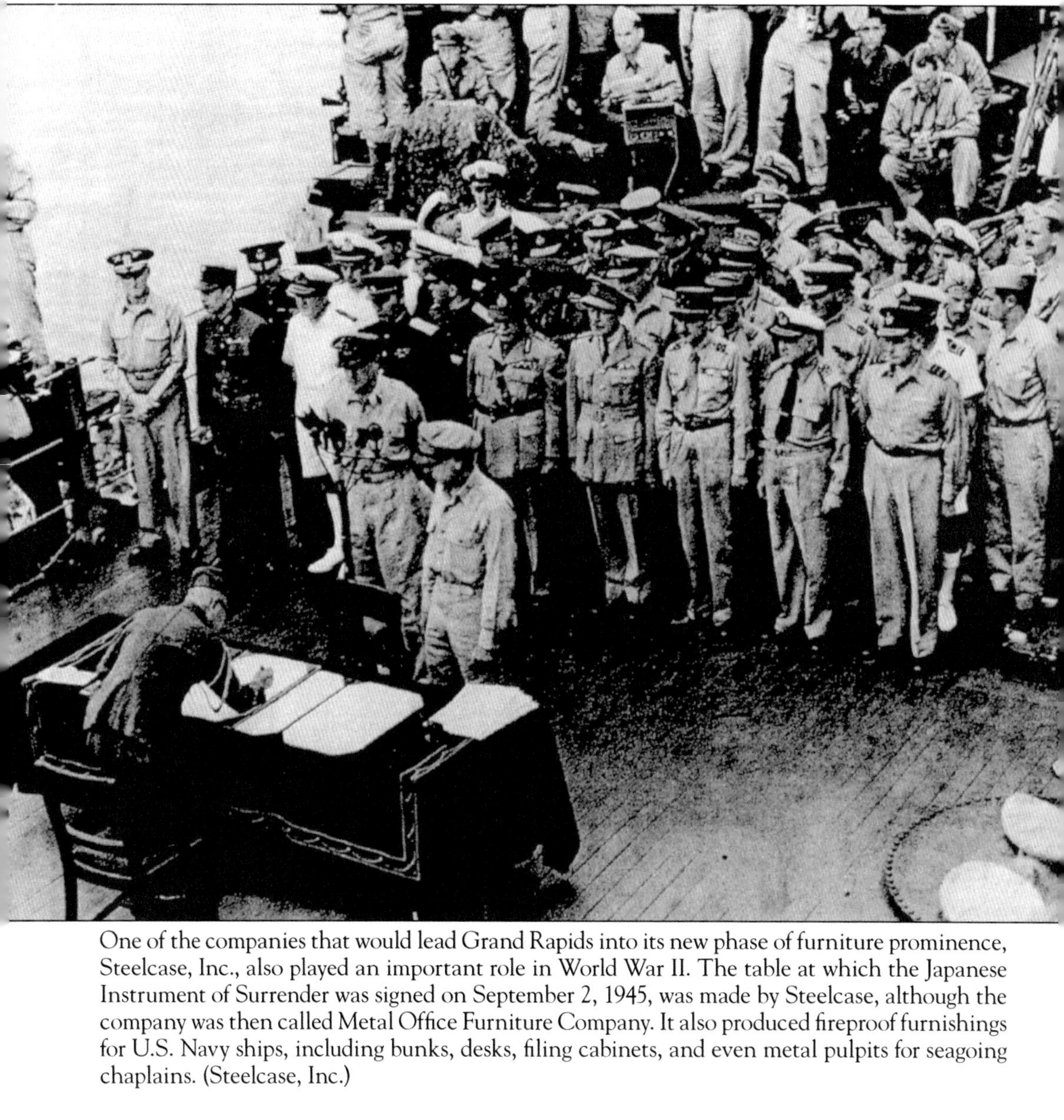

One of the companies that would lead Grand Rapids into its new phase of furniture prominence, Steelcase, Inc., also played an important role in World War II. The table at which the Japanese Instrument of Surrender was signed on September 2, 1945, was made by Steelcase, although the company was then called Metal Office Furniture Company. It also produced fireproof furnishings for U.S. Navy ships, including bunks, desks, filing cabinets, and even metal pulpits for seagoing chaplains. (Steelcase, Inc.)

Four

The Transition

In the end, neither strikes nor natural disasters nor national disasters defeated the Grand Rapids home furnishings industry. North Carolina did. The state lured companies south, offering cheaper nonunion labor in a milder climate.

The features that originally made Grand Rapids a perfect locale no longer applied. The vast forests were depleted, and the Grand River was no longer needed for transportation and for power. Also many of the factories had become obsolete. Starting over allowed the owners a chance to build more efficient, sprawling one-story buildings. Of all the companies once operating in Grand Rapids, only Kindel still produces home furnishings in the city today.

Perhaps the furniture makers themselves can take a part of the blame. Fine furnishings that lasted for generations did not foster repeat business. Also American tastes and buying habits changed. The old-fashioned ornate pieces fell out of favor. Too many people bought into the mind-set of "if it is new it is better," and companies that mass-produced cheaper products flourished. Furniture was no longer a major investment but rather something to replace periodically. By the post–World War II years, the country was well on the way to becoming a throwaway society.

But that did not end the area's furniture production. American Seating Company and Irwin Seating Company still manufacture sports, entertainment, and transportation seating. Anyone who has gone to a concert hall, attended a stadium sports event, or ridden a subway has sat on a Grand Rapids seat. Most students probably stashed their schoolbooks in Grand Rapids desks.

Grand Rapids and nearby Zeeland and Holland now lead the office furniture industry. Giants Steelcase, Inc., Herman Miller, Inc., and Haworth, Inc., became the "big three" and continue to dominate. Their modular office components meet today's efficiency needs and can be reconfigured as requirements change.

While many home furnishings companies remain headquartered in North Carolina, furniture is no longer made there. Company owners who fled south have now shifted their production to Asia, once again seeking lower labor costs.

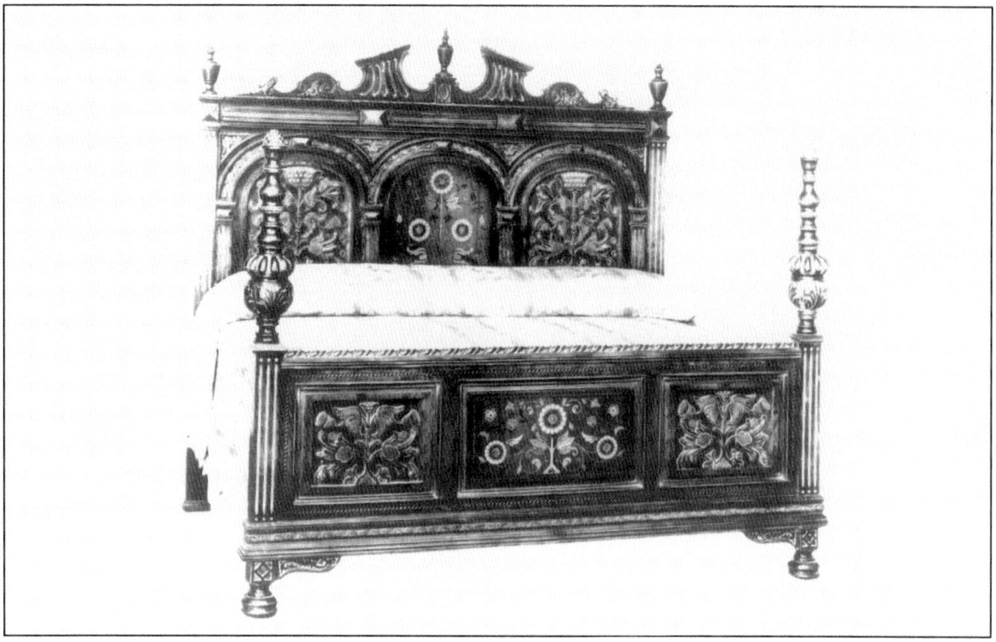

Star Furniture Company began production in 1905 and specialized in traditional bedroom suites like the painted and carved example in the photograph above. By 1919, sales declined and new management changed the direction of the company. In 1923, the new president, D. J. DePree, with his father-in-law, Herman Miller, became majority stockholders, and DePree renamed the company Herman Miller. Designers Gilbert Rohde, Charles and Ray Eames, and George Nelson favored modern furniture in light wood and simple shapes as shown in the photograph below. The new designs were an overwhelming success and determined the company's future. (Herman Miller, Inc.)

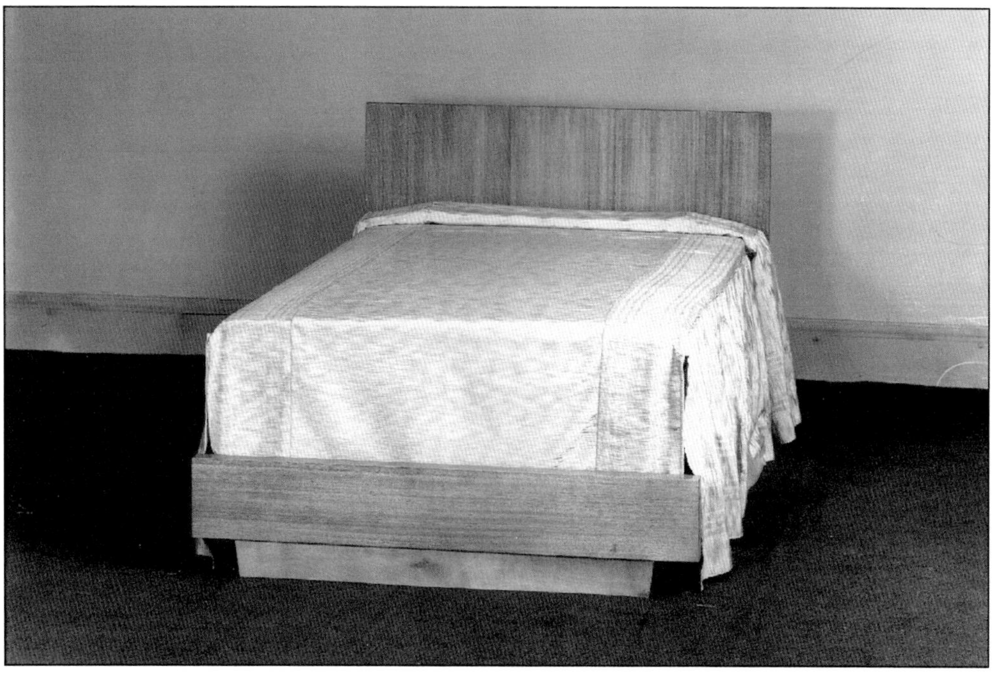

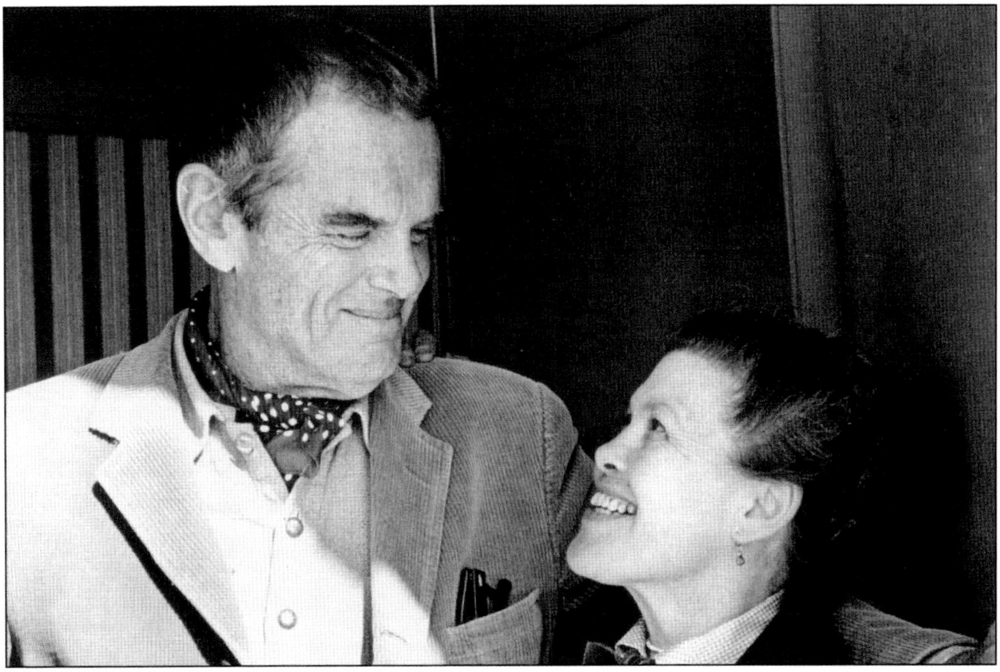

Charles and Ray Eames have been called the most successful husband-and-wife design team ever. He studied architecture and she studied art. Their collaborative efforts won the coveted Royal Gold Medal for Architecture, a recognition started by Queen Victoria in 1848 and considered the most prestigious international award in the industry. Theirs was a happy personal and professional union as evidenced here in 1969. (Herman Miller, Inc.)

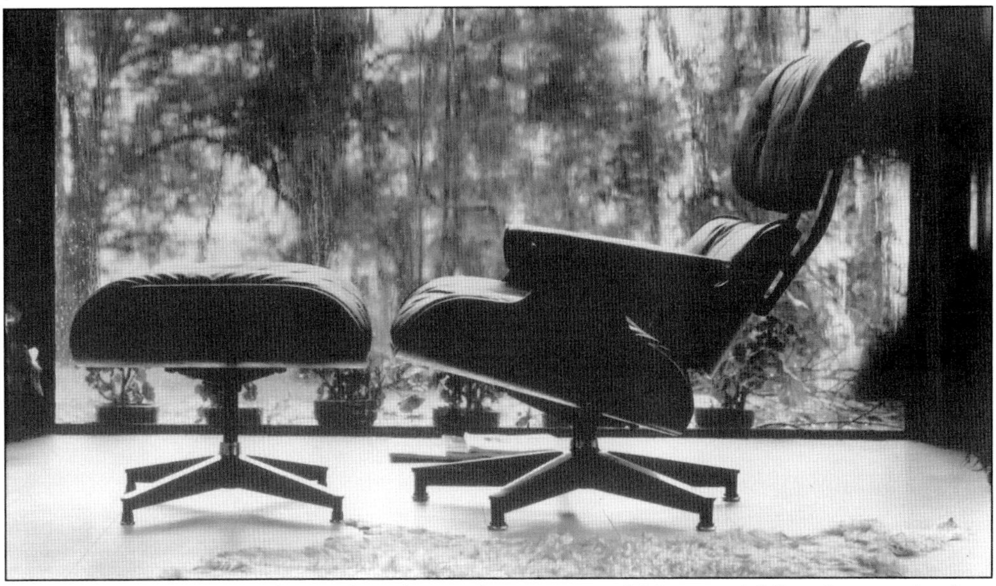

The Eameses contributed significantly to the success of Herman Miller, Inc., with their innovative and award-winning designs. Their Eames Lounge and Ottoman is a perfect pairing of sophistication and comfort. Designed in 1956, it is still sought after today. This photograph was taken in the Eameses' California home by Deborah Sussman. The couple began working with Herman Miller's design director in 1946. (Herman Miller, Inc.)

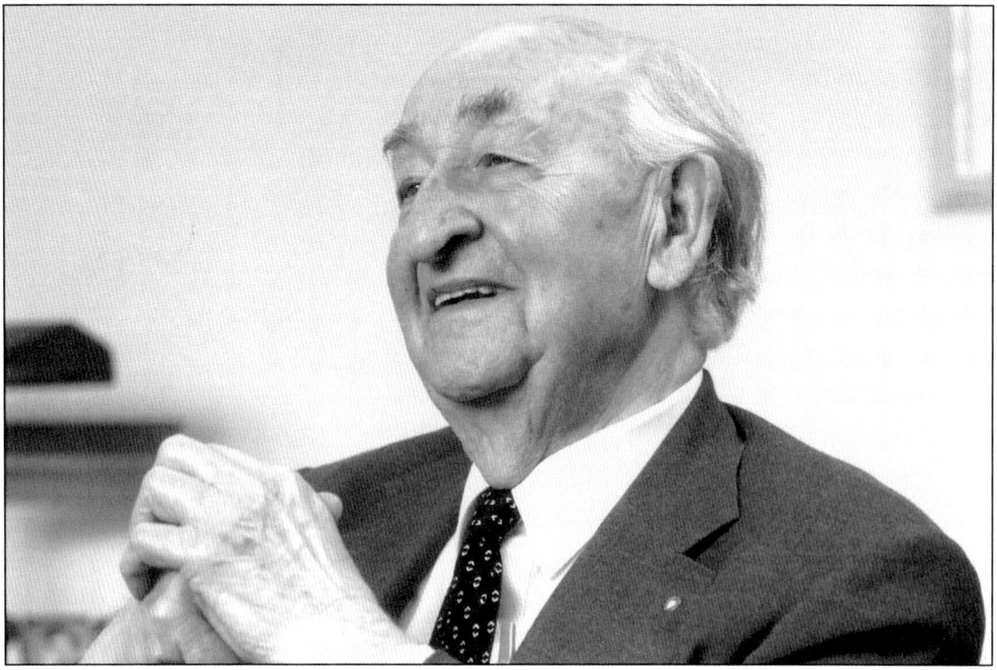

Dirk Jan DePree joined what would become Herman Miller, Inc., in Zeeland in 1905. By 1919, he had risen from clerk to president. DePree, who preferred to be called D. J., remained president until his son took over in 1962. At that time, DePree became chairman of the board. (Herman Miller, Inc.)

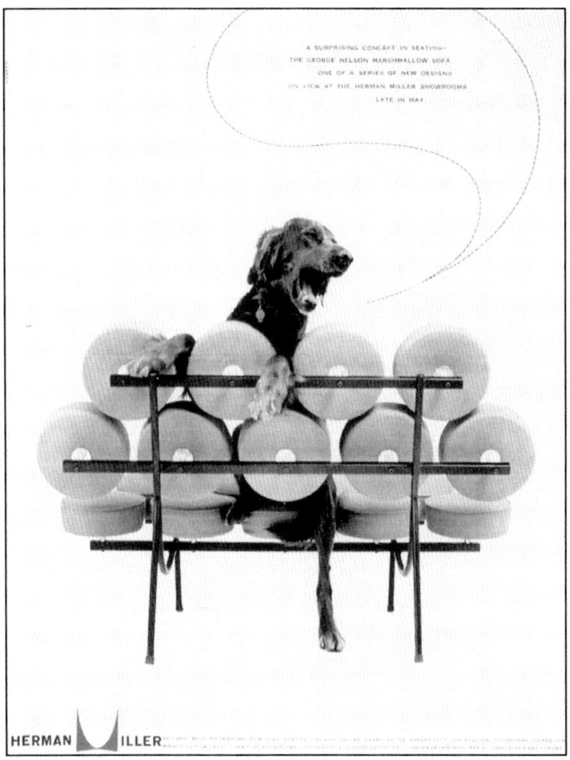

Design director George Nelson created the Nelson Marshmallow Sofa for both home and office use. Its playful shape made it a favorite with everyone, even the family dog as shown in this 1956 advertisement. Initially only 186 were produced, but the sofa was reintroduced in 1999. Some sofas had all marshmallows the same color, others were multicolored. (Herman Miller, Inc.)

Irwin Seating Company built these high school auditorium seats for Hillside High School in Hillside, New Jersey, in the 1930s. The assembly hall is typical of what was found in schools countrywide. (Irwin Seating Company.)

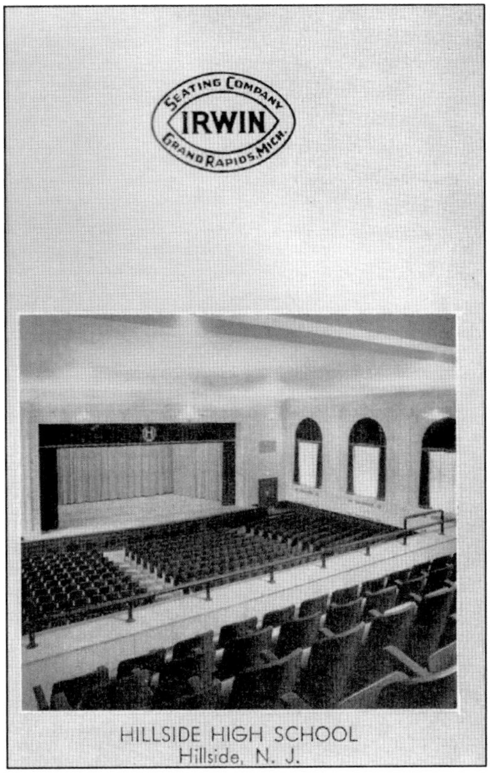

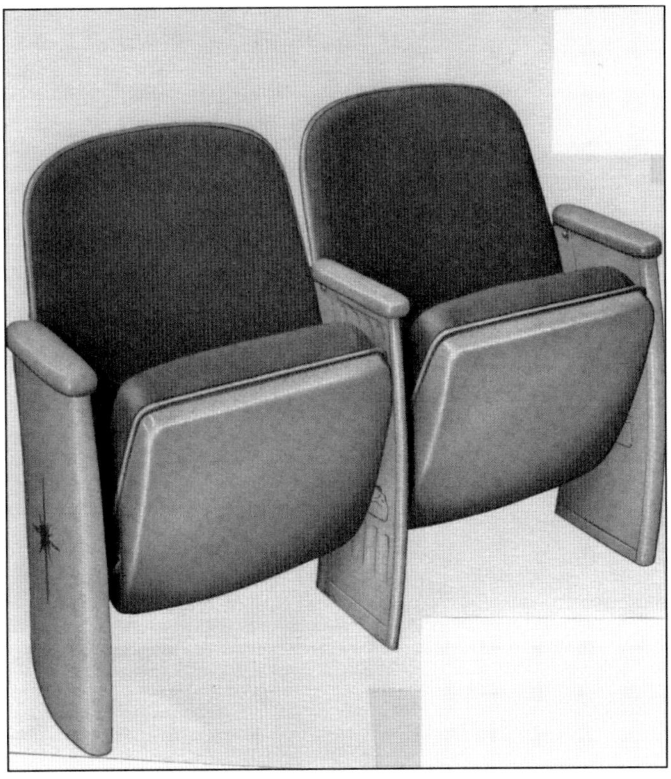

A perennial top seller for Irwin was its Comet theater seat, available in numerous colors and upholstery choices. A movie theater staple, it conjures memories of first dates or family nights out. It was comfortably padded, and the seat automatically folded upright when not in use. (Irwin Seating Company.)

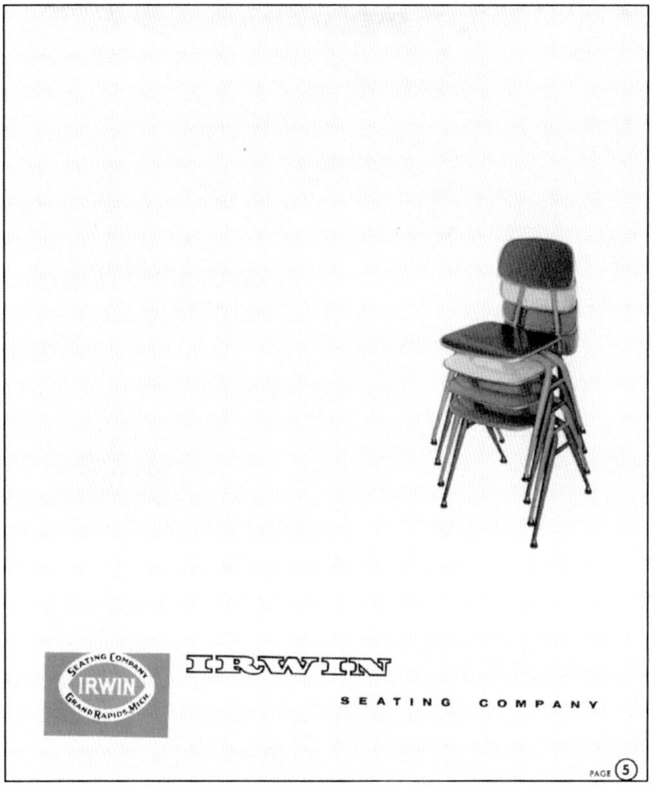

Another useful Irwin Seating Company product was the chair at left. Chairs could be placed wherever they were needed, then stacked for easy storage. (Irwin Seating Company.)

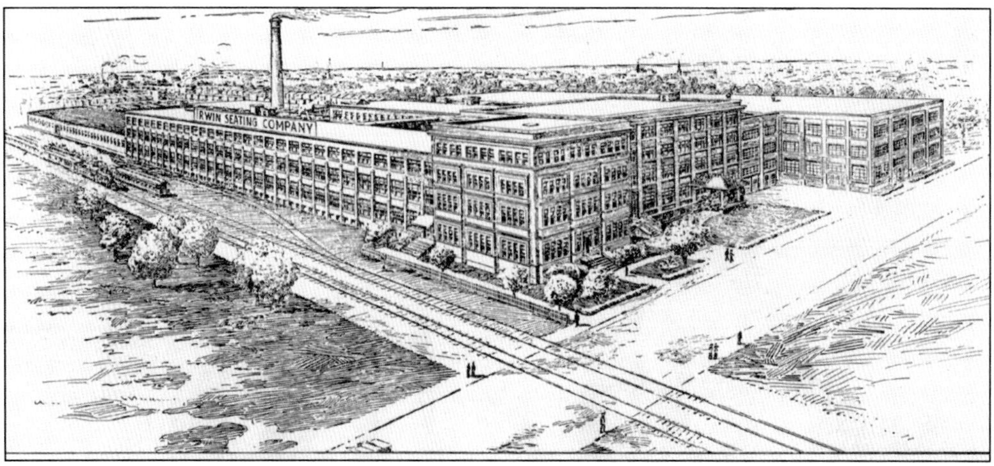

The Steel Furniture Company was founded in 1908 by five investors that included three Irwin brothers, Earle, Eber, and Robert. They bought out the others in the 1930s and renamed the company Irwin Seating. This is an artist's rendering of an early Irwin Seating factory, dating back to the 1930s. In 1968, the company moved to its current headquarters on the northwest side of Grand Rapids. (Irwin Seating Company.)

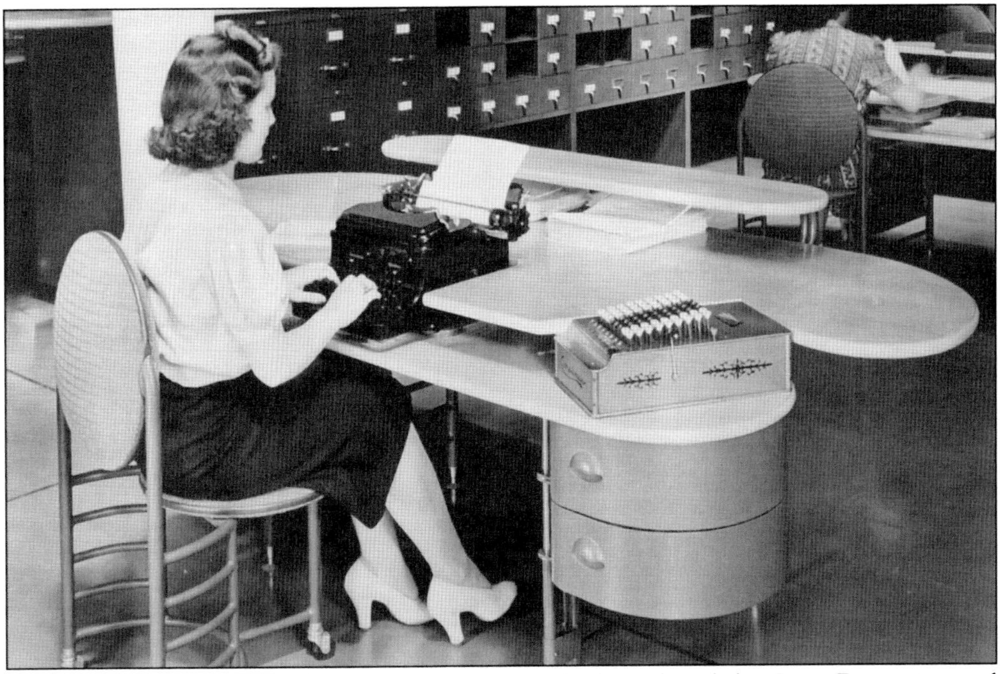

By the late 1930s, Metal Office Furniture Company had weathered the Great Depression and was looking to the future to determine what new products to bring to the market. The consensus was that design would become as important to buyers as function. Who better to collaborate with than Frank Lloyd Wright? Wright needed a company to produce the desks he designed for S. C. Johnson and Company in Racine, Wisconsin. The resulting desk is shown above. (Steelcase, Inc.)

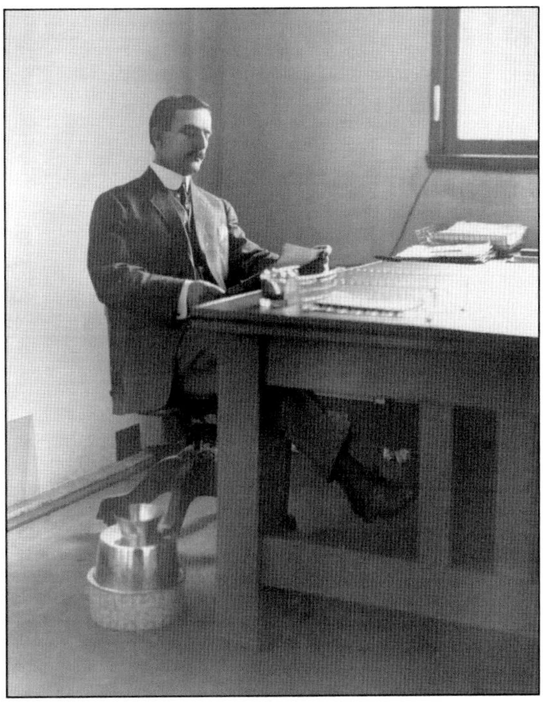

Before smoking at one's desk became verboten, men like one of the Steelcase, Inc. founders, Peter Wege (right), caused countless wastebasket fires. Although Wege is trying to avoid that calamity, not everyone was as careful. Thus came the Steelcase rectangular metal wastebasket, an office mainstay since it first appeared in the 1930s. (Steelcase, Inc.)

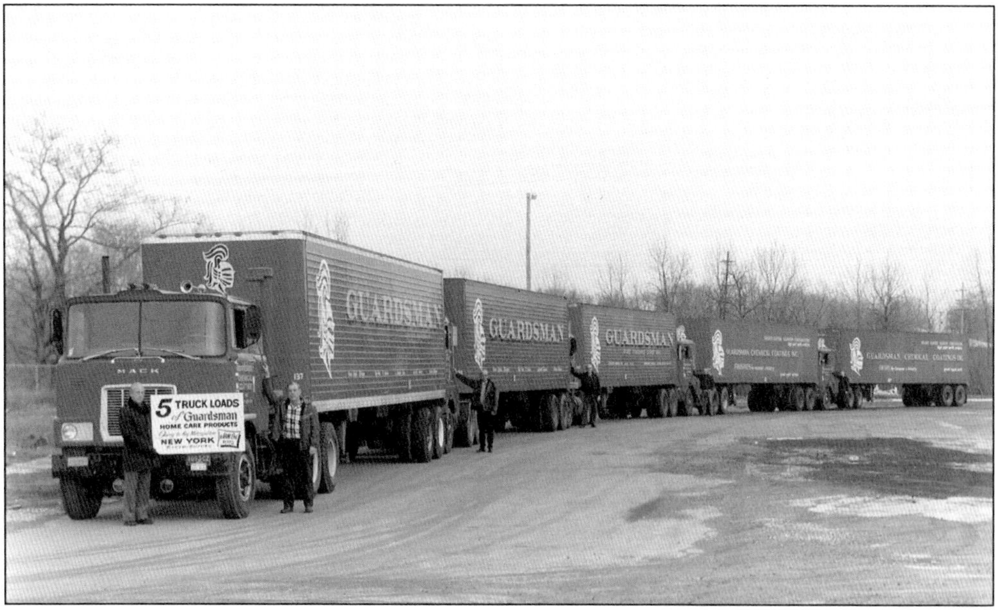

This gleaming Guardsman fleet heads for New York in 1972. A leader in the furniture-finishing and wood-care product industry, the company is sending these trucks to supply its New York distributors, which will in turn sell to both manufacturers and consumers. (Guardsman Products.)

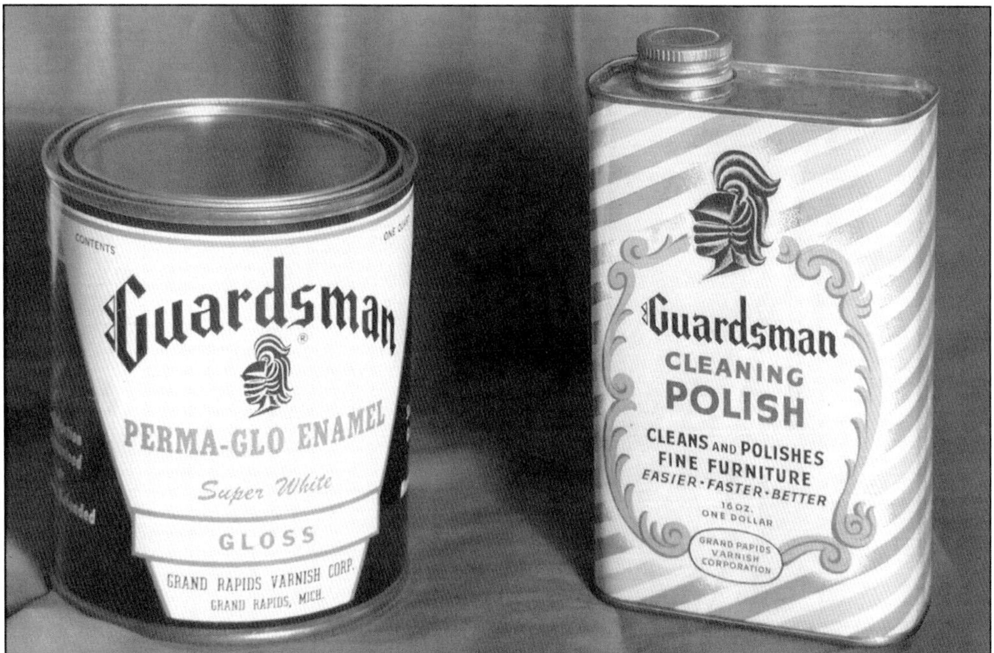

Products like these have enhanced, protected, and maintained fine wood finishes since Guardsman Products opened its doors in 1915 as Grand Rapids Varnish Company. The corporate name changed in 1966 to Guardsman Chemicals and to the present name in 1985. (Guardsman Products.)

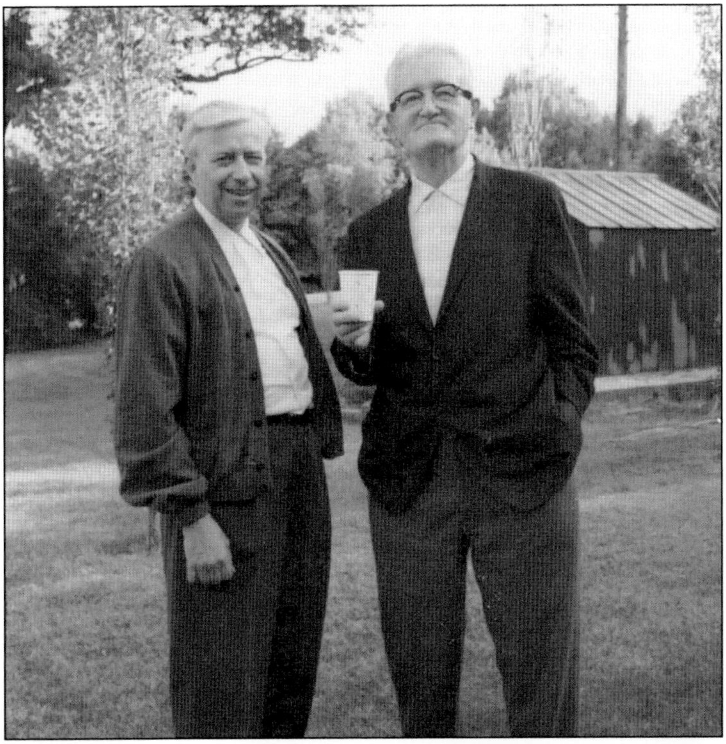

An important part of any salesman's job is attending sales meetings periodically in a casual setting for a combination of learning and fun. The Hekman Furniture Company team was no exception. Here company president Adrian Vanden Bout (left) relaxes with Harry Noonan, a salesman based in New York. (Charles Hekman.)

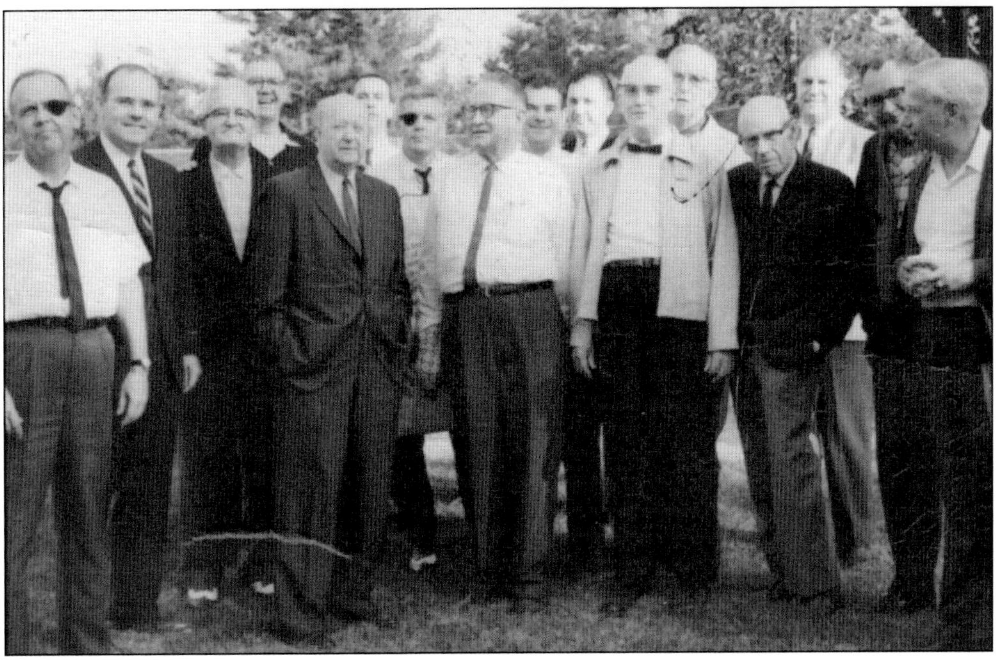

Such gatherings require a bit of clowning around. Note the eye patches. From left to right are Ralph Thompson, Les Stevenson, Harry Noonan, Gabe Hekman, Lynn Livesey, unidentified, Alan Doezema, John Hurley, Curtis Williams, Ray Sabota, two unidentified men, Dudley Dewey, Henry Boss, unidentified, and Adrian Vanden Bout. The action took place at the Hekman cottage in 1966. (Charles Hekman.)

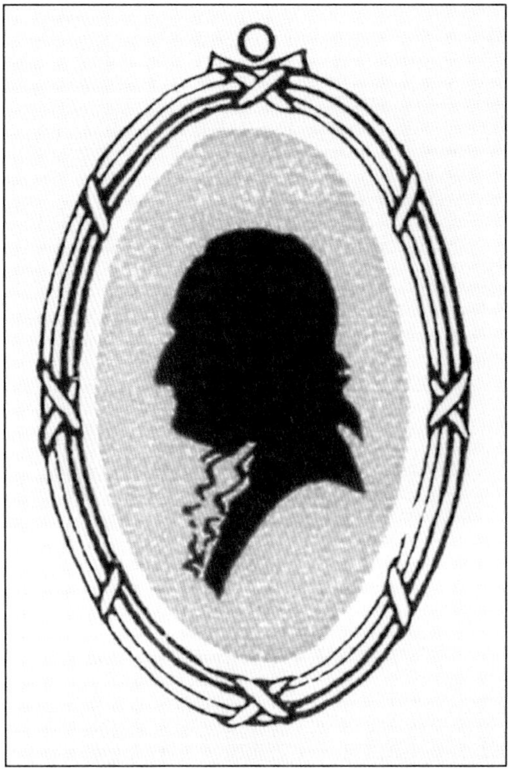

George Washington in profile graces the Kindel Furniture Company logo and has since 1930. (Kindel Furniture Company.)

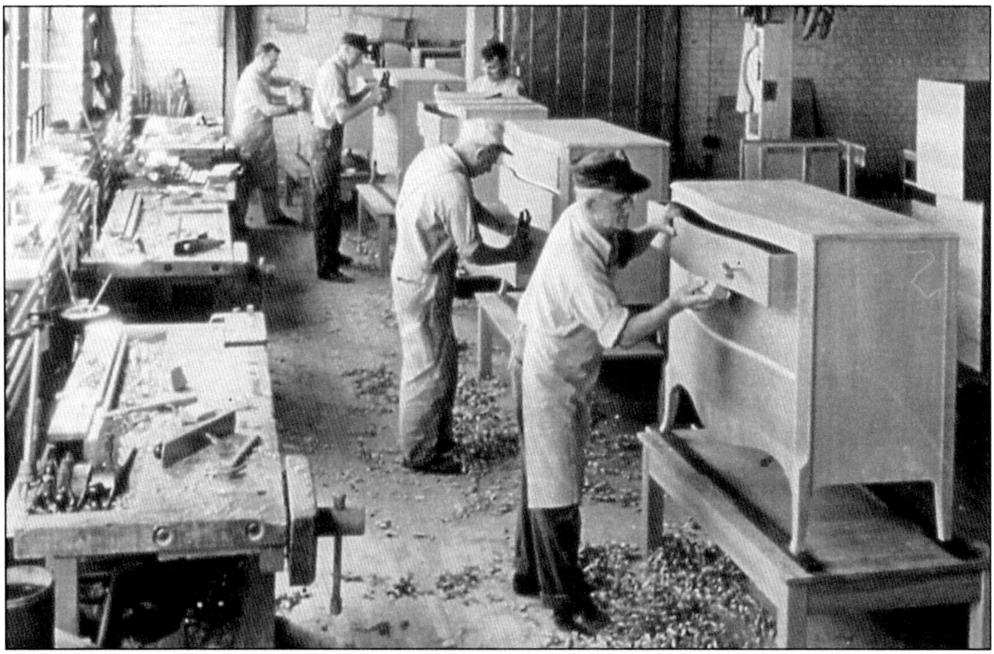

One feature of Kindel furniture is that all drawers are built oversize. Then each is hand fit to its opening. The drawers are dovetail constructed and made of sycamore, a wood known for stability—just one of the many touches separating Kindel pieces from the mass-produced offerings making up the bulk of the market today. (Kindel Furniture Company.)

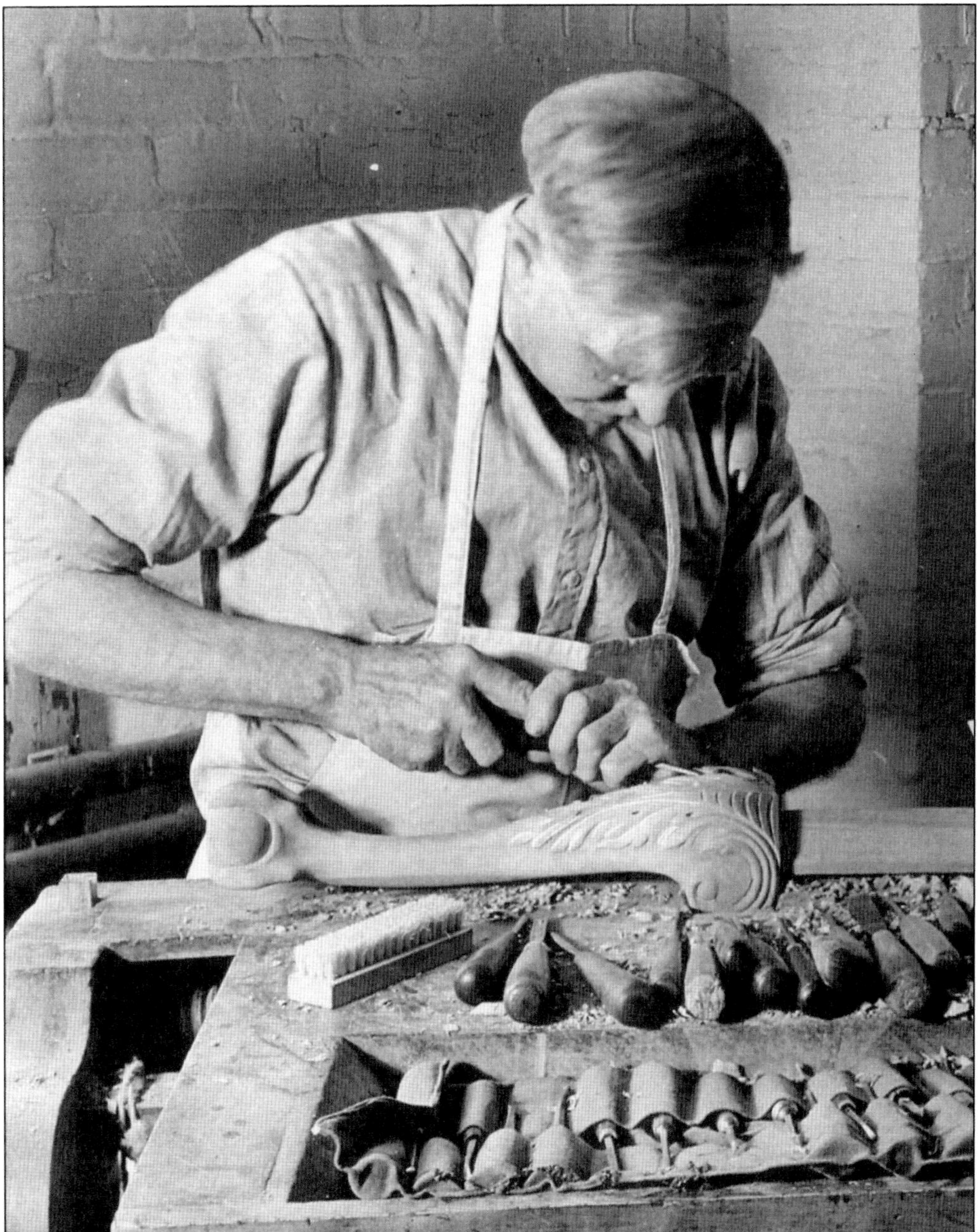

One of Kindel's master carvers carefully defines his work on the spindle carving machine—one of the many steps involved in creating furnishings that are partially machine made but detailed and finished by hand. (Kindel Furniture Company.)

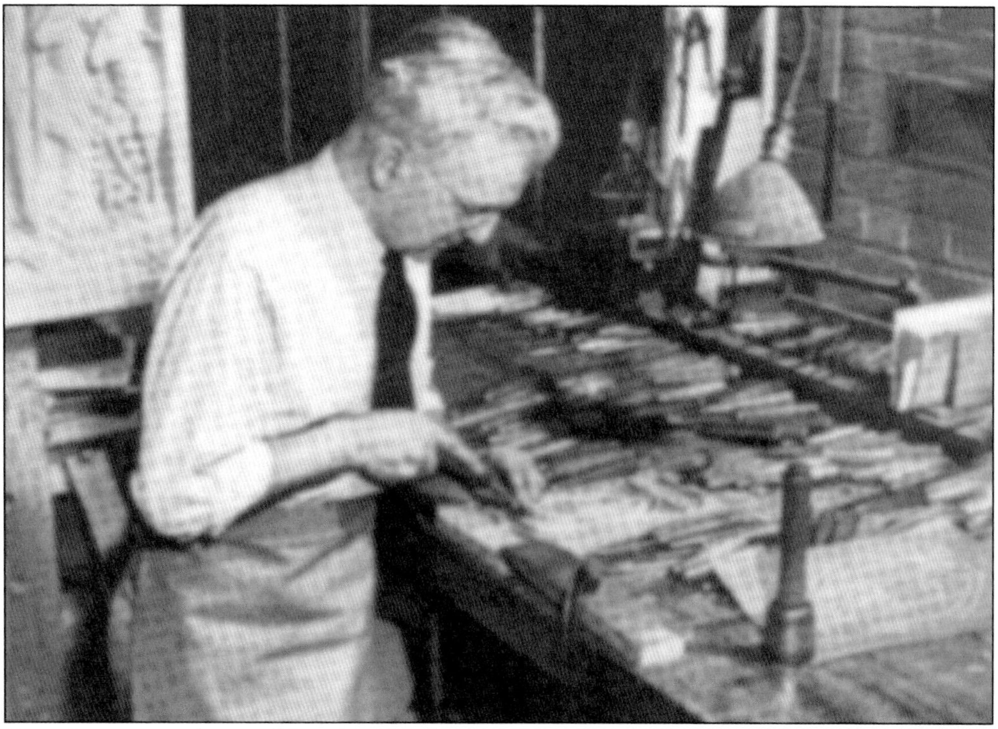

Churches are another market served by the American Seating Company. Master carver Joseph Wolters is seen at his workbench where he created decorative works based on Bible symbols. (American Seating Company.)

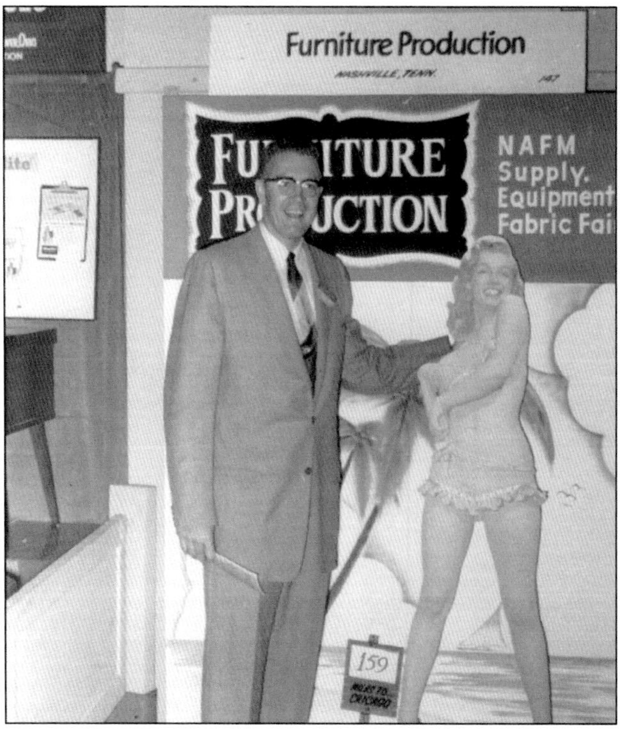

The Hekman Furniture Company was founded in 1922 by brothers Henry, Jelle, and John Hekman, and leadership of the enterprise was passed down through the next generation. Gabe Hekman, Jelle's son, poses playfully with a cardboard glamour girl cutout at a furniture manufacturers' convention in Nashville, Tennessee, in the 1950s. (Charles Hekman.)

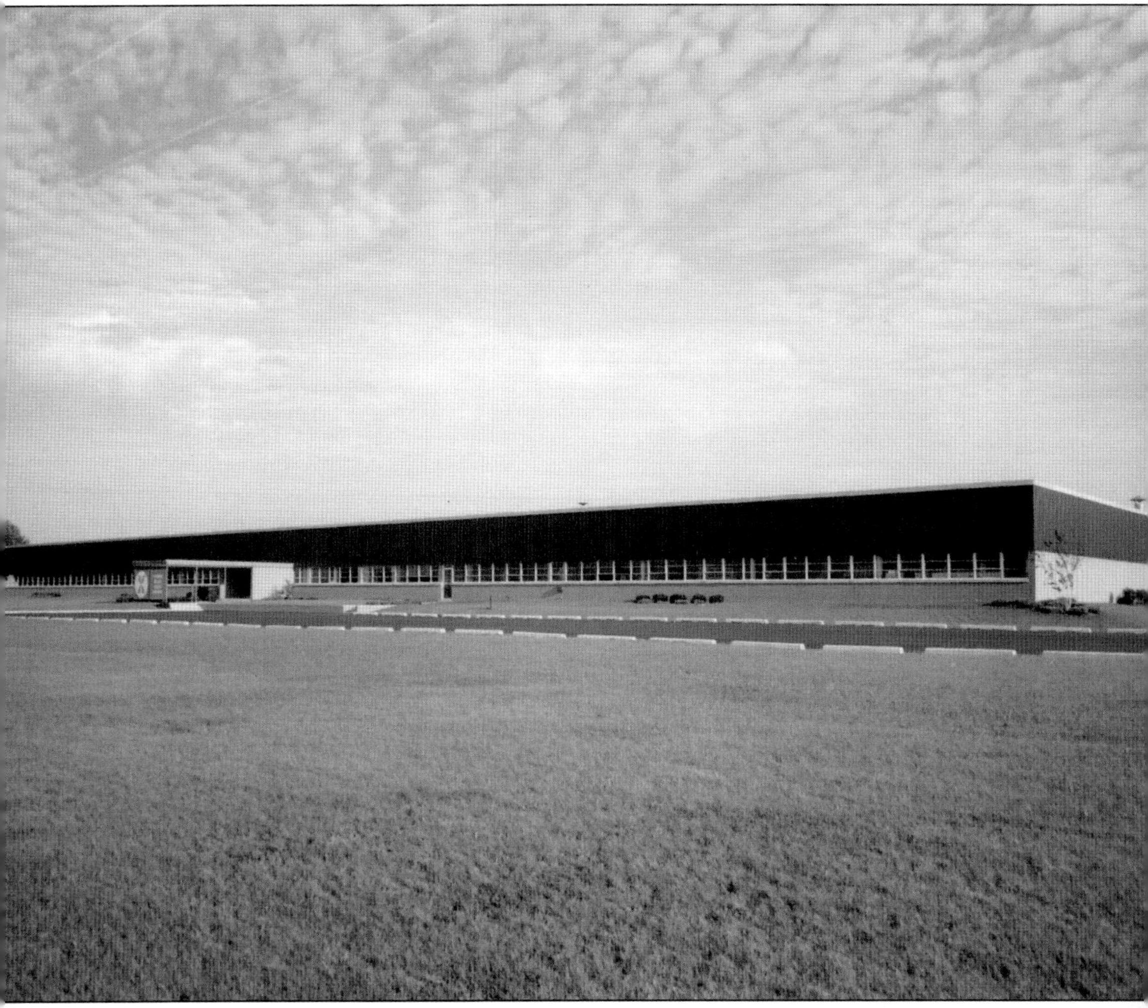

This is the Howard Miller factory as it looked in Zeeland in 1975. The company has since outgrew this facility and built anew. Its product line remains the same—clocks, quality-made clocks of timeless style. (Howard Miller Clock Company.)

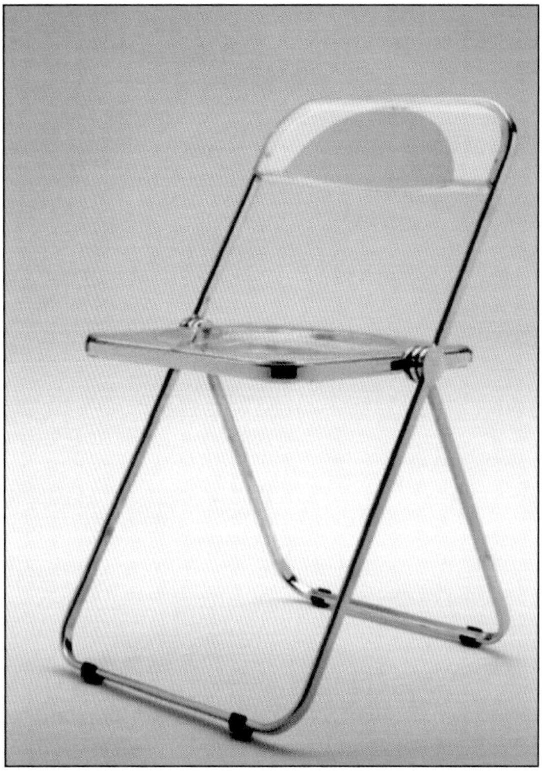

Haworth, Inc., designer Giancarlo Piretti's Plia chair exemplifies the manufacturer's focus in the 1960s on creating a modern, sophisticated product line. The chair received widespread acclaim and is now on permanent display at the Museum of Modern Art in New York. (Haworth, Inc.)

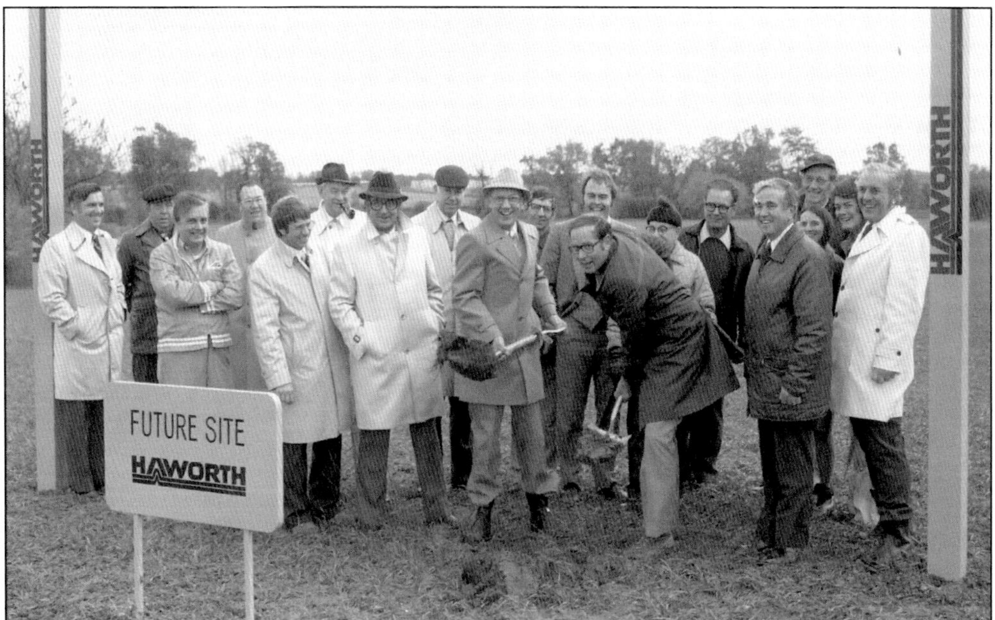

In 1976, Haworth, Inc., introduced the world's first pre-wired modular panel and changed its name from Modern Products to Haworth. That marked the beginning of the company's exclusive focus on office furniture systems. At around the same time, the company moved into its world headquarters building in Holland, Michigan. (Haworth, Inc.)

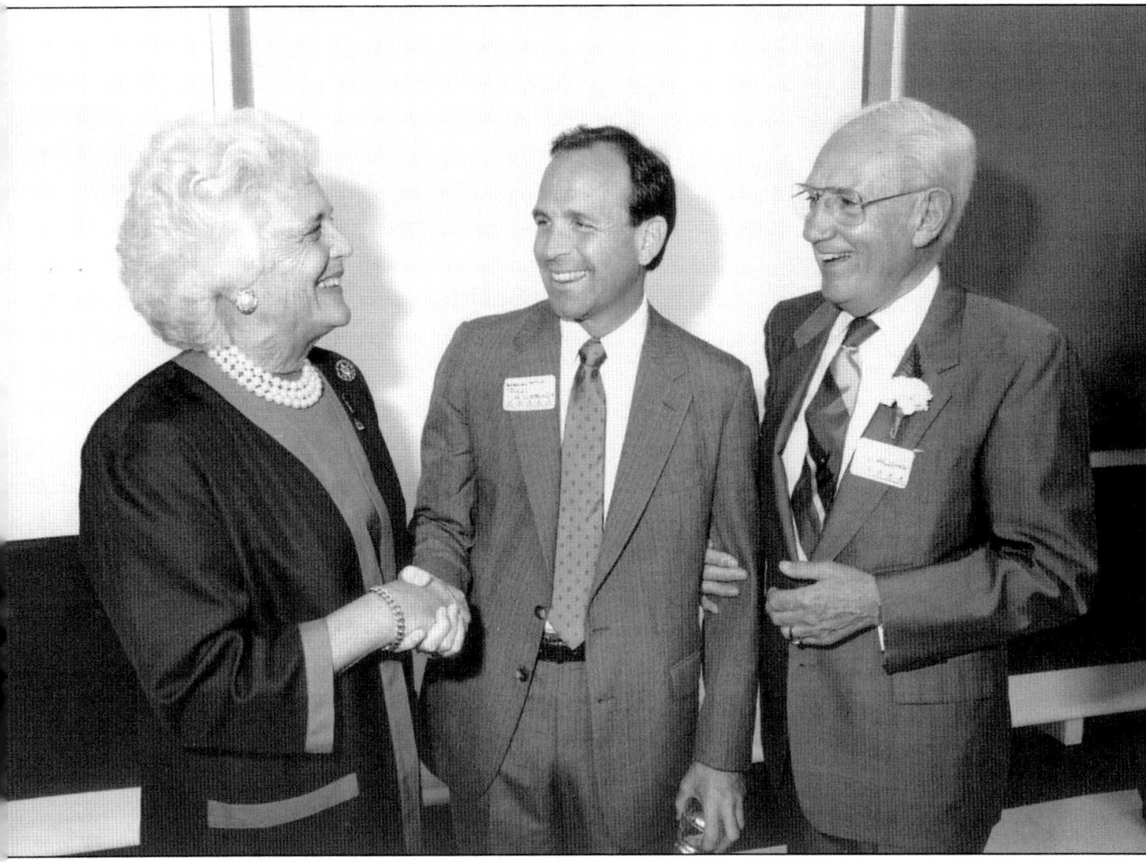

While serving as first lady, Barbara Bush visited the Haworth, Inc., plant accompanied by Paul Hillegonds (center), former speaker of the Michigan House of Representatives. Giving them the VIP tour is company president G. W. Haworth. (Haworth, Inc.)

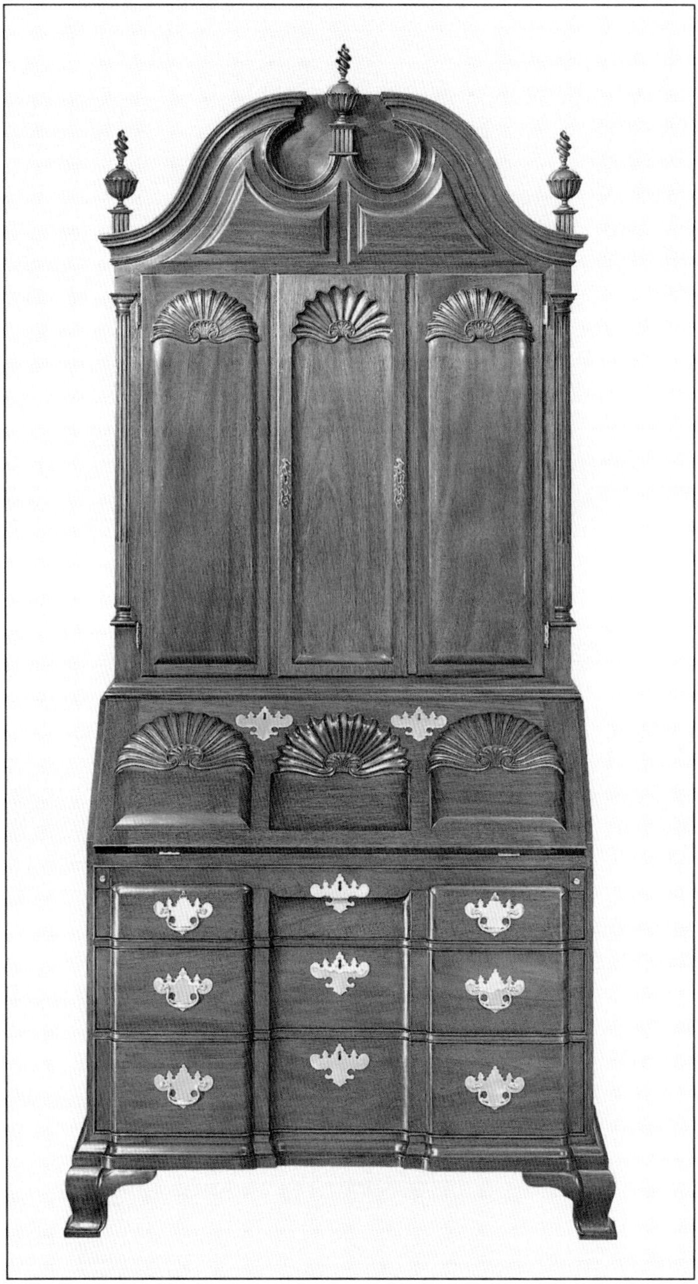

The Henry Francis DuPont Winterthur Museum awarded Kindel Furniture Company a license to reproduce pieces from the world's most important collection of American decorative arts and furnishings. To be called a *reproduction* rather than an *adaptation*, the Winterthur definition requires "a line-for-line copy of the original object, using the same primary and secondary materials." One of Kindel's reproductions for the collection is the Townsend and Goddard desk-and-bookcase shown above. The original was made in the 1770s. Christie's sold the privately owned piece in 1989 for $12.1 million. Grand Rapids' only remaining home furniture manufacturer continues adding to its Winterthur collection that was first introduced in the 1980s. (Kindel Furniture Company.)

When the United States government needed a building to represent America's Colonial period at the French International Colonial and Overseas Exposition in Paris in 1931, George Washington's home, Mount Vernon, immediately came to mind. Washington's great-great-great-grandniece Anne Madison Washington decorated the replica and turned to the Kindel Furniture Company for help. One of the six beds she chose is the canopied four-poster at right. (Kindel Furniture Company.)

The Washington Family Again Furnishes MOUNT VERNON

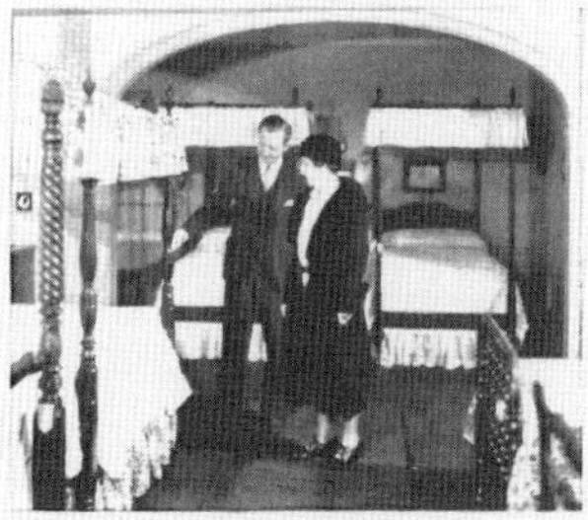

Miss Anne Washington personally selecting Kindel beds for the French International Colonial and Overseas Exposition. The selection was made from regular Kindel stock.

Mount Vernon, America's best-loved historical show place, has again been furnished by a member of the Washington family!

At the great French International Colonial and Overseas Exposition in Paris, this historic old mansion was reproduced by the United States Government to represent the Colonial period, as the outstanding American exhibit.

The important task of selecting furniture and decorations for this replica was entrusted to Miss Anne Madison Washington, a great, great, great grandniece of General George Washington, and daughter of the distinguished antiquarian, Lawrence Washington.

Miss Washington was singularly fitted for this appointment, not only because of her ancestry, but because of her intimate acquaintance with Mount Vernon and her thorough knowledge of Colonial architecture and furnishings acquired through life-long study. This knowledge, as well as her understanding of present furniture sources, qualified her as an invaluable aid in the successful re-creation of the Mount Vernon interior.

As her first move, Miss Washington journeyed to the furniture style center of the world, Grand Rapids. Here she confidently turned to Kindel for

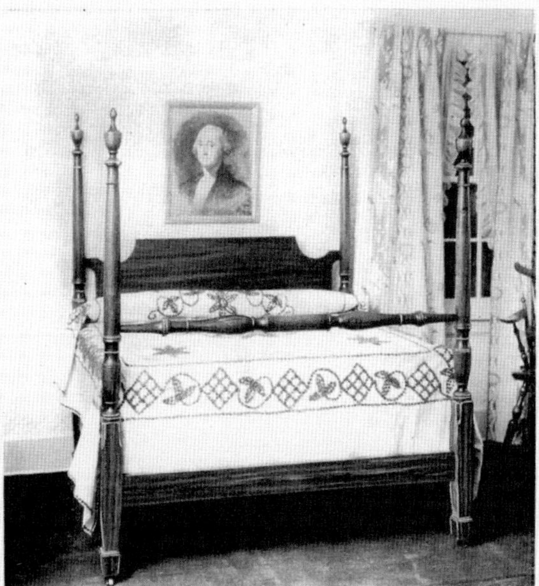

George Washington Memorial Bicentennial Bed

(Not offered for sale)

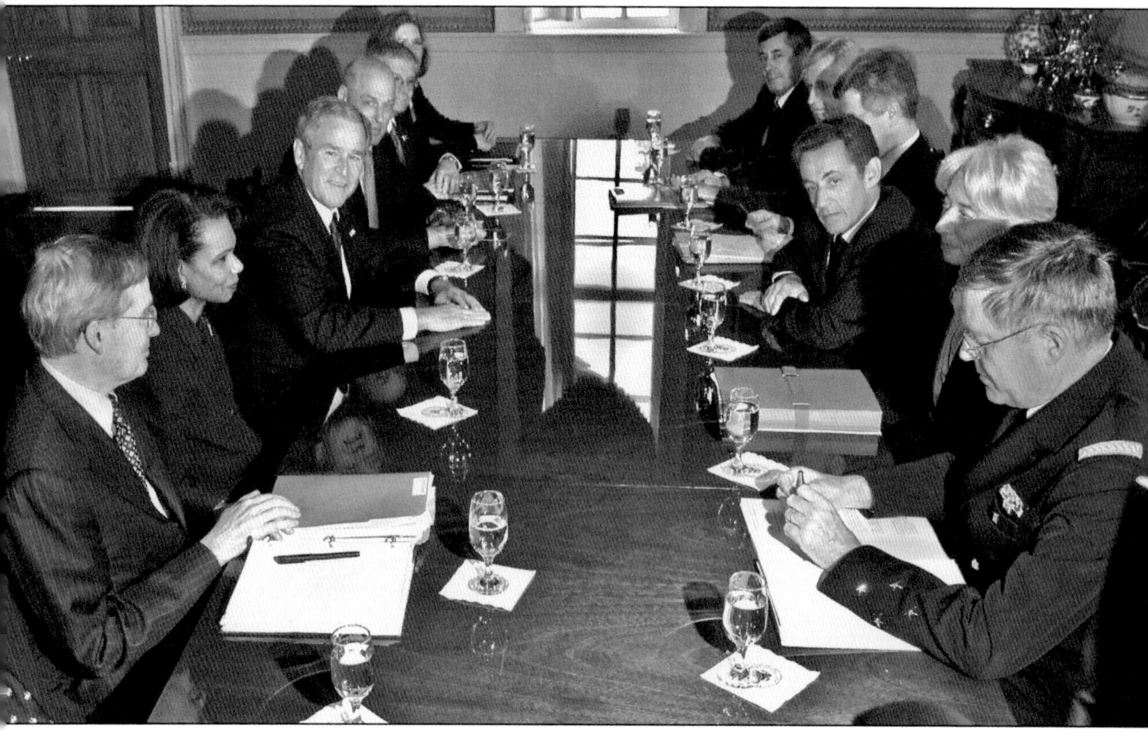

This gleaming 23-foot-long mahogany table was also produced by Kindel for the Mount Vernon replica. It was used for the meeting between French president Nicolas Sarkozy and United States president George W. Bush in November 2007. While most residences cannot accommodate a table of that size, it provides ample room for the leaders along with their aides and secretaries. (Kindel Furniture Company.)

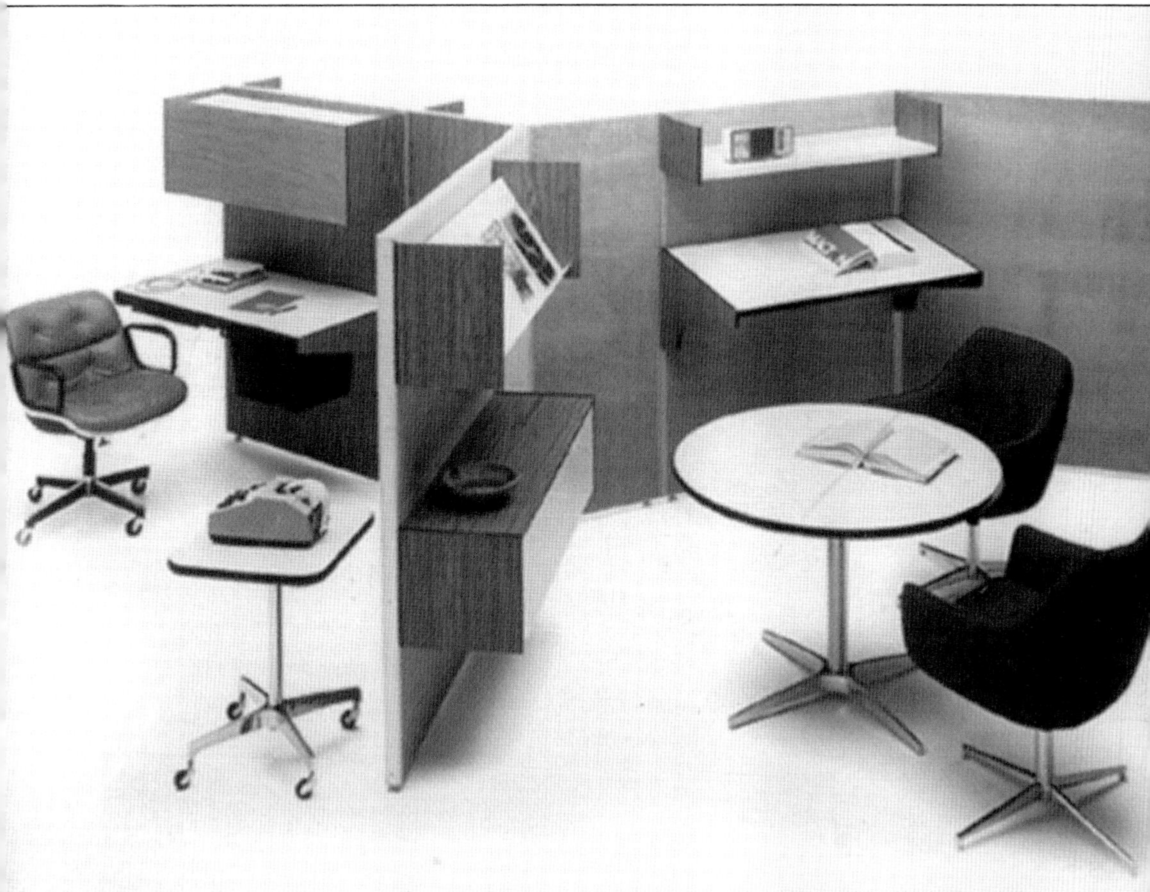

In the 1950s, Haworth, Inc., decided its future lay in office systems. That led to configurations that included pre-wired panels, the industry's first. The risk paid off; the company has enjoyed enormous success over the following decades and remains one of three industry leaders. (Haworth, Inc.)

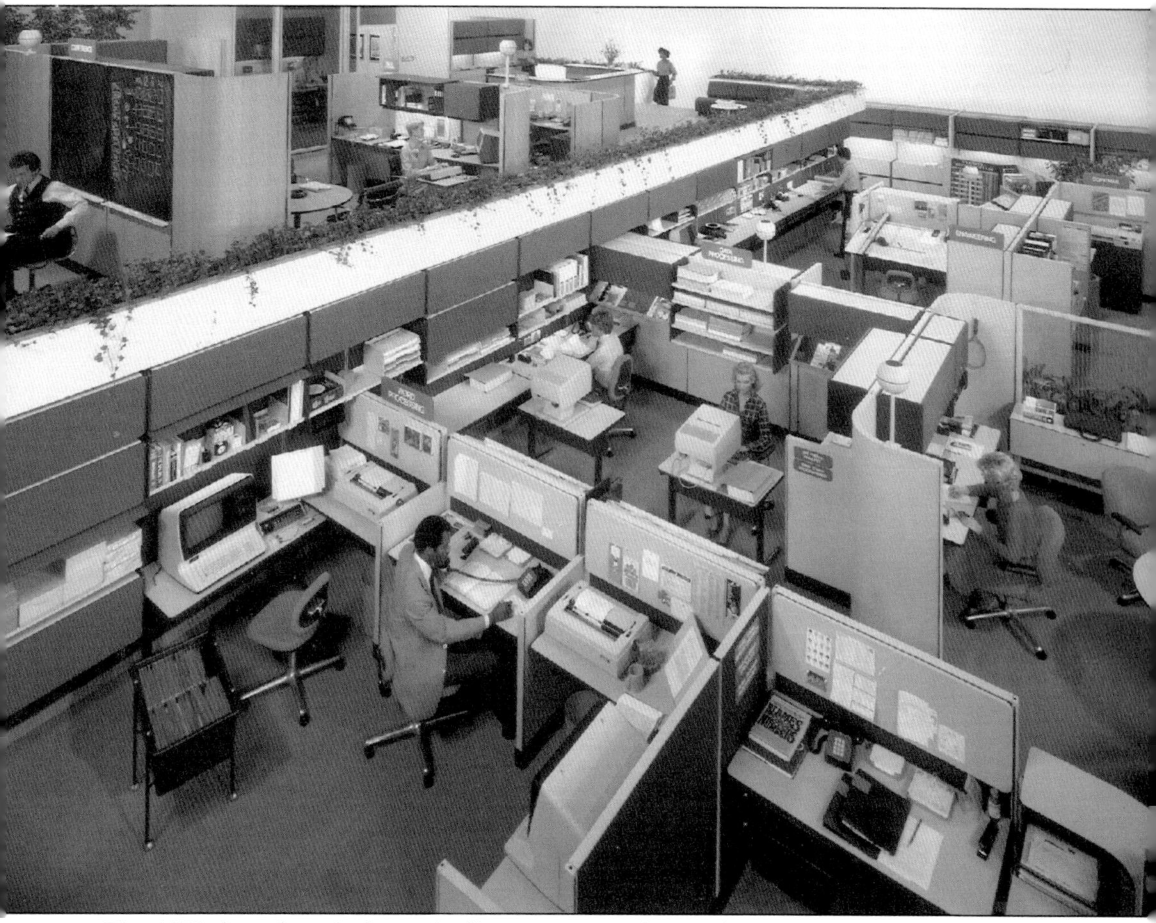

The 1970s brought cubicles and office systems made up of moveable components that could be reconfigured as needed. The Action Office system of Herman Miller, Inc., shown in sales brochures in 1978, featured red and brown upholstery with neutral laminate panels and surfaces. (Herman Miller, Inc.)

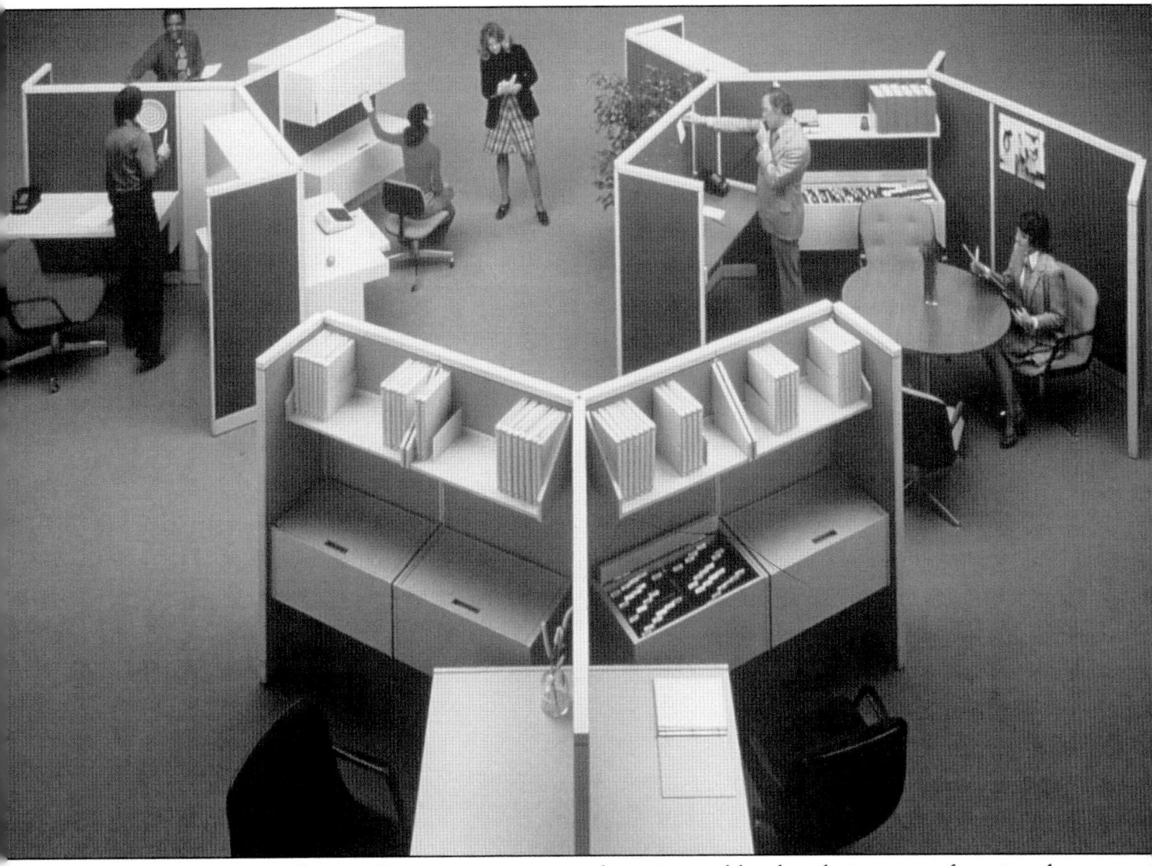

This Steelcase, Inc., office configuration proves anything is possible when laying out a functional office plan. Instead of lining up side by side, in the conventional cubicle format, these components accommodate a more creative layout. (Steelcase, Inc.)

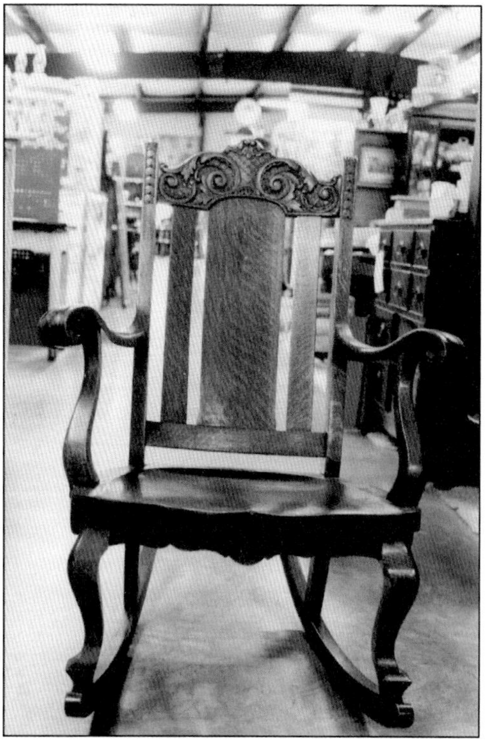

While some Grand Rapids furniture remains in the families that originally bought it, astute antiques buyers can still find treasures like this rocker made by the Grand Rapids–based Michigan Chair Company. It was found at the West Michigan Antiques Mall on Highway 31, about halfway between Grand Haven and Holland. (Norma Lewis.)

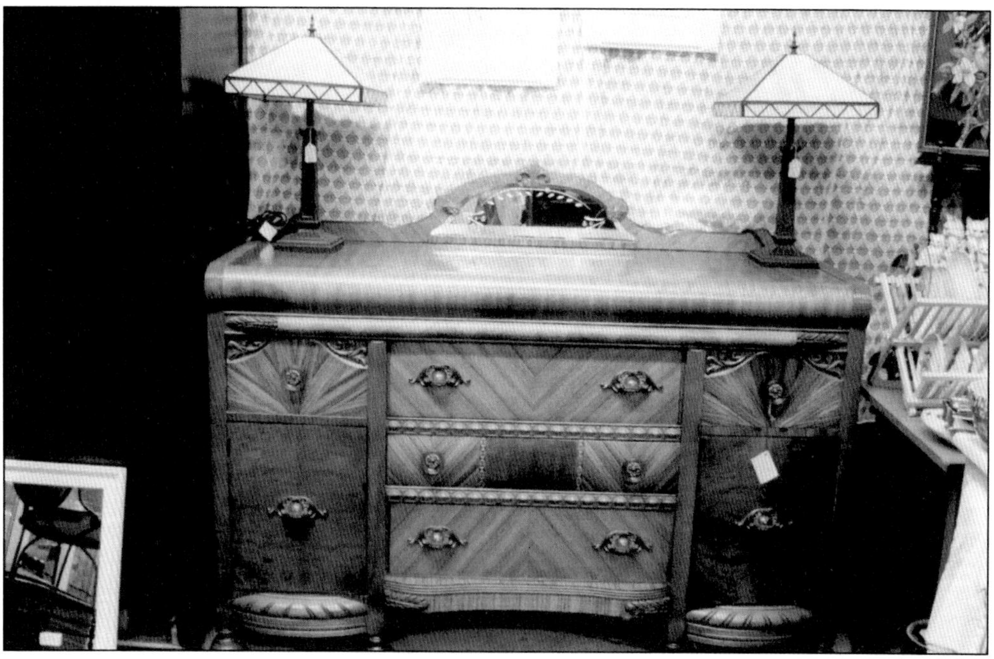

The "waterfall" style of this buffet enjoyed enormous popularity, and while there are still many to be found, not all are in as good condition as this example. It is displayed here at the West Michigan Antiques Mall on Highway 31 in Grand Haven. It is identified as coming from the Harris Sample Furniture Company, Grand Rapids, and dates back to the 1920s–1930s. (Norma Lewis.)

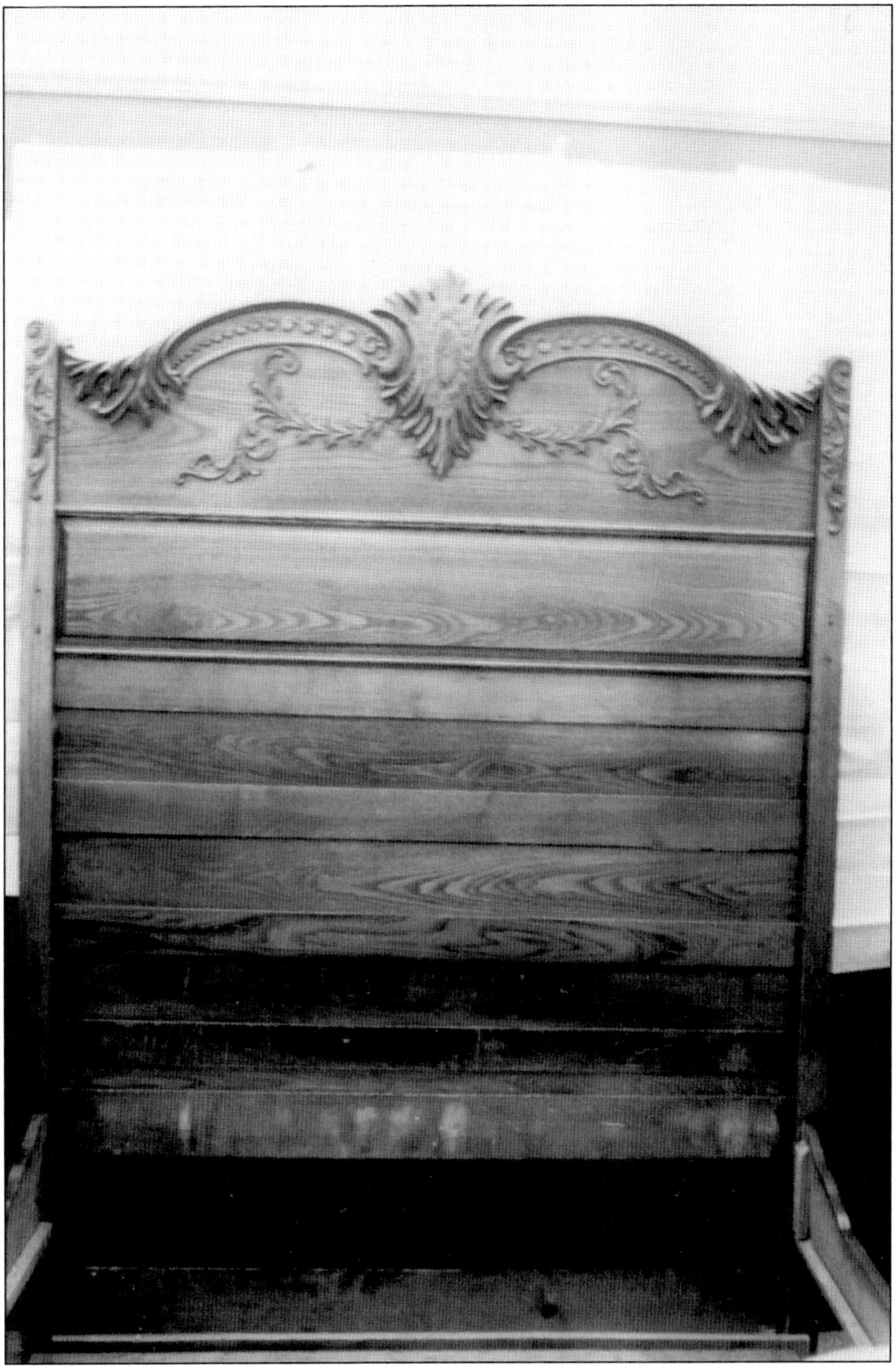

This carved headboard is part of a bedroom suite purchased in 1884 by a bride and groom. It was delivered to their farm where it remained until they built a new house on the same property. Both the farm and the furniture remained in the family through four generations. The last owner moved into an assisted care facility and placed it for sale at Somewhere in Thyme in Grandville. It is known to be Grand Rapids–made and is in the style of several manufacturers of that year, including Berkey and Gay, Widdicomb, and Nelson Matter. (Norma Lewis.)

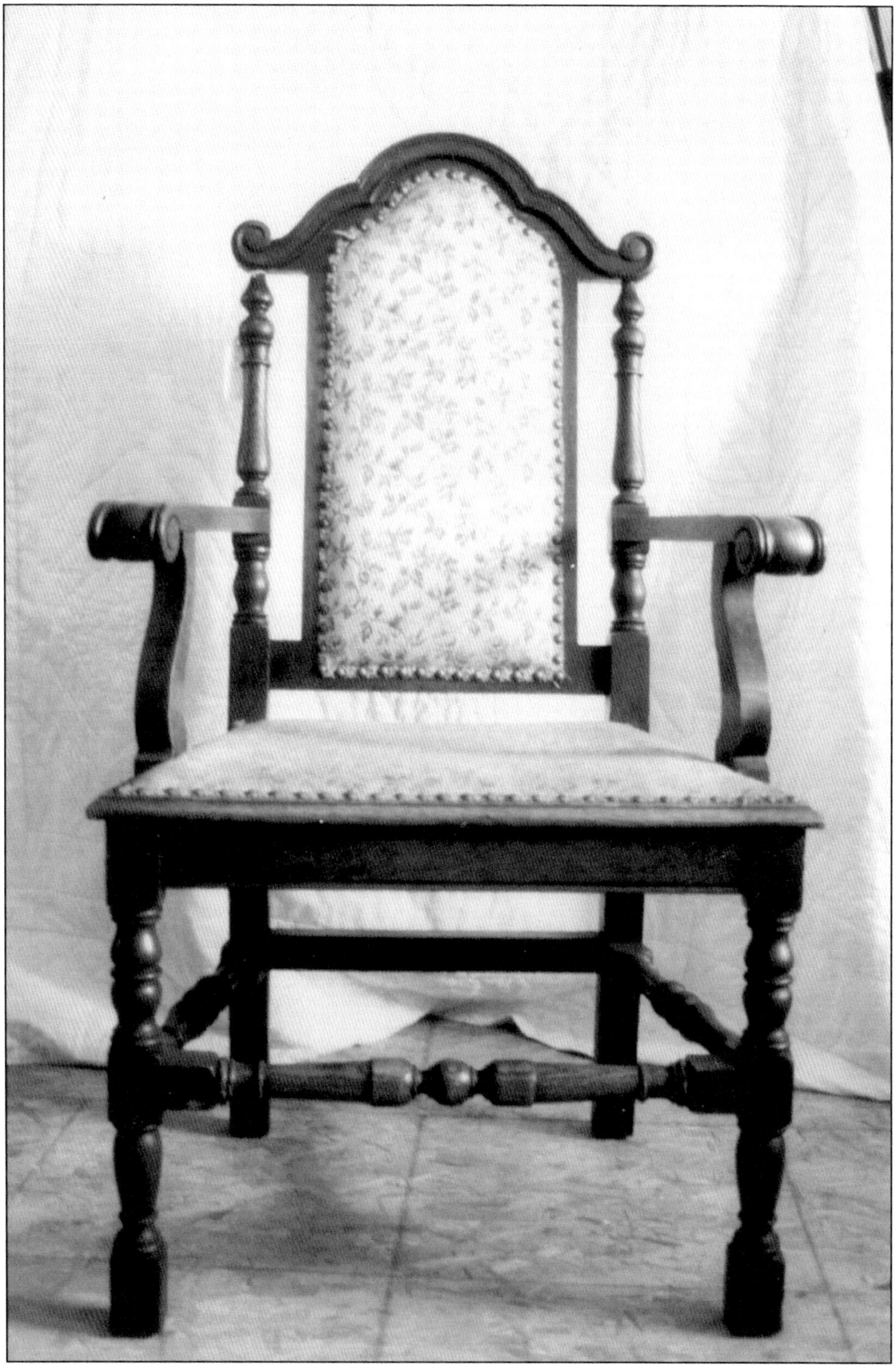

This upholstered Berkey and Gay armchair, made sometime between 1905 and 1929, will be a lucky find for someone. Note the graceful curve crowning the back. It is not known if the upholstery is original. The chair was found at Light House Furnishings in Grand Rapids. (Norma Lewis.)

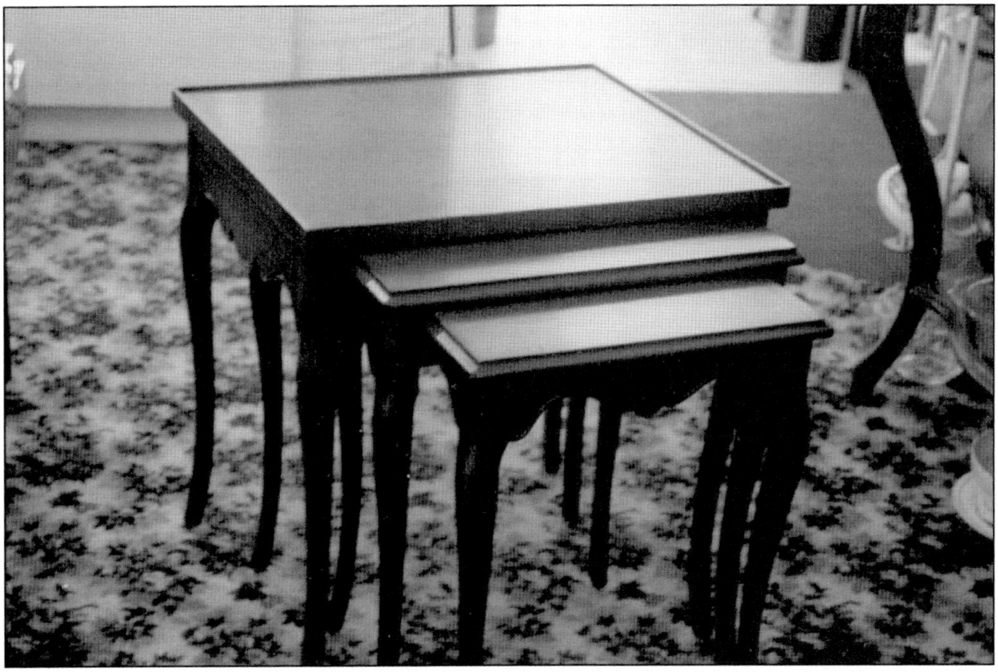

These mint condition Imperial Furniture Company nesting tables would work well with almost any style of decor. The company specialized in tables, usually made of walnut or mahogany. These tables were probably made in the early 1950s, before the company was sold to Bergsma Brothers. (Norma Lewis.)

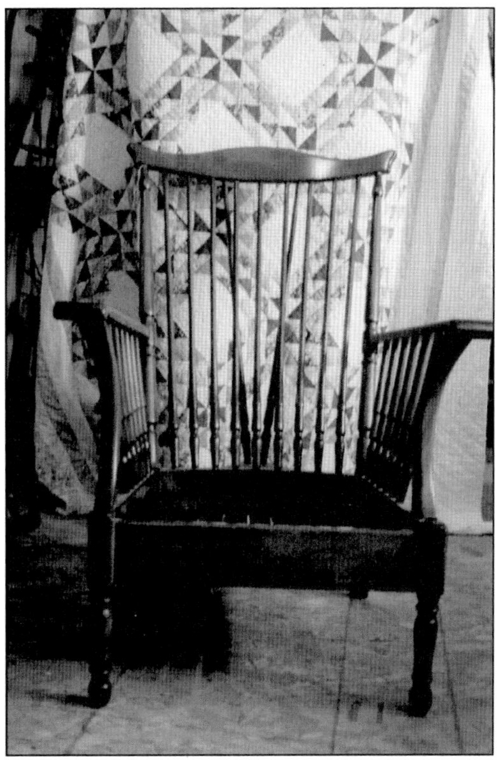

Stickley furniture remains popular and sells quickly. This chair is missing its cushion but is otherwise in good condition. The Stickley Brothers Furniture Company operated in Grand Rapids, while Gustav Stickley opened a factory in New York. L. and J. G. Stickley Furniture Company was yet another New York company. The five Stickleys were brothers. Both the chair and the nesting tables above were found at Light House Furnishings in Grand Rapids. (Norma Lewis.)

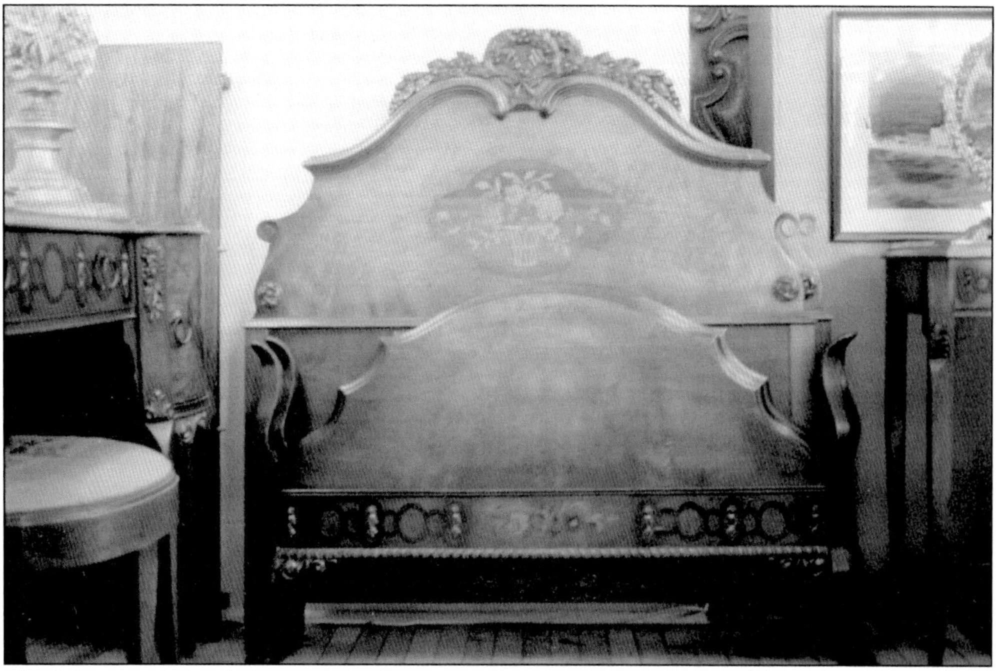

The Johnsons behind the Johnson Furniture Company were Carl, Axel, and Hjalmar, three brothers who immigrated from Sweden. Above is a bedroom suite. The carved and painted bed is flanked by a vanity, left, and nightstand, right. Also included are a dresser and mirror. Along with the painted design and carving, note the detail at the bottom of the footboard. The photograph below is a Johnson chest. The top is plain, but the signature decorative painting and carving are evident on the front. All the pieces on this page are from around 1910–1920. They were found at Eastown Antiques, on the corner of Lake Drive and Wealthy Street in Grand Rapids. (Norma Lewis.)

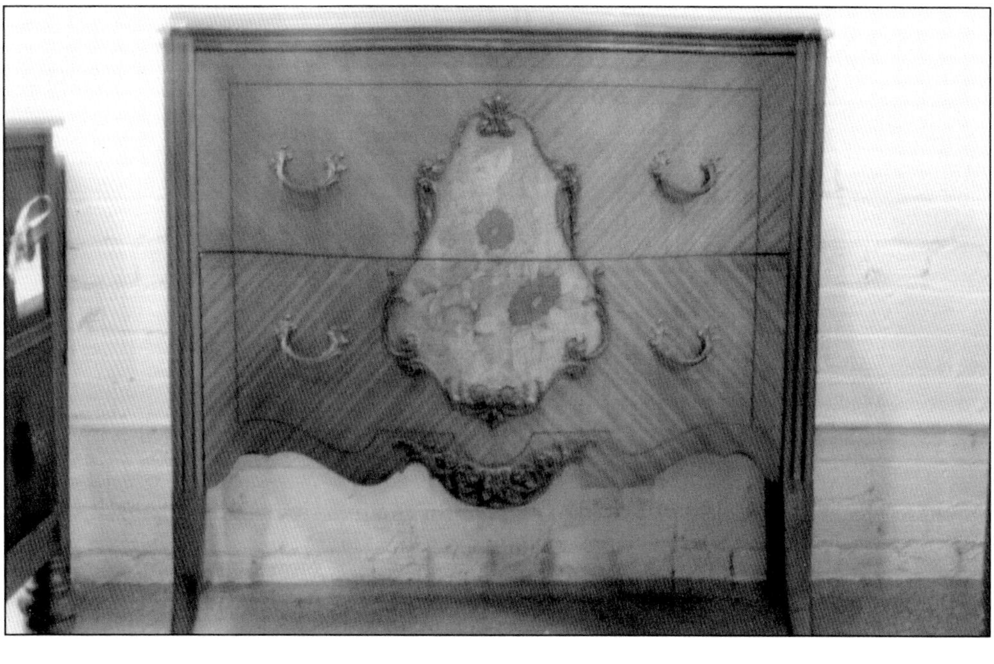

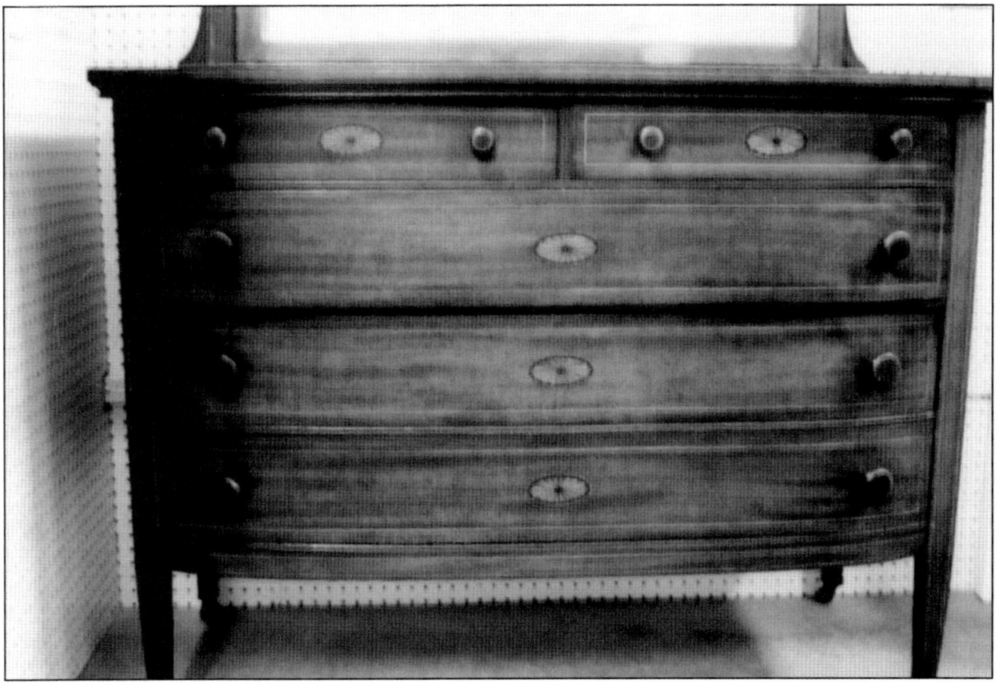

This dresser was part of a three-piece bedroom suite manufactured by the Luce Furniture Company in the 1930s and found in the Great Lakes Antique Mall, Highway 31, Holland. While many pieces are not so easily identified, the dresser still had the registered triangular red and white logo in one of the drawers. (Norma Lewis.)

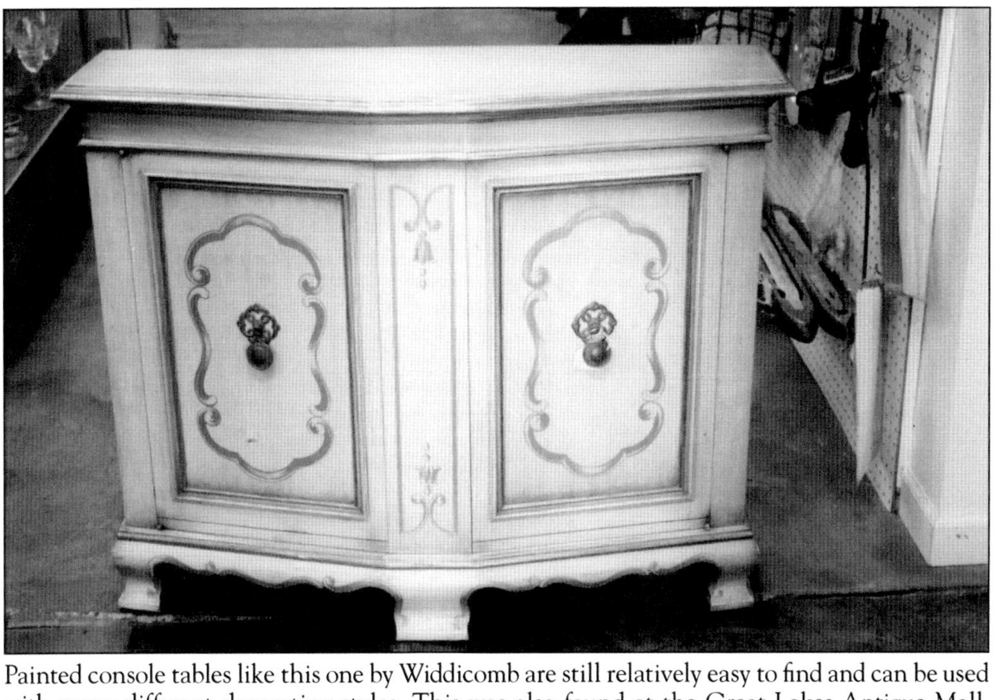

Painted console tables like this one by Widdicomb are still relatively easy to find and can be used with many different decorating styles. This was also found at the Great Lakes Antique Mall. (Norma Lewis.)

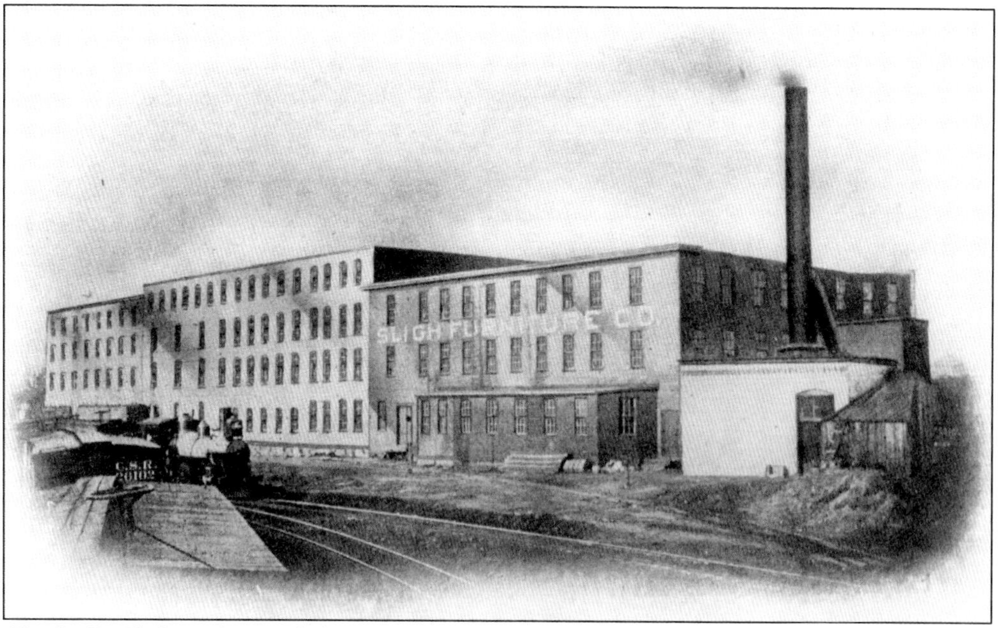

Charles R. Sligh Sr. first made his mark on the furniture industry with a convertible bed. Later he decided his company should make "everything for the bedroom." In a time when the city boasted the Grand Rapids Chair Company, the Grand Rapids Desk Company, the Grand Rapids Brass and Iron Bed Company, and the Grand Rapids Bookcase Company, among others, it was thought quite innovative and was one of the reasons he was nominated for, and inducted into, the Furniture Hall of Fame. (Norma Lewis.)

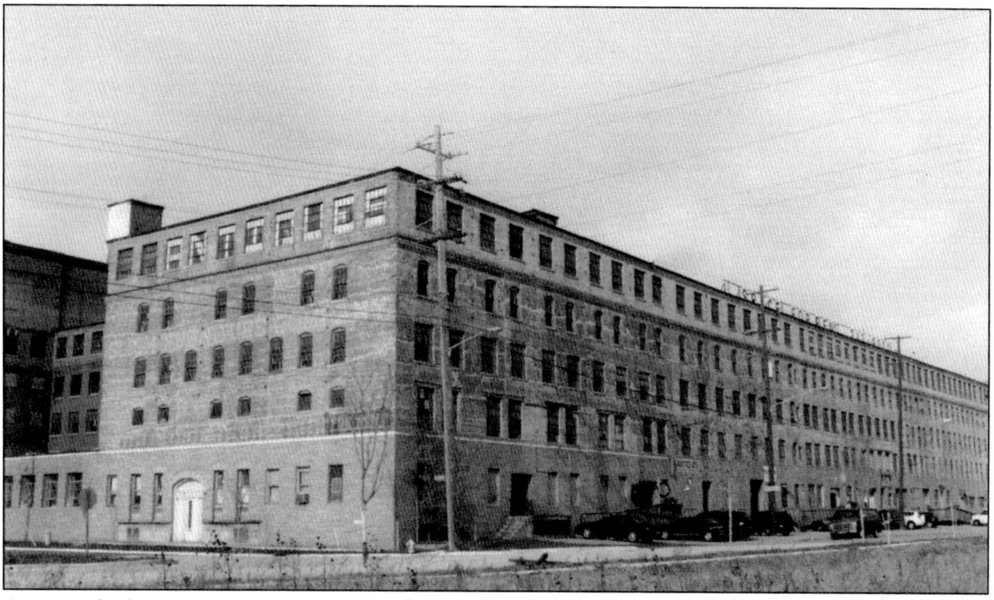

Among the businesses now occupying the former Sligh factory are two antiques malls, Victoria's Warehouse and Century Antiques. Savvy shoppers may be lucky enough to find a Sligh piece returned to where it was produced. Almost always, Grand Rapids–made furniture can be found here. Both owners are knowledgeable and will happily help find treasures with a local origin. (Norma Lewis.)

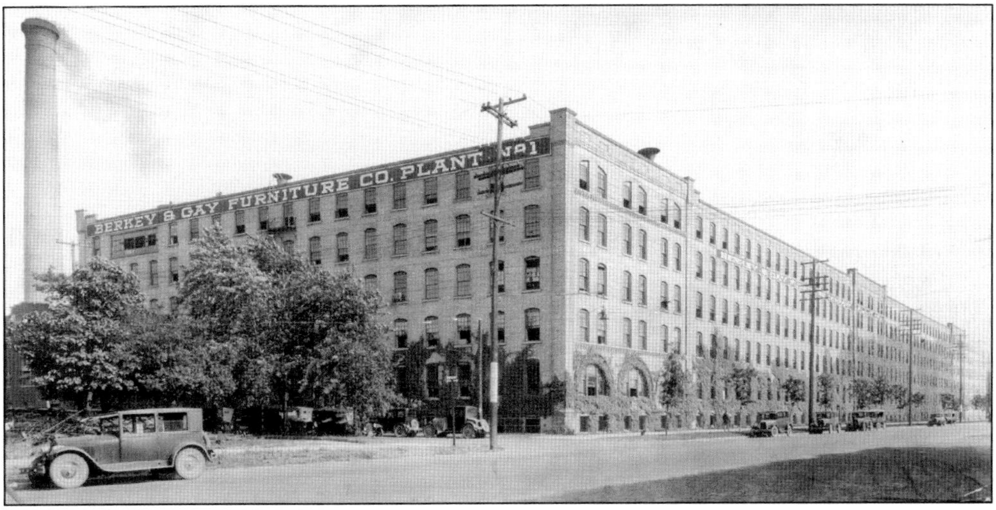

The Berkey and Gay Furniture Company's plant No. 1 on Monroe Street is seen as it looked in the early 1900s. At that time, the company still produced large and heavily carved parlor and bedroom suites, although the arts and crafts movement was coming into favor. (Grand Rapids Public Library.)

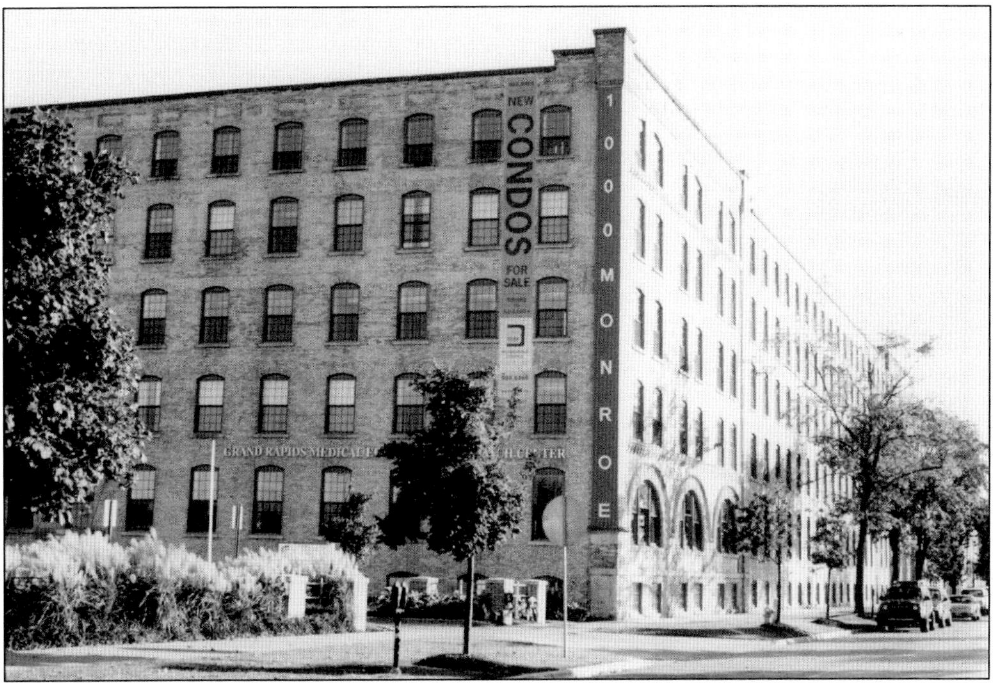

Today plant No. 1 contains a restaurant and a few businesses. Most of the facility has been renovated into the upscale Boardwalk Condominiums, complete with pool, rooftop gardens, and exercise facilities. The Grand River, once needed for power and transportation, now provides a scenic view for some condominium owners joining the wave of those choosing city life. (Norma Lewis.)

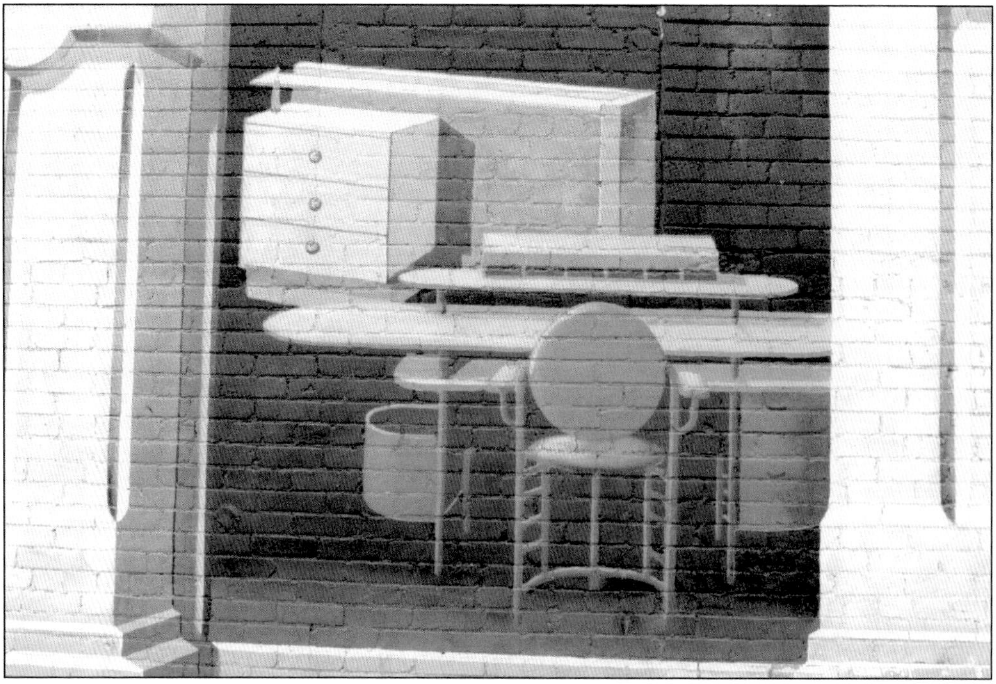

The mural on the following page is a celebration of the Grand Rapids furniture and logging industries. It is a signature piece by Richard Haas and was done for the Dwelling Place, a local nonprofit organization dedicated to creating low- to moderate-income housing in the area. The close-ups seen here are depictions of the marshmallow sofa from Herman Miller, Inc., (shown on page 100), and the Frank Lloyd Wright desk manufactured by Steelcase, Inc. (seen on page 103). (Norma Lewis.)

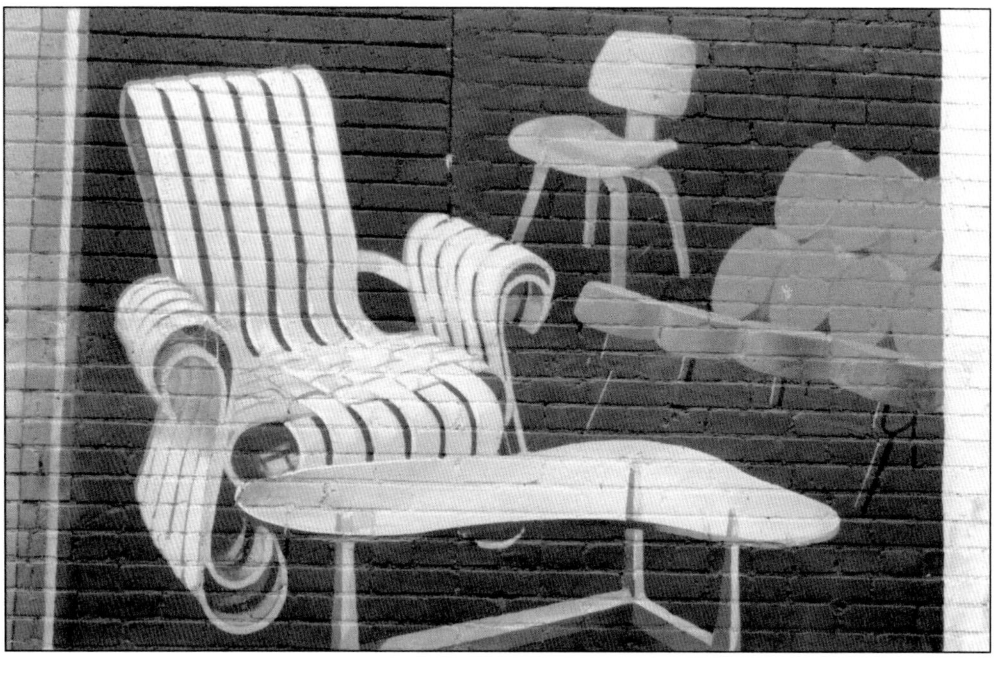

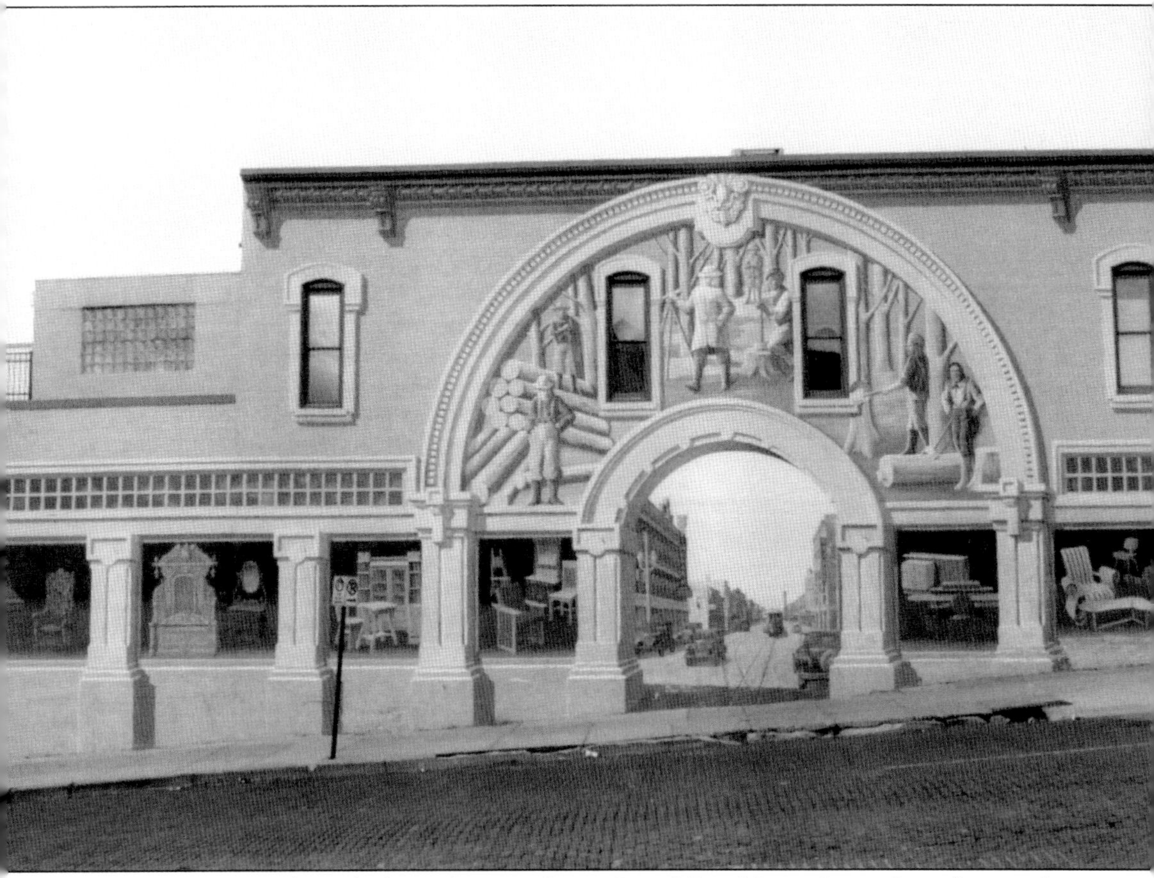

One can almost step through the archway and into Grand Rapids' proud past from the mural on the northwest corner of Division Avenue and Cherry Street in the city's Heartside area. The ornate bed on the left depicts one made by Berkey and Gay for the 1876 Philadelphia Centennial Exposition. Through the arch is Division Avenue, looking north, as it appeared in the early 1900s. The Winegar Furniture Store was in the building on which the mural is painted. The store's fire sale is described on page 83. (Norma Lewis.)